THE CHIEF LEARNING OFFICER

Driving Value Within a Changing Organization Through Learning and Development

TAMAR ELKELES, Ph.D.
JACK PHILLIPS, Ph.D.

Routledge
Taylor & Francis Group

LONDON AND NEW YORK

First published by Butterworth-Heinemann

This edition published 2011 by Routledge
2 Park Square, Milton Park, Abingdon, Oxon OX14 4RN
711 Third Avenue, New York, NY 10017, USA

Routledge is an imprint of Taylor & Francis Group, an informa business

Library of Congress Cataloging-in-Publication Data
Application submitted

British Library Cataloguing-in-Publication Data
A catalogue record for this book is available from the British Library.

ISBN 13: 978-0-7506-7925-1
ISBN 10: 0-7506-7925-5

Contents

Foreword

THE CLO'S CRITICAL ROLE

In many circles, the rise of chief learning officer (CLO) as a senior corporate position is seen as a recent phenomenon. True, the title doesn't have the celebrated history of the chief executive officer (CEO) title, and to those unfamiliar, it may not carry the obvious clout that comes from some other "C" level titles.

In the span of mankind, the CLO role is a fairly new one for business, but historically speaking the same could be said about television. It's only when you put it all in context that the uninitiated realize the value that learning and the CLO bring to the corporate table.

Officially, you could find CLO on the corporate reports going back to the mid-1990s. That's when Jack Welch, the fabled CEO of General Electric, worked with his team of innovative learning leaders to define the value of education to the business world and deemed it to be of strategic importance to the business objectives of GE.

A good idea catches on, and before long organization after organization was setting off down the trail GE blazed and recognizing the benefits achieved when corporate learning is in tune with the overall business plan. The twentieth century ended on an educational high note, with a record number of companies realizing workforce management was about more than compensation and benefits. As it turns out, even the thought leaders of that recent past had yet to scratch the surface.

Today, education is everywhere, delivered adroitly through technologies that sometimes replace the classroom and sometimes augment it. Learning takes place on the job and on the go, leveraging technologies from the Internet to the iPod to deliver just-in-time learning just where and when it's needed. The CLO has taken on a more critical role than even Jack Welch envisioned, now that learning is more readily available and more instantly applicable than ever before.

But the changes go beyond delivering media and learning styles. Today's CLO orchestrates education that's more strategic than tactical, another major shift in corporate learning. Just as the personnel department morphed into Human Resources (HR) to recognize the expanded role of those corporate agents, learning today is less about specific job skills or application training and more about the capture, dissemination, and application of knowledge. The result is an army of corporate learners ready to assess situations, identify solutions, and overcome obstacles. It's the CLO's role to create the opportunities for such personal growth, and to ride the ripple effect of skills and potential the new-fashioned learner offers.

Necessity, it seems, really is the mother of invention. Even as the numbers of CLOs continue to grow worldwide, learning executives are devising new strategies, leveraging new technologies, and realizing new visions in education. Companies are reaping immense cost savings and productivity surges, and workers are engaged again in building their employers' businesses. The message on the critical importance of workforce development has infiltrated, maybe even inundated, the boardrooms and executive suites. Technology and tools have advanced to a state of reliability, making it possible to fuel existing programs and pave the way for future needs. The learning departments, which have historically been seen as the starting point for budget savings, are suddenly viewed as the strategic partners capable of guiding the corporate ship through rough waters or of navigating into uncharted territories offering unrealized rewards. In times both lean and boom, education's role is becoming clear.

The fact that you're holding this book attests to the new reality. Over the past few years, corporate education has grown as an industry, as a solution, as a vision. What once was the poor stepchild of enterprise budgeting is now a relied-upon avenue for innovation. Corporate universities and learning departments are standing on their own as corporate partners, working separately but equally with HR executives, finance leaders, CIOs, CEOs, and board members. New support industries are popping up daily, offering everything from expert consulting to the latest technological widget, all designed to support the intrinsic value of education.

In less than a decade, education went from fad to fashion, from an afterthought item on corporate planning sheets to a sought-after solution with a funding formula all its own. Learning is claiming higher percentages of corporate revenues as business leaders see the wisdom and necessity of investing back in the business, earning returns and rewards both tangible and otherwise. Corporate education has even moved beyond workforce development to encompass not just employees but also customers, suppliers, and partner organizations. Lifelong learning has become the main mantra, and businesses are pursuing success with an unparalleled passion.

Naturally, fueling that passion is one of the missions of today's CLO, as well as our mission at *Chief Learning Officer* magazine. With that in mind, always in mind, it was my honor to author this foreword when asked by Jack Phillips and Tamar Elkeles, two of the industry leaders who are giving root and rise to this happy revolution. Both Jack and Tamar became instant supporters of *Chief Learning Officer* magazine and the work we're doing to create a community and support its ongoing needs. The strength of this book is the strength of their years of experience, when they were building the CLO role around the world without benefit of a title or even a defined job role, not to mention the benefits of the increased visibility learning leaders enjoy today.

Jack is a regular columnist in *Chief Learning Officer* magazine, contributing "Business Intelligence" columns in every other issue. Jack has also spoken at our CLO Symposium series of business conferences, connecting first-hand with learning executives around the globe. His work determining return on investment (ROI) has made his ROI Institute the leading resource for learning measurement.

Tamar's story is really reflective of the rise of the learning industry itself. She started working with QUALCOMM, the international communications company, as a part-time student intern. Leveraging technology, grant money, and a passion for education, Tamar quickly climbed the corporate ladder, and today her role as vice president of learning and development is crucial to the organization's growth strategies. In short, with their unique combinations of insight and experience and drive and determination, you couldn't find better guides to the critical role of the CLO than Jack and Tamar.

What lies ahead for the CLO position? Certainly those in this position will continue to create value for their organizations, shall continue to empower and inspire the workforce, and must continue to use education as a tool both internally and externally to advance the business of business.

What's more, the current crop of learning leaders stands now at the head of a long succession of future CLOs. The next generation is now learning the role directly from the original innovators, adding their own special perspectives. As the role continues to gain importance from headquarters to home offices, new crops of leaders will refine old ideas, enact new scenarios, and impart new wisdoms. Change is the one constant in life, the old saying goes, and change for the better will continue to be the mantra for corporate education.

CLOs have come a long way in a short time, a march ahead fueled by the best practices of fellow learning leaders, the support of expert resources, and the sense of community that comes with a shared mission that transcends corporate competitiveness. It's an exciting time in an exciting industry, and with guides like Jack and Tamar, you'll enjoy learning your way up the line.

Norm Kamikow
President/Editor in Chief
Chief Learning Officer magazine
norm@clomedia.com

Preface

New business realities and customer demands, coupled with new technologies in a changing competitive landscape are causing corporate learning departments to rethink their value, role, and impact in the organization. Added to this changing environment is an increasing level of business uncertainty that causes managers to question the investment in learning. They are focusing increased attention on trying to understand the value of learning and deciding the appropriate level of investment. In a world of limited resources and tight budgets, learning must be viewed as essential to a successful achievement of business goals. The individual driving this function, the chief learning officer (CLO), is in a unique position to add significant value to the organization.

A critical role of the CLO is to drive value, focusing on issues such as business alignment, managing resources, innovation, return on investment (ROI), and customer service. The challenge is to show value to the organization in terms that business leaders and other stakeholders can understand and appreciate. Written from the perspective of the CLO, this book discusses nine important value-adding strategies that make up this critical role of the CLO of the future:

- Show how the learning and development function is an important part of strategy (and often significantly influences strategy).
- Invest heavily in learning and development and have a mechanism to show the value of this investment.
- Take extreme measures to ensure that programs are linked to the business and that they are addressing business issues routinely.
- Recognize the shift to performance. Many go beyond the traditional learning solutions to provide a variety of nonlearning solutions.
- Focus on delivering learning, at the right time and at the right place, efficiently.

- Manage the function effectively and efficiently, understand the costs, work within budgets, and essentially run the learning enterprise like a business.
- Show the success of major programs, demonstrate value, and communicate value to a variety of stakeholders ensuring that senior executives and stakeholders understand the value of learning and development.
- Recognize that talent management is an important responsibility, and manage it, often from the recruiting process to managing retention.
- Secure tremendous support from executives and, in most cases, the CEO. Make them involved and committed and have them serve as role models.

An important focus of this book is the input from successful CLOs. While dozens of CLOs provided informal input to this book, 17 very high-profile, very successful CLOs agreed to be interviewed to offer their insights in this area. Collectively, their input in this book represents a tremendous amount of current CLO thinking.

WHY THIS BOOK AT THIS TIME

The CLO is challenged with the responsibility of making a difference in the organization or failing and diminishing the opportunity. Successful CLOs recognize the opportunity to add value and come up with specific strategies to develop and demonstrate value in the organization. Unsuccessful CLOs struggle to align with the organization, offering all types of programs that are often disconnected from the realities of the workplace. Consequently, learning is diffused, disorganized, and disconnected. The result is that the learning function misses a great opportunity to add value to the bottom line.

This book remedies this problem by showing how to connect the learning enterprise to the business using a variety of strategies. This connection is critical to the success of learning and the CLO's role in the learning enterprise. No other book addresses this issue, focusing directly on the nine strategies just outlined, written from the CLO perspective.

TARGET AUDIENCE

First, this book is designed for the CLO who is struggling to show the value of and connect learning to the business. Current CLOs will find this book to be an important and useful tool to drive business value. One of the most important challenges for the CLO is to constantly improve, update, and stay ahead of the curve. This requires learning from many others who are in similar jobs. Consequently, this should be a great addition, reminder, refresher, and enhancer for all CLOs.

The next audience is those individuals who aspire to be CLOs in the future. This book provides these individuals with a road map to success as they build expertise in making the learning enterprise successful. No other book can provide the insights, challenges, and opportunities for this important function. This is a must-read for anyone considering the opportunity of leading a learning enterprise in any organization, in any industry—be it in the private sector, in the government, in a non-profit, or in a nongovernment organization.

The third group is made up of the CLO's team members who must be aligned with the overall direction of the learning enterprise. Learning professionals need insight into the strategies required to add value to the business. The best way to support a CLO is to think like a CLO. This book helps staff members think the way most successful CLOs are thinking. It is an absolutely essential read for all staff members in the learning and development enterprise.

The fourth audience is those leaders in the organization who demand that learning add the necessary value to the enterprise. This book shows the value that can be achieved in the organization if it is managed and organized properly and the appropriate leadership is provided. We fully expect many organizations to purchase this book to give to their key leaders so that they understand what the CLO challenge is all about.

Acknowledgments

FROM TAMAR ELKELES

This book is dedicated to CLOs around the world who are making a contribution to the learning profession and positively impacting business performance. Keep the momentum and continue your very important work. We all benefit from your leadership.

Special thanks to my colleagues who were interviewed for this book: Frank Anderson, Susan Burnett, Tim Conlon, Bob Corcoran,Pat Crull, Fred Harburg, Ted Hoff, Steve Kerr, Michael Lee, Donna McNamara, Rick O'Leary, Donnee Ramelli, Bonnie Stoufer, Dave Vance, Allan Weisberg, Bill Wiggenhorn, and Kevin Wilde. I am grateful for your time and appreciate your significant contributions to this book. Without your valuable insights and perspective, this book would not be possible.

I would also like to thank Ed Betof, Ed Cohen, Cheryl Getty, Cindy Johnson, Lynn Slavenski, and Karie Willyerd for allowing me to share their wisdom with you via the quotes at the beginning of this book.

All of you are an inspiration to me as well as to all current and future CLOs. You are at the forefront of the profession and are forging a path for others to follow. I am so grateful for your wisdom and friendship. I commend your leadership in our profession and feel fortunate to have had the opportunity to learn from you.

My heartfelt thanks go to Jack Phillips who encouraged me to collaborate with him on this book. I am honored to be your coauthor. When we first embarked on this journey together, I was unsure of what would be ahead. Thank you, Jack, for your constant reassurance and for taking the initiative to put pen to paper. The more I learn about you, the more I am impressed. I have tremendous respect for your knowledge, passion, and dedication to the learning profession. You are an amazing author, a respected leader, and a wonderful friend. There is so much I learned from you during this process. I will always value our across-all-time-zones conversations about learning, ROI, and the CLO's role. You left a lasting impression on me that will forever shape my thinking and my future contributions. I look forward to future collaboration and continued friendship.

This book would not be possible without the tireless efforts of my assistant, Laurie Mee. While her words are not on the pages of this book, her tremendous support, dedication, and exceptional follow-through are reflected throughout. She has typed, collated, copied, e-mailed, coordinated, and revised numerous times to make this book become a reality. Thank you, Laurie. You have been an instrumental part of this endeavor.

Special thanks to all of my staff at QUALCOMM who challenge me daily to become a better CLO. Your individual and collective efforts continue to elevate QUALCOMM's performance. I am so proud of your accomplishments.

I am grateful to all of the staff at the ROI Institute who assisted with this book. You added tremendous value to this publication. We could not have done this without you. I especially appreciate the patience of everyone at Butterworth-Heinemann and Elsevier as we wrote this book. We believe it was worth the wait.

During the writing of this book there were many sleepless nights. Thank you to my husband, Larry, for waking up for those middle-of-the-night discussions and for making such significant contributions to my life. I cannot thank you enough for your support of my career and this book. I appreciate your keeping my nonwork life together. It's not always easy. Thanks for hanging in there.

To my daughter Mia, who teaches me more each day than I could ever teach her. She is my true "chief learning officer." Thank you for enriching my life and for your unconditional love. I hope one day you will read this book and understand why I go to work each day. You will always be my greatest contribution.

Thanks to my mother, Fran Elkeles, who encouraged me to write and taught me to have an opinion. And special thanks to my grandmother, Sylvia Adelman, who unfortunately passed away during the time I was completing this book. Your wisdom and strength will always be an inspiration.

And finally, thank you to my father, Gidon Elkeles, who encouraged me early on to work in the corporate world and to pursue my dreams. He taught me to work hard and to always add value to an organization. Thanks, Dad. Your memory lives forever within me.

From Jack J. Phillips

I would like to thank the many CLOs I have had the pleasure of working with over the past 15 years. When we provide consulting services to organizations all over the world, our principle contact is the CLO. We have worked with hundreds of CLOs, and on every occasion we have learned from them. To this important group of clients I extend a personal thanks for what they have taught me over the years. They are truly a very capable and impressive group.

Special thanks go to our staff at the ROI Institute, who provided excellent support to make this book a reality. Thanks to Margaret Marston, who coordinated and provided input on this book from inception to completion. Jaime Beard made the final push required to get the book to the publisher. Joyce Alff, our long-time editor, provided her usual great editing and coordination. And finally, thanks to Kathy Porter, who directs our publishing program. To all on this top-notch support team, we greatly appreciate your efforts.

We are constantly indebted to Butterworth-Heinemann and Elsevier for their continued support of our work on this series and on other publications. Ailsa Marks has been very patient through this process, allowing us to push deadlines as we continued to capture additional content. Ailsa is a very professional, highly respected, and productive editor. Thanks to Ailsa.

It has been a pleasure to work with Tamar Elkeles on this project. Tamar is the most admired and most effective CLO in the business. While I have worked with hundreds of CLOs, I have found no one as impressive as Tamar. Her long tenure at QUALCOMM has been an important part of her success. I am amazed at the executive support that she enjoys and the influence that she commands within QUALCOMM. She is indeed a role model for CLOs. Much of this book represents her thinking, her experience, and her tolerance for working with me. Thanks, Tamar, for a great coproduction.

And finally, thanks go to my partner, spouse, and special friend Patti, CEO of the ROI Institute. Although Patti is not one of the listed authors, she provided much insight, input, and some final editing to make this book a reality. She always contributes significantly to our work, and has done a marvelous job of pushing the ROI Institute to the forefront of the assessment, measurement, and evaluation field. To Patti, we owe you much, and we'll continue to owe you much more. Thanks.

Author Biographies

Tamar Elkeles, Ph.D., is vice president of Learning and Development at QUALCOMM. In this role she is responsible for defining the overall strategic direction for employee development across the company. Her scope of leadership includes company-wide professional and technical development, executive/leadership development, internal communications, organization development, and learning technology for more than 11,000 QUALCOMM employees worldwide.

Elkeles created the Learning Center within QUALCOMM in 1992 to meet the learning and development needs in a rapidly growing and changing high technology environment. Today, the focus of her organization is to continually bridge the gap between training and information to improve both individual and organizational performance. In 1999, the Learning Center evolved into an internal consulting function within the organization, which provides business divisions with innovative solutions in training, organizational development, talent management, onboarding, internal mobility, and communications that impact business results.

Since 2000, QUALCOMM has consistently ranked in the top 50 in *Training* magazine's list of Top 100 Training Organizations. In

2002, QUALCOMM was ranked as "best in class" in telecommunications. In both 2000 and 1994, QUALCOMM also earned the Organization of the Year Award from the American Society of Training and Development (ASTD) San Diego for exceptional training and development programs. In 2005 and 2006 QUALCOMM was named one of ASTD's BEST award winners for demonstrating enterprise-wide success as a result of employee learning and development.

Elkeles' extensive focus on alternative delivery methods enabled QUALCOMM to begin development of online learning in early 1995. As a result of these progressive efforts, QUALCOMM was awarded the ASTD Best Practice Award for the Use of Technology for Learning in 1996, and in 1998, it was honored with an ASTD Best Practice Award for Web-Based Learning. She has been featured in both *Chief Learning Officer* magazine, *Training* magazine and *T&D* magazine for her leadership and contributions to the learning profession.

Nationally, Elkeles is a member of the Conference Board Council for Training, Development, and Education as well as a member of the *Chief Learning Officer* magazine editorial board. She also served on the board of directors for ASTD, the world's premier professional association and leading resource on workplace learning and performance. She holds both an M.S. and a Ph.D. in organizational psychology.

Jack Phillips, Ph.D., is a world-renowned expert on measurement and evaluation and chairman of the ROI Institute. Through the Institute, Phillips provides consulting services for Fortune 500 companies and workshops for major conference providers throughout the world. Phillips is also the author or editor of more than 30 books and more than 100 articles.

His expertise in measurement and evaluation is based on more than 27 years of corporate experience in five industries (aerospace, textiles, metals, construction materials, and banking). Phillips has served as training and development manager at two Fortune 500 firms, senior HR officer at two firms, president of a regional federal savings bank, and management professor at a major state university.

His background in learning and HR led Phillips to develop the ROI Methodology—a revolutionary process that provides bottom-line figures and accountability for all types of learning, performance improvement, human resources, and technology programs.

Books most recently authored or coauthored by Phillips include: *Return on Investment (ROI) Basics*, ASTD (2005); *ROI at Work*, ASTD (2005); *Investing in Your Company's Human Capital: Strategies to Avoid Spending Too Little or Too Much*, AMACOM (2005); *Proving the Value of HR: How and Why to Measure ROI*, SHRM (2005); *Make Training Evaluation Work*, ASTD (2004); *The Leadership Scorecard*, Elsevier Butterworth-Heinemann (2004); *The Human Resources Scorecard: Measuring the Return on Investment*, Butterworth-Heinemann (2001); *A New Vision for Human Resources: Defining the Human Resources Function by Its Results*, Crisp Learning (1998); *Managing Employee Retention*, Butterworth-Heinemann (2003); *Retaining Your Best Employees*, ASTD (2002); *Return on Investment in Training and Performance Improvement Programs, 2nd Edition*, Butterworth-Heinemann (2003); *The Project Management Scorecard*, Butterworth-Heinemann (2002); *How to Measure Training Results*, McGraw-Hill (2002); and *The Consultant's Scorecard*, McGraw-Hill (2000). In addition, he is a regular contributor to *Chief Learning Officer* magazine.

Phillips has undergraduate degrees in electrical engineering, physics, and mathematics, a master's degree in decision sciences from Georgia State University, and a Ph.D. in human resource management from the University of Alabama. He can be reached at jack@roiinstitute.net.

A Note on the Position of the CLO

In the knowledge economy, CEOs and business leaders are focused on organizational growth. They understand the key to growth and sustaining competitiveness means developing and retaining a highly skilled, knowledgeable workforce. How do they make this happen? By engaging their senior workplace learning and performance executives—business partners who understand the strategic link between employee learning and the performance measures that impact organizational results.

These senior executives, often called chief learning officers (CLOs), serve at the highest level of their organizations to direct and manage the learning, performance improvement, talent management, career development, and organizational knowledge functions.

To better understand the profile of today's CLO, ASTD recently partnered with the University of Pennsylvania to analyze CLOs' current positions, career histories, educational backgrounds, and the competencies they believe are critical for success. Data from 92 CLOs, with learning budgets greater than $1 million in companies with more than 100 employees, were included in the survey results.

The survey results show that CLOs spend most of their time on strategy and communication up and down their organizations to align learning requirements with business goals, and to deliver learning opportunities in the most efficient manner. While multiple career paths can lead to the position of CLO, the key competencies required to be successful are leadership and the ability to articulate the value of learning in business terms.

The survey results also show that the new breed of learning executive has or wants a dual competency in learning and business, and a dual mandate to improve the performance of the business and the productivity of the learning function. To carry out this complex role, a CLO must be a skilled learning professional and a capable business person, and able to speak the language of both.

Our survey showed that the role of the CLO today is quite similar to that of the first CLO, Steve Kerr, when he was at General Electric. These results also echo Timothy Baldwin and Camden Danielson's 2000 report in *Business Horizons* of interviews with 10 CLOs. They concluded that the role was largely strategic, linking learning priorities and initiatives to the strategic direction of the firm, with increased pressure on CLOs to produce tangible value from learning investments.

Does this mean that the more things change, the more they stay the same? I guess it depends on your perspective, but one thing is for sure—an organization's ability to grow and compete is wholly dependent on the knowledge and skills of its people. Professionals in workplace learning and performance—and especially CLOs and senior learning executives—are responsible for developing and increasing the capacity of an organization's human capital. While this responsibility is broad and deep, it presents an exciting opportunity to make a significant impact on individual and organizational success. For learning professionals, there has never been a time when the path to being a true strategic business partner was clearer.

Tony Bingham
President and CEO, ASTD

In the Beginning...

...From an interview with Steve Kerr, the founder of the Chief Learning Officer title and the first "CLO". Steve created Crotonville, General Electric's (GE) Management Development Center.

Tamar Elkeles: So Steve, we understand the inception of the CLO title began with you at General Electric.

Steve Kerr: Yes, I originally came up with the name Chief Education Officer (CEO), but Jack Welch said there was only room for one CEO and that title was already taken. Jack thought the title should be reflective of what people do (learning is a verb) in the organization instead of what they are (Chief Human Capital Officer is a noun). Hence, the title CLO.

1

CHAPTER 1

The Chief Learning Officer: Trends and Issues

> *The easiest way for a CLO to demonstrate value and business relevance is to connect learning solutions to strategic direction. Helping leaders deal with what change needs to take place to move themselves, their people, and organizations from their current state to where they need to be in the future can demonstrate clear business linkage.*
>
> Tim Conlon, Director of Learning and
> Chief Learning Officer, Xerox

Much has changed in the world of learning and for the individuals who lead the learning enterprise. Recent trends and developments show that the Chief Learning Officer (CLO) is gaining the attention and respect needed to be successful in the organization. The most pronounced trend is that the CLO must constantly add value to ensure success in the organization. There are numerous opportunities for new CLOs and those aspiring to be CLOs. For seasoned CLOs, these opportunities represent challenges that must be addressed to sustain the growth and development of the learning enterprise.

The Evolution of the CLO

Challenges and Changes

To begin examining important trends and issues, one needs to explore how top executives view the CLO position and the chal-

Financial Challenges	Globalization Challenges
• Understand the products of the company. • Understand the company's business issues. • Facilitate business model changes.	• Understand the company's culture.

Recruiting Challenges	Customer Challenges
• Increase workplace learning to attract new people to the organization. • Schedule job fairs designed to educate the community about the organization.	• Regularly consult with customers. • Keep customers in the forefront of planned learning.

Technology and Internet Challenges	Corporate Knowledge Challenges
• Evaluate technological trends. • Use the trends to help change the business. • Communicate the trends to the organization.	• Manage company-wide transitions. • Create a continual learning environment. • Provide mentoring.

Figure 1-1. CLO roles to meet business challenges.

lenges facing organizations. Figure 1-1 provides roles for CLOs to help them meet the six most important business challenges they face. These challenges are taken from a study of CEO perceptions about competencies of workplace learning and performance professionals (Lindholm, 2000). These six business challenges may come as no surprise to CLOs who routinely develop talent, serve customers, manage knowledge, and use technology appropriately. Being able to handle all of these in a global environment, within precise financial targets and constraints, is what makes the CLO role dynamic in today's business world of today. The CLO is in an excellent position to demonstrate progress in each of these areas.

In a follow-up effort to this study, the CEOs identified the competencies needed by CLOs to assist the organization in meeting these challenges (Rothwell *et al.*, 2004):

- *Business knowledge.* Aligning programs to company strategy, keeping abreast of industry trends and company performance, and demonstrating transfer of learning to individual performance
- *Communication.* Communicating effectively throughout the organization and becoming an advocate on behalf of the organization, individual, and groups
- *Broad perspective.* Assimilating numerous experiences into learning approaches, demonstrating open-mindedness, viewing employees as assets, possessing empathy, and possessing an awareness of the organizational culture
- *Assessment skills.* Measuring improvement, assessing needs and guiding both individual and organizational workforce learning needs, forecasting and preparing analyses, and identifying performance problems
- *Delivery systems.* Assessing, designing, and implementing effective delivery mechanisms for classroom, e-learning, blended, and other formats
- *Innovation.* Conceptualizing, designing, developing, and applying new learning interventions to business needs, while simultaneously modeling strong values and openness to change
- *Drive.* Demonstrating energy and enthusiasm for programs, projects, and initiatives and building bridges across barriers to learning program acceptance

These seven areas are the CEO-identified competencies to achieve success in meeting the challenges facing organizations today and in the future.

A total of 464 learning executives, many holding the official title of CLO, responded to these issues and other questions as a part of the CLO Futures Survey to determine current and future trends related to both the position of the CLO and the issues that concern the individuals who have that position (L'Allier, 2005). To determine competencies considered most important to CLO success now and in the future, respondents to the survey were asked to rate a set of seven CLO competencies from "not critical" to "very critical." These were the top four competencies:

- Demonstrated leadership skills.
- Possessed experience with strategic planning.
- Commanded knowledge of the learning and development process.
- Demonstrated impact on business performance.

Clearly, these competencies help the CLO to add value.

To understand the evolution of the CLO, it might be helpful to consider how the job of chief information officer (CIO) has evolved. It took 10 years following the debut of *CIO Magazine* for chief information officers to be declared "as vital as any other top-level executive." This statement appeared in the September 15, 1997 issue of the magazine (Bauer, 2004). Yet just two years prior, *InformationWeek* published an article titled "Left-Out CIOs," widely chastising technology managers for their lack of responsiveness and leadership. In the January 16, 1995 issue of *InformationWeek*, information technology (IT) analysts speculated on the future of the CIO position, warning that "top technical officers who are going to stand the test of time are those whose number one asset is that they understand the business well." Clearly, by the time *CIO Magazine* issued its declaration, CIOs had gotten the message that their success was tied to understanding the technology needs of the business and delivering business solutions to address those needs.

So what conclusion can be drawn by CLOs reflecting on the early learning of CIOs? Bauer provides a vision for vital CLO accountability and a road map for executing that vision based on five best practices witnessed in leading organizations in which learning strategy and operations are governed at the executive level.

Best Practice 1: Move Beyond Traditional Boundaries When Defining Audiences

Best Practice 2: Develop Individual Agility to Enable Organizational Agility

Best Practice 3: Reduce Time-to-Proficiency and Time-to-Mastery

Best Practice 4: Measure and Communicate Vital Metrics

Best Practice 5: Fix the Process, Then Technology-Enable It

The Changing Landscape for Learning and Performance— What's in a Name?

Perhaps the changes in workplace learning are best illustrated by the name associated with learning in organizations. The profession itself struggles with what to call the learning function and its various derivatives, including the individual who is in the top leadership role responsible for providing learning initiatives and programs. Some prefer to use the term *learning and development*, to reflect that some programs are designed to help individuals learn skills for current jobs or jobs that are changing or evolving, or to learn skills for new jobs that may appear on the near horizon. Development is more incremental and long term and is often associated with cultural changes as well as perceptions and mindset adjustments. Some organizations still use the word *training* to reflect skills needed immediately to improve job performance. Some use the term *education and training* in the learning context, having the perspective that education is preparing an individual for a future job, while training is focusing more on the skills needed for performance on the current job. A variety of terms are emerging as the function evolves.

The CLO is expected to address performance issues from two perspectives. First, some of the solutions needed are not traditionally learning; they represent performance improvement and may involve solutions such as job aids, coaching, organization development, performance management, and reward systems. The other perspective is that learning should lead to performance enhancement; that is, learning must be transferred to the job and translated into individual performance if the learning is to be considered successful. Consequently, the term *performance* often appears in the CLO's function. Sometimes it is labeled *learning and performance*; sometimes it is *learning and performance improvement*; while in some companies it is *training, learning, and performance improvement*. The performance dimension represents an important shift in the CLO's role. Some may say that learning professionals have always been in the performance business, while for others this is a new opportunity to add value. Consequently, one of the critical areas for adding value is in the performance space, and a complete chapter is devoted to it.

The word *technology* is sometimes also used to describe the CLO's role, such as in *human performance technology* (HPT). This term has often been promoted by the International Society for Performance Improvement (ISPI). A certification has been developed on HPT recognizing the systematic approach to improving performance that includes specific techniques. This translates into a structured methodology for technology to improve performance. Some professionals prefer to use *human performance improvement* (HPI) instead of HPT; however, the approaches are similar.

Location has become an important issue. Thus, the term *workplace* enters the learning world. This is where the American Society for Training and Development (ASTD), the world's largest professional association of learning and development professionals, places its stake in the ground. ASTD's logic for adopting workplace learning and performance (WLP) as the official term for learning functions follows a logical path (Sugrue, Driscoll, and Blair, 2005). According to ASTD, the workplace specifies the context for learning and performance. The W in WLP also acknowledges the role of workplace variables such as goals, systems, resources, and incentives. Learning, as described earlier, is a surrogate of the term *training and development*. Learning shifts the focus from external activities to what is happening for the individuals who are "trained and developed." Using the term *learning* broadens the scope of CLO's responsibilities to include all opportunities—formal and informal, planned and unplanned, on the job and off the job—that lead individuals to learn and develop new knowledge and skills, as well as change their perceptions, attitudes, and behaviors.

According to ASTD, the word *performance* has multiple meanings in WLP. First, performance is the outcome of learning and can be viewed at three levels: individual, group, and organization. Second, performance is a perspective or mindset that leads one to see learning as only one of many interactive variables that influence individual, group, and organizational performance. Also, a performance mindset leads to analysis of performance gaps, prescriptions, and solutions that go beyond learning. ASTD concludes that the term WLP explicitly connects learning, and all the activities that support learning, for the improvement of the individual, group, and organization. Figure 1-2 shows the complete workplace learning and performance value chain.

Evolution of the CLO's Role

Aligned with the variability of the name of the learning function is the title of the person leading the charge. The title and the corresponding role have evolved considerably in the last half century. Initially, the title Training Director was used to reflect the individual in charge of training employees. The American Society of Training and

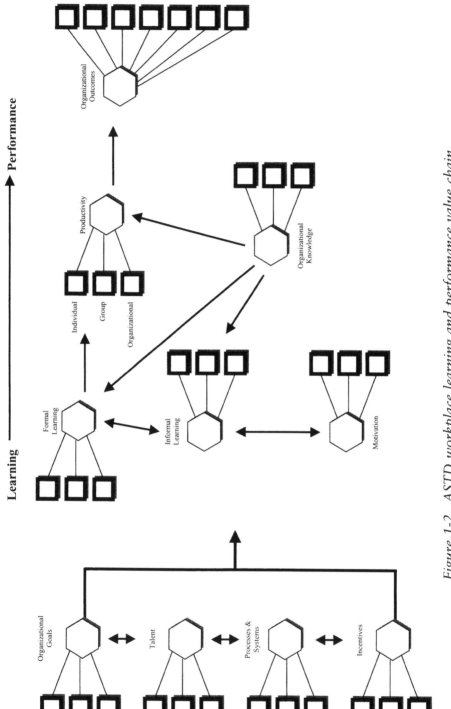

Figure 1-2. ASTD workplace learning and performance value chain. (Source: © ASTD, 2004. Used with permission.)

Development was originally known as The American Society for Training Directors, and their initial publication was the *Training Director's Journal*. Although this term appears to be outdated for many, it is still in use. For example, the Training Directors Forum offered by VNU Learning (*Training* magazine) is still considered to be one of the premier events for CLOs. This conference is designed for the top training or learning executive with a particular absence of commercialism (in the exhibits), entry level issues, and mundane routine topics. Instead, it attempts to reflect the changing needs and roles of the CLO to offer high-level programming from well-known leaders in this important area.

The title Training Director was gradually replaced by Training Manager, assuming a title that was the same as other managers in the organization. This eventually evolved into the Training and Development Manager, recognizing that not only is the person responsible for job-related skill training, but many developmental efforts including leadership development, management development, and executive development. As the status of this function grew and the importance of learning, training, and development evolved, the title was upgraded to Vice President of Training and Development or Learning and Development. This action began to position the top learning leader in the role of an officer in the organization, parallel with other functions such as Vice President of Marketing, Vice President of Research and Development, and Vice President of Manufacturing. In the late '80s and early '90s, the term Chief Training Officer began to evolve, reflecting a "C" level job to position this function at the same level as a Chief Marketing Officer, Chief Operating Officer, Chief Technology Officer, Chief Information Officer, and Chief Financial Officer. Because of the limitations in the word training and the emerging role of the Chief Technology officer, CTO eventually was replaced by CLO (Chief Learning Officer) retaining the "C" level designation, but focusing on learning with learning taking on a broader context because of the vast number of opportunities, activities, programs, and processes—both on and off the job—available 24/7 to satisfy employee learning needs. (See "In the Beginning" of this book.) Today there is a magazine devoted to CLOs. *Chief Learning Officer* magazine has earned its reputation as a premier resource for worldwide learning professionals.

As the CLO's title and role have changed, so has the learning enterprise's relationship to the organization. Figure 1-3 provides an excellent summary from The Concours Group (Gratton, 2004). Clearly, the focus is only creating value, the focus of this book.

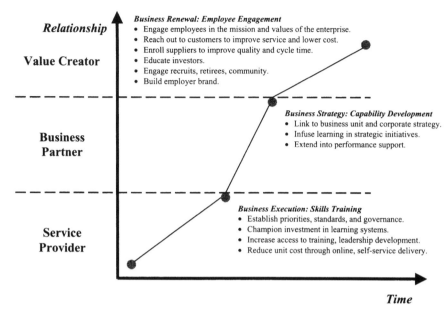

Figure 1-3. The maturity of the learning enterprise.
(Adapted from Gratton, 2004.)

CURRENT STATUS OF THE CLO

The New CLO

The new CLO is perhaps best described by those individuals charged with recruiting candidates for this important role. The recruiters are seeing important changes in the requirements for this job. The critical characteristics for success were recently detailed in an article in *Chief Learning Officer* magazine (Bongiorno *et al.*, 2005). CLOs are often recruited externally, based on a perception that someone new and different is needed to drive this critical function in the organization, particularly as this function is more aligned with creating value.

The search for CLOs, or similar titles, now comprise almost 20 percent of HR searches and often contain a broad set of specifications. Clients want individuals who are seasoned, with successful assignments leading the learning function. Talent management, succession planning, and organizational development experience top the list of specifications. Process improvement experiences or similar credentials also figure prominently into the equation. Recruiters suggest that the C not only stands for chief—bringing it to the "C" suite—but also for commitment.

Top executives who recognize the value of learning avoid jetti-soning staff in economic downturns and hiring them back as the economy improves. They take a more moderate approach, recog-nizing the value of people and their performance. They recognize that sometimes the time to invest in learning is when the economy is not so good. For example, rather than pulling the plug on recruit-ing trips to universities during recessions, these companies maintain their presence at top business schools and undergraduate programs through both up and down cycles. These companies are also the ones that are inclined to use the "C" title to mean a leader in charge of learning. According to these researchers, retail and banking compa-nies tend to understand the value of learning and hire CLOs to run that function of the business. Wal-Mart, Home Depot, and Bank of America are all recognized for their sophisticated learning and devel-opment capability. GE and IBM are two companies that have main-tained their focus on this issue.

The CLO position rarely exists without the blessing of the CEO. By appointing the CLO, the CEO communicates to internal and external audiences that the organization is making a long-term investment in organizational learning. In essence, the CLO functions as a translator for the CEO. The CEO relies on this individual to not only address the traditional issues of learning and performance needs, but be, at times, a sounding board for organizational issues, problems, and the barriers to achieving many of the goals of work-place performance. Sometimes these barriers are not only systems and procedures, but individuals. Today's CLOs often take responsi-bility for all development and effectiveness functions including recruitment, training, succession planning, retention, and enterprise-wide process improvement. This broadens the traditional role of the learning professional or learning leader. According to these recruiters, recent executive search specifications have also included technology and performance improvement experience. These are critical components to adding value.

The current responsibilities of CLOs highlight the issue of creating and adding value. When the work of Bongiorno is combined with the CLO interviews in this book, at least 10 ways are identified in which CLOs are addressing the issue of creating value:

1. Exploring, implementing, and gaining financial commitment for performance initiatives where individual compensation is tied to clearly specified performance goals, not only with high-level employees but lower levels, as well.

2. Serving as a partner with key executives, particularly the CEO and executive team. Working diligently and proactively to develop a productive partnership, even in times when the executive may not want to partner with the CLO.

3. Ensuring that the organization is in compliance. Compliance training comprises a significant part of the budget and sometimes the top executives are looking to the CLO to ensure that regulatory compliance is achieved.

4. Extending the learning enterprise beyond the traditional target groups of employees to include customers, suppliers, and the community as well.

5. Strengthening customer service. Many of the problems with failed customer service delivery are either lack of skills and appropriate talent, or attitudes and perceptions. All of these are key areas for the CLO. Increasingly, the CLO is held at least partially accountable for customer service delivery.

6. Developing stronger links between learning and the bottom line. The learning function is evolving from a traditional back office support function to a mainstream activity that is adding to the bottom line. CLOs are beginning to show many successes for their particular measured programs including the actual ROI. According to the recruiters, "Measure, measure, measure serves as an appropriate mantra to guide the CLOs as they strive to master the challenge of assuming a more strategic role." (Bongiorno, 2005, pp. 52–58)

7. Developing and improving the organization through a variety of organization development initiatives extending from organizational assessment and effectiveness processes.

8. Managing the talent in the organization from attraction and selection to development and retention. This includes talent reviews and succession planning.

9. Supporting the mergers and acquisition integration by ensuring that teams are integrated, new members are provided with appropriate onboarding, and critical competencies are maintained.

10. Growing leaders in the organization through a variety of on- and off-the-job developmental experiences that are effective and results based.

These critical CLO roles appear in many reports. In November 2004, Accenture surveyed 285 companies about CLO specifications.

Accenture's reports identified several capabilities that leading learning organizations deliver and measure.

1. Aligning learning initiatives to business goals.
2. Measuring the overall business impact of the learning function.
3. Extending learning to customers, suppliers, and business partners.
4. Supporting the organizations' most critical competencies and jobs.
5. Integrating learning with functions such as knowledge and talent management.
6. Using technology to deliver learning.
7. Delivering leadership development programs.

In short, the role of the CLO has evolved. The new CLO is expected to do much more than design, develop, and deliver learning solutions. He or she must be the catalyst to bring change and create value in the organization. This is the goal of this book.

The Consequences of Failure

As new CLOs are recruited, the consequences of failure are often underscored. Some recruiters suggest that the turnover rate of high-profile top CLOs is very high. An individual is recruited with high hopes, only to be disappointed with what is delivered. Thus, the future of the CLO becomes questionable and the impact can be disastrous.

Consider a particular case in point of a recruited CLO on the job for about a year. "Cathy" was recruited to head a major learning organization. (The real name of the individual and the organization are not revealed for obvious reasons.) The staff represented one of the most high-profile learning organizations in the United States, with a full-time professional learning staff that numbered over 500. Cathy not only had the title of Chief Learning Officer but was labeled president of the corporate university. With a high salary and a corresponding employment agreement, she attempted to build the desired learning organization. The individual who recruited Cathy was a very progressive, newly appointed senior officer responsible for Human Resources. This HR executive could see the value of having a professional, experienced CLO to unite all the learning functions, avoid duplications, and, more than anything else, create value for the organization. This would ensure that learning and development needs were met in a fast, changing, growing, and highly competitive business. Unfortunately, Cathy was resented by many staff members who were overlooked for this opportunity. Cathy increased her staff at a time when other support staffing units were unable to do so. New processes were implemented, new contracts were drawn, new consultants were brought in, and skills were improved—but all of this represented additional expenditures. The direction of the corporate university and the learning function was being radically changed, yet the staff resistance continued. And to make matters worse, successes were not materializing.

Meanwhile, the senior HR executive who recruited Cathy left the organization and was replaced by an internal candidate who did not have the same view of the value of learning. This new HR executive forced Cathy out and began to dismantle much of what had been accomplished. All in all, this was very painful for the organization, representing much expenditure, wasted efforts, and confusion as the learning process endured a major change. The consequences of this debacle were devastating, causing some key learning and development team members to leave. One of the existing staff members was appointed to the CLO position and the organization essentially returned to its status of ineffectiveness and ineptness. While there are many lessons in this case, it illustrates the tremendous pain when there is failure in this role.

Clearly, in this organization, the top executives do not understand the CLO function or the value that the CLO can bring. The challenge is to show senior executives the value of learning and development and the importance of the CLO role. Until this occurs, these missteps will continue to be made, costing organizations tremendous amounts of money. More important, many opportunities are lost as the attention is focused in other places.

The Rewards of Success

While the consequences of failure are great, the rewards of success can be even greater. When a CLO is allowed to develop and evaluate effective learning solutions and programs, the successes can be tremendous, but only if the CLO is adding value to the organization. This value must be measured, reported, and perceived as important to key stakeholders. How is value defined? Unfortunately, the traditional approach is to report value in terms of the number of programs, initiatives, and solutions in place. Measurable data consisted of the number of learning hours multiplied by the number of learn-

Level	Measurement Focus	Key Questions
0 Input	Measures input such as volume and efficiencies.	What are the number of participants, hours, and programs and what are the costs?
1 Reaction and Planned Action	Measures participant satisfaction with the project and captures planned actions.	Was the learning relevant, important, useful, and helpful to the participant and the job environment?
2 Learning	Measures changes in knowledge, skills, and attitudes.	Did participants increase or enhance knowledge, skills, or perceptions and have confidence to use them?
3 Application	Measures changes in on-the-job behavior or action.	What did the participants do differently in the job context?
4 Business Impact	Measures changes in business impact variables.	What are the consequences of the application in terms of output, quality, cost, time, and satisfaction?
5 ROI	Compares project benefits to the costs.	Did the monetary benefits of learning exceed the investment in the program?

Figure 1-4. The learning value chain.

ers, along with the number of topics and the delivery systems. Efficiency was often the measure—how many could be trained in a certain period of time.

While these are important measures that often define the commitment and inputs to the process, they fail to represent learning outcomes. What is needed is a clear, up-front definition of value and program success as well as benchmarks along the way to show success. Figure 1-4 shows the learning value chain, which is often accepted as showing the various ways in which value is categorized for learning initiatives. This learning value chain is based on the fundamental works of both Kirkpatrick (1994) and Phillips (1983) to define a series of measurement categories that reflect learning success.

This value chain could represent the success of an individual program and can be integrated across programs. Coupled with this is the realization that not all programs would be taken to the higher level values through the chain. Some would stop with learning assessments to see the extent to which skills and knowledge are enhanced. In a few others—often 20 to 30 percent of programs—some type of application or behavior change would be tracked. Still a few others—often 10 percent of programs—would be connected directly to business impact, showing the contribution of the program linked directly to business. Others, often around 5 percent of programs, would be selected for ROI analysis.

For a CLO to show value to the organization, there must be integration of this data—using technology—into a meaningful report to reflect what is being achieved and contributed. This can be achieved in a learning scorecard format—a tool that reflects combined measures along each of the value chain measures. This is not easy, but it represents a major shift. Chapter 8 is devoted to this key issue.

Success is also defined by the ability to adjust to needs and accomplish certain projects. For example, when implementing a major software change, a large banking unit had less than a month to train almost 10,000 employees on critical skills needed to use the software effectively. Thus, the learning had to be presented in an e-learning format. The learning organization was successful at developing, implementing, and training all the employees in the specified period of time. This is success, but only if the success is achieved with the outcomes in the appropriate learning value chain level.

Success is sometimes defined by the number of awards an organization receives. While important, this is often a misplaced or inappropriate measure of success. In almost any direction a CLO or other corporate professional turns, there is a professional organization eager to hand out awards. For example, global awards are available in the top 100 training organizations in *Training* magazine, the Building talent, Enterprise-wide, Supported by the organization's leaders, fostering a Thorough learning culture (BEST) training organizations presented by ASTD, the top CLO awards from *Chief Learning Officer* magazine, or the Corporate University Best in Practice (CUBIC) awards offered by HR Events. While these awards are well meaning and their criteria important, too often success depends on who is willing to put in the effort to get the award. Some of the best organizations do not allocate the resources to apply for these awards, resulting in a lower quality of applications and a misrepresentation of the industry stars.

The Cost of an Unprepared Workforce

Regardless of the approach taken to measure success, nothing is more devastating to an organization than not having a fully prepared workforce to address all the changes and issues they must face. Workforces are extremely dynamic, fast-paced, and rapidly changing; technology is changing by leaps and bounds, and the importance of customer service is critical. These challenges are often addressed through a variety of learning initiatives. Not providing the right learning initiatives at the right time to the right group may leave the workforce unprepared for these challenges. An unprepared workforce can reduce profits, impede market share, create inefficiencies, lower morale, and/or increase attrition. More importantly, it can affect the quality of the service provided to business customers.

Customer service has deteriorated in recent years; a lack of continuous learning and poor performance are the most prominent reasons for the situation. Some organizations choose not to invest in extensive customer service training because of the high turnover rate of the frontline customer service employees, believing that investing heavily in this area would be a waste of time. "Why should we train these employees when they will probably be gone in the next few months?" The more important question is, "What happens if we don't train them and they stay?" The consequences of having an unprepared workforce may be more devastating than the inefficiencies incurred by employee turnover.

From the other perspective, there is a huge payoff for developing the workforce on an accelerated basis. The success of having a prepared workforce is priceless. The CLO's support of the organization's goals to achieve the desired standards of service, quality, efficiency, and productivity can, in some cases, make the difference between success and failure of the organization. This can be achieved only when executives realize what is needed and have a clear understanding of the value that learning delivers. Consider, for example, a press release from Belk Stores based in Charlotte, NC. Belk is a large department store chain operating primarily in the southeastern United States. Belk attributed its jump in quarterly earnings to very successful sales and customer service training. The executives acknowledged that the learning function was the primary factor for improved performance in the organization. This acknowledgment is the ultimate definition of success, and it can be achieved once there is a clear connection between learning and business success that is recognized by executives.

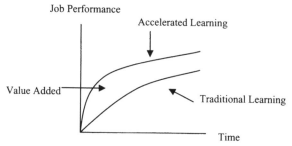

Figure 1-5. The payoff of a prepared workforce.

The problems associated with an unprepared workforce versus the rewards of having a prepared workforce can be illustrated best when how employees learn and adjust to their job and to the organization is examined. Figure 1-5 shows the impact of fast-paced programs delivered to employees as needed for new assignments. In traditional learning, it may take a longer period of time for employees to learn and adjust and then deliver performance. With focused learning on an accelerated basis—perhaps using technology and e-learning delivered just in time to the target audience and tailored to the individual ("just for me")—not only can the performance be achieved much sooner, but often higher levels of performance can be achieved and sustained. The difference in accelerated, targeted, fast-paced learning compared to the traditional method is the value added and can be highly significant for an organization.

CHALLENGES IN LEARNING

The CLO

The ROI Institute has supplied consultants to some of the world's largest organizations, developing a unique vantage point within the learning and development community. In that role, the Institute has assisted hundreds of organizations with measurement and evaluation, helping to bring accountability to learning processes. As a result, the Institute has had the opportunity to examine the success (and failure) of major learning and development programs in all types of settings. While there are numerous successful learning functions and CLOs around the world, there are still challenges for many professionals in the learning field. The following reasons explain why learning and development sometimes fail to deliver the expected results or the results that are possible.

Lack of Alignment with Business Needs

The payoff of a learning program comes from business measures driven by the program. If the program is not aligned or connected to the business, no improvement can be linked to the training program. Too often, a learning program is implemented for the wrong reasons based on a trend, desire, or perceived need that may not be connected to a business initiative. For example, consider the need to develop leadership behaviors in an organization. If a senior executive requests the implementation of a particular leadership program, the request may be based on a perceived behavior need and not necessarily on a business need. If the executive cannot articulate specifically which business measure should change as a result of the new leadership behavior, then a lack of alignment to the business strategy may exist. This is not to imply that specific leadership behaviors are not important. They are. However, at least for most situations, they should be driven by the need to improve the business—if they are expected to add value.

A major telecom firm faced this lack of alignment as they reviewed the major programs in their corporate university. One of the first steps they needed to take to check for business alignment was to attempt to connect core courses to some business outcome or business need based on the perceptions of the corporate university staff. If the staff could not readily make the connection, it was determined that the linkage did not exist. A more detailed up-front analysis was required to identify the needs. This leads us to the next reason for program failure.

Failure to Recognize Nonlearning Solutions

If the wrong solution is implemented, little or no payoff will result. Too often, learning is perceived as a solution for a variety of performance problems when it is not an issue at all. A recent evaluation of a major learning program for a leading US bank clearly identified this problem. The bank was attempting to prepare the commercial loan officers (relationship managers) to sell products other than commercial loans. They wanted the relationship managers to push the bank's capital market products and cash management services. However, the learning actually produced very little change in the managers' behavior. The study subsequently revealed the culprit—the compensation arrangement. When probed to find out the reason for lack of results, the commercial bankers quickly indicated that unless their compensation system changed to take into account the new product lines, they would not change their behavior. They would continue to sell only the products on which their commissions were based.

This simple example points to a very serious problem: attempting to solve performance issues with learning solutions when other factors-such as reward systems, job design, and motivation-are the real issues. To overcome this problem, the learning and development organization must continue to focus on methods to analyze performance rather than conduct traditional needs assessments. This is a major element of the shift to performance improvement that has been developing across the training function for many years. The up-front analysis should be elevated from needs assessment, based on skills and knowledge deficiencies, to a process that actually begins with the business need and works through to learning or performance needs.

Lack of Specific Direction and Focus

The learning and development process should be a focused process so that all stakeholders are aligned with the desired results. Otherwise, the results may be less than desired. The focus on results begins with the actual objectives for learning and development, which should be developed at higher levels than traditional learning objectives.

When developed properly, these objectives provide important direction and focus for a variety of stakeholders at different time-frames. For the performance consultant who analyzed the problem and recommended the solution, objectives provide a summary of what the solution is intended to provide. For designers and developers, the objectives provide insight into the types of examples, illustrations, role plays, case studies, and exercises needed to focus on application and impact—not just learning. The facilitators need detailed, higher levels of objectives so they can prepare the individuals for the ultimate outcomes of the learning experience—performance change. Participants need the direction provided by these higher objectives so that they will clearly see the outcomes of the learning solution. Otherwise, they have difficulty understanding how this program will actually help them or the organization. The sponsors of learning solutions—the key clients who pay for and support the program—need higher level objectives to recognize the connection between the solution and important business outcomes or performance. Finally, evaluators need this type of direction so they know exactly what type of data to collect to determine if the program has been successful.

Recognizing the importance of multiple levels of objectives up to and including business impact, a major package delivery company addressed this issue with a policy change. The corporate learning and development function decided not to develop any new programs without higher level objectives built into the programs. The CLO posed an important question, "How can we expect our management team to support a program when we cannot define the behavior expected from participants and the subsequent business impact driven by the program?" While this seems a logical argument, it does require additional up-front analyses, and not all programs should be subjected to detailed analysis.

The Solution Is Too Expensive

When the fully loaded costs for learning and development are considered, the program may not generate enough monetary value to justify the high cost of the solution. Consequently, from an ROI perspective, the program is unsuccessful. It is important to note that a negative ROI is not always a sign of failure. Many programs may add enough perceived value through intangibles and significant behavior change in the short term to overcome the negative ROI. The important point is that if a positive ROI is expected, then a negative ROI shows failure and is unacceptable.

In a recent impact study, a large bank's executive leadership development program was evaluated. The program offered an impressive design from a learning perspective, and included project assignments for the participants, mentors, and learning coaches. Unfortunately, the program proved too expensive for the monetary value that it added, even in multiple years of a benefits stream. When the fully loaded costs of the four weeks of formal learning in major cities around the world were added to the costs of consultants (to help with the projects), personal learning coaches (for each executive), and the designer, development and facilitation team, the total costs were high—almost $100,000 per participant—and the program was unable to deliver what management expected.

The good news is that many very effective learning solutions can be implemented with low costs; they don't have to be expensive to drive business results. Some of the most successful training programs have very low costs. For example, in a sexual harassment prevention workshop conducted at a hospital chain, the fully loaded cost per participant (managerial level) was $424. The ROI was 1,052 percent (Phillips, Stone, and Phillips, 2001). It is possible.

Regarding Formal Learning as an Event

A positive business impact must come in the form of behavior change from the individual participant, and behavior change does not easily take place. When a formal learning program is considered a one-time event (e.g., a three-day workshop), the odds of changing behavior are slim. Without the behavior change, the business results are not generated. A major physician malpractice insurance provider offered a variety of seminars for physicians to help them adjust their approach, procedures, and behavior regarding certain medical procedures. The programs were usually offered in four-hour or full-day programs, with no prework and no follow-up reinforcement. The seminars provided very little change in behavior, if any. This is not surprising.

Sometimes it is helpful to consider behavior change as body-building. An occasional visit to the gym will have little impact on the body. It requires a continuous process of working out, along with the proper motivation and support to make it happen. Learning new skills is the same. It must be a continuous process, not an event.

Participants Are Not Held Accountable for Results

Participants in learning programs must drive performance change if the program is to be successful. Without their individual efforts, the program will not be successful. When pressed for reasons for *not* applying new behaviors, participants are quick to blame others, usually the immediate manager. But that may not be the real issue. Figure 1-6 illustrates the groups or individuals who are held responsible for results. The participant is one category that is often overlooked and deserves more attention. Participants don't see their own change in behavior as their responsibility. Historically, when there is a lack of results, the learning and development staff comes under fire, as do immediate managers. What we often don't see is a focus on the role of the participant in the process.

This issue was underscored in a recent impact study involving a technology firm based outside the United States. When the impact of several leadership programs designed for different levels in the organization were reviewed, the results were not what were

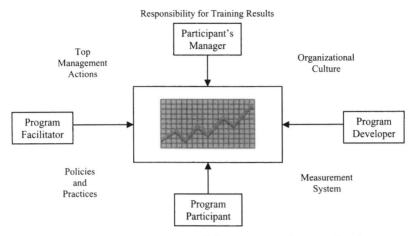

Figure 1-6. Major responsibility groups for results from learning programs.

expected. One of the major barriers was that each group of participants always identified lack of support from their immediate managers as the problem. Ironically, each level blamed the next level. The CEO commented that somewhere along the chain of authority a person has to accept responsibility and make things happen.

This situation underscores the fact that many participants can achieve success with learning if they are properly motivated to do so and are held accountable for their results, even in the face of an unsupportive manager. Typically, people manage the way they are managed, unless they are given new skills or provided with new examples to follow. Traditionally, the role of participants in a formal learning program is usually limited to attending the program and learning the skills and knowledge offered. Sometimes they are asked—even required—to apply the new skills on the job. While this creates additional expectations, this role has now been expanded. Not only should the participants apply what is learned, but they should ensure the consequence of the application reflects business results *and* report those results. Thus, their role is elevated from attending, learning, and applying to actually achieving results and reporting the data. This shift is accomplished through developing expectations for learning solutions, defining the roles of employees, and providing specific expectations of a person's role. With this approach, participants understand that the success of any program rests largely with them and disappointing results may be their responsibility.

Failure to Prepare the Job Environment for Learning Transfer

Without the transfer of learning to the job, there will be no performance change, and the learning program will fail. The learning transfer problem has been an important issue in learning and development for many years. Unfortunately, studies continue to show that as much as 60 to 90 percent of what is learned is not transferred to the job. The reason for this lack of transfer is a very complex issue involving many different barriers. While multiple barriers always exist, little attention is provided until it's too late. The result—the barriers interfere with the success of an otherwise successful program.

It is important for barriers to be understood in the beginning, as part of the needs assessment and analysis. When workplace inhibitors are identified early, they can be addressed in the design, development, delivery, and implementation of the solution. Efforts to minimize, if not eliminate, the barriers before the learning solution is implemented will pay off significantly.

Lack of Management Reinforcement and Support

Without management encouragement and support, participants will rarely implement new skills and knowledge in the workplace. Consequently, the expected results may not be realized. The manager's role is critical in the learning process. Most studies have shown that the two most powerful opportunities for transfer are the interaction between the learner prior to the training solution and after the training. If there is a lack of management support, it is a harder path for employees, but one that is necessary for improved individual and organizational performance.

Managers do not usually realize their influence; more actions are needed to ensure that managers understand their influence and what they can do to make changes. Some managers push back on this issue. Because their employees work in an empowered environment, managers should not have to probe and pry into the learner's individual application of skills. Participants should be empowered to use what they have learned, and they should feel free to do so without encouragement from management. However, learning new skills is a different situation. A new process implemented into the workplace, particularly one involving a significant departure from previous approaches, has more success with encouragement and support from the immediate manager. Just a simple inquiry about the success of the program and how it will be implemented into the work unit is often sufficient. The bottom line is simple—no comment sends a strong message.

Lack of Commitment and Involvement from Executives

Without the critical commitment and involvement from top executives, the learning and development function will not be effective; major programs will fall short of their expectations. There are many different ways for executives to demonstrate their commitment and involvement. Passive support or active support—both are effective in varying degrees based on company culture and leadership. Commitment equates to resources allocated to the learning and development function and specific programs. Involvement is the actual presence and actions—the active role of the individual executive in the process. The business literature is laced with examples of top executives taking active roles. Andy Grove, former chairman of Intel, sees learning and development as one of his key responsibilities. Jack Welch, former chairman of GE, devoted a prescribed number of days per month at the GE management development center in New York. Bill Gates, Microsoft chairman, allocates time to conducting a portion of the orientation for new employees as part of a rotating assignment with senior executives. Active roles by senior managers are critical and can be accomplished in a variety of ways.

Failure to Provide Feedback and Use Information About Results

Employees often need feedback about their performance. Developers and designers need feedback about program design. Facilitators need feedback to see if adjustments should be made to delivery. Clients need feedback about the success of the program. All stakeholders need feedback. Without it, the program may not reach expectations. The challenge is to provide a stream of information, as data are collected, to a variety of audiences. Reaction data and learning data are used to improve learning design and facilitation. Application data should be provided to those who are involved in the implementation of programs so that adjustments can be made. Business impact data need to be communicated to clients and others so that the entire group can see the value.

Learning from Disappointment

As the earlier reasons for failure illustrate, there are many issues that cause a lack of success with learning programs and the function overall. These issues have confronted this field for many decades and leave an important question: "Why do dysfunctional approaches still exist in learning?" We don't seem to have these repeated mistakes and dysfunctional processes for other areas in manufacturing, production, distribution, marketing, research and development, and so on.

Several reasons explain why we do not learn from disappointment. First, the field has not always been perceived as a legitimate function in the organization. Obviously, people need to learn, but is it necessary to really have a systematic, methodical process with principles and standards and operating procedures? Only in larger organizations was this ever considered a possibility in the past.

Second, learning is a small part of the total cost of operating a business. In the United States alone, organizational learning is responsible for $100 billion of direct expenditures, and that's just the formal and direct expenditures! While it is huge, this expenditure is a small part of the organization—on average it represents about 1.2 percent of payroll. For an organization spending 30 percent of revenues on payroll, formal learning represents an investment of only about 0.36 percent of revenue. That's not enough for many executives to be concerned.

Third, until recently there were not very many formal degree programs preparing individuals for the learning profession. Consequently, those who entered the profession were often ill-prepared and committed the same mistakes as those who came before, who were also ill-prepared. This is changing as degree programs—bachelors, masters, and Ph.D. levels—are now sprinkled through the landscape of the educational community.

Fourth, individuals who move to formal learning roles in many cases do not stay there for any length of time. By design, they are rotated through learning assignments even at the CLO position. This may be considered a developmental opportunity for some while a special assignment for others. Still others provide subject matter expertise needed to train others. Consequently, they are not interested in, nor do they have time to develop, standard processes.

Fifth, the profession has struggled with the issue of standards. Not until 2006 was there a certification offered by the field's largest professional society. In that year, ASTD launched a certification process to build critical competencies and certify that individuals possess these competencies.

Fortunately, things are changing in all of these areas. Executives are beginning to realize that learning is an important issue, demanding their attention. It also needs resources that are, in some cases, becoming significant. For example, IBM and General Motors (GM) spend over $1 billion a year on learning. They are realizing that the consequences of failed efforts are monumental. If a significant program is unsuccessful, not only is the expense generated, but precious time is unnecessarily expended, and the original goals for implementing the learning initiative still exist.

FINAL THOUGHTS

This chapter explored the trends emerging in learning and development and how they affect the CLO. Major changes have taken place in the last decade, placing more emphasis on learning and creating more opportunities to add value. These changes provide the CLO with the enviable opportunity to make a significant contribution to the organization. But to do so, he or she must focus on results, as well as select and execute plans and programs that are designed to enhance the success of the organization. When this is achieved, the CLO will also be successful. The ultimate measure of success would be no need for the CLO role or a separate learning function because learning would be fully embedded in the organization and into all organizational elements. The remaining chapters focus on the individual elements that make up the value adding roles for the CLO.

> *In my experience, the most effective CLOs are those who are passionate about their work, have a clear vision of learning, and work collaboratively to carry out their vision. They care deeply about people development, individually and collectively.*
> Pat Crull, Vice President and CLO, Time Warner Cable

REFERENCES

Bauer, Diane. "The Vital CLO: Accountability to the Enterprise and Beyond," *Chief Learning Officer.* April 2004, 24–47.

Bongiorno, George, *et al.* "Critical Characteristics for CLO Success," *Chief Learning Officer.* April 2005, 52–58.

Gratton, Linda. *Aligning Corporate Learning with Business Strategy.* Kingwood, TX: The Concours Group, 2004.

Kirkpatrick, Donald L. Evaluating Training Programs: The Four Levels. San Francisco, CA: Berrett-Koehler, 1994.

L'Allier, James J. "The CLO's Role: Preparing for Future Challenges," *Chief Learning Officer.* March 2005, 26.

Lindholm, John E. "A Study of CEO Perceptions of the Competencies of Workplace Learning and Performance Professionals." Unpublished doctoral dissertation. University Park, PA: The Pennsylvania State University, 2000.

Phillips, Jack J., Ron D. Stone, and Patricia Pulliam Phillips. *The Human Resources Scorecard: Measuring the Return on Investment.* Boston, MA: Butterworth-Heinemann, 2001.

Phillips, Jack J. *Handbook of Training Evaluation and Measurement Methods.* Houston, TX: Gulf Publishing, 1983.

Rothwell, W.J., *et al. What CEOs Expect from Corporate Training.* New York, NY: Amacom, 2004.

Sugrue, Brenda, Tony O'Driscoll, and Daniel Blair. "What in the World Is WLP?" *T&D Magazine.* January 2005, 51–52.

CHAPTER 2

Developing the Strategy

> CLOs *need to convince leaders that learning opportunities are a place to communicate their message. Use learning programs as a pulpit, signify the importance of them, and get information to employees so programs will be a beneficial use of time. The CLO's role is to move ideas, to create a boundaryless organization. CLOs need to prepare people to move information and barriers. They should create processes to enable decisions and ensure employees are well informed.*
>
> Steve Kerr, Managing Director and
> Chief Learning Officer, Goldman Sachs

The first step in examining the CLO's ability to create value for an organization is to review strategy. This chapter explores a variety of issues involved in linking learning to the strategy of the organization, and it includes current trends, processes, and successes. The focus throughout this chapter is on how to develop a strategy to create value and drive results for the organization. Because of the importance of determining the investment in learning as a part of strategy, Chapter 3 is devoted to various strategies for setting this investment level.

THE IMPORTANCE OF LINKING LEARNING TO STRATEGY

The Challenge

Connecting learning to organizational strategy has been a developing trend for many years. Learning was originally initiated in organizations because business strategy determined that learning was critical. The level of CLO participation in the corporate strategic

29

planning process has been increasing, and there is evidence to suggest that the CLO's role as strategic partner in learning and development will be increasingly important in the years to come. This conclusion is based on how the CLO responds to three basic questions that surround the strategic planning process:

- What is our business?
- What will our business be?
- What should our business be?

Learning is an important part of framing the appropriate responses to these questions. The CLO, as part of top management's strategic planning effort, can provide the knowledge and vision necessary to make decisions and take action that will provide employees with the opportunity to achieve success.

Learning is being completely transformed in many organizations. The result is a creation of strategic, value-added, critical business processes within the organization. To achieve value, the learning and development function is creating business results, assisting in strategy implementation, and helping in strategy formulation.

Determining exactly how learning is connected to strategy is difficult. Many CLOs have been successful in achieving the appropriate connection. There is more evidence of success than CLOs are willing to admit or divulge. They view the success as a strategic advantage and are unwilling to discuss it, much less publish it. In addition, some CLOs are attempting to make the connection, but they do not feel comfortable reporting the results because they are concerned that their process may not be perceived as adequate or effective.

When it comes to connecting learning with strategy, the role of human resources (HR) enters the picture. From the context of strategic direction, learning and HR are very closely aligned. Today, the CLO is focusing more on organizational performance, human capital development, organizational productivity, talent management, succession management, and intellectual capital. The role is shifting to one of a strategic business partner where professionals provide internal consulting on business unit and corporate performance.

Influences

The major influences connecting learning and development to strategy cover several areas. Although the connection seems to be a logical, rational evolution of the field, several important influences emerge. For learning and development to become more effective and produce the desired results, it must be closely linked to the strategic objectives of the organization. Otherwise, it may not add the appropriate value and move the organization in the desired direction. Thus, providing the right learning at the right time for the right individuals to generate the desired results requires a close alignment with strategic business objectives.

At the heart of any strategic direction of an organization is change and change management. Change is the only constant in most organizations, and learning and development is often seen as the driver for the change process. This requires the learning function to be more closely aligned with strategy as the CLO organizes, coordinates, implements, evaluates, and leads organizational change.

Recent interest in the return on investment (ROI) in learning and development has brought more attention to the strategic connection. As senior executives and internal clients demand a measurable return, the learning and development function must design programs with specific business objectives. These objectives are derived from an analysis of the business needs of the organization, which are usually defined by the strategic direction. Thus, the requirement to produce business results from learning is driven by business objectives, which come from business needs, which are connected to strategy. This chain of events links learning to the key strategic objectives of the organization.

As the learning and development function becomes more sophisticated, CLOs are planning strategically. Learning and development functions have mission statements, vision statements, and their own strategic plans, which, must support the strategic plan of the organization. Thus, as the learning and development department plans strategically, it becomes more closely aligned with the organization's overall strategy.

Top executives recognize the importance of learning and the necessity to use it in a strategic role. In some situations, top executives are applying top-down pressure to link learning and development to strategic direction. For example, some organizations have developed a strategy to transform customer service into a strategic and competitive weapon. Learning is one of the most effective processes to achieve excellent customer service. Consequently, learning is an important tool to fulfill a major strategic objective.

Finally, with increased concern about intellectual capital, knowledge-based organizations, and human capital development, some top executives are realizing that to sustain their competitive advantage, they must acquire, develop, and retain effective human capital. To do so, the CLO must connect the learning process directly to the strategic direction of the organization.

Overall, these major influences have placed considerable pressure on organizations to connect learning and development more closely with strategy. The evidence is impressive, and the progress has been significant. However, there are still more advances to be made as more organizations attempt to make this dramatic shift.

Influence of Corporate Universities

Perhaps no influence in the evolution of learning and development and its connection to strategy is more pronounced than the growth of corporate universities. Some argue that the corporate university is just another label in the traditional learning and development function; it is just renaming the process to enhance its image. Others argue that the corporate university is much different—designed to be more of a strategic approach to learning than traditional learning and development. Although definitions may vary, three definitions for corporate universities are offered here:

- A centralized strategic umbrella for the education and development of employees, which is the chief vehicle for disseminating an organization's culture and fostering the development of not only job skills, but also core workplace skills (Meister, 1998)
- A central organization serving multiple constituencies that helps the organization develop the employee capabilities required for successes (Moore, 2001)
- An educational entity that is a strategic tool designed to assist its parent organization in achieving its mission by conducting activities that cultivate individual and organizational learning, knowledge, and wisdom (Allen, 2002)

Whatever the definition, clear-cut differences between traditional learning and development with corporate universities are beginning to emerge. Table 2-1 shows these comparisons (Veldsman, 2005). Unmistakably, there are differences between the corporate university and the traditional university. The corporate university represents a new and improved version of the traditional university, reflecting a more strategic position for learning and development. Although many learning and development centers in organizations subscribe

Table 2-1
Comparison of Traditional Learning and Development, Corporate University, and Traditional University.

Traditional Learning and Development Department	Corporate University	Traditional University
• Operational needs	• Business needs	• General educational needs
• Reactive: present, "fix-it" orientation	• Proactive: Future, improvement/renewal orientation	• Reactive/proactive: past, present, future oriented
• Fragmented, learning events (the course/program)	• Integrated, on-going action learning/ teaching process (enhanced performance)	• Teacher-led/mediated process (the certificate/diploma/ degree)
• Short-term focus on programs (less than 2 years)	• Medium-term focus on programs (2 to 5 years)	• Long-term focus on programs (5 to 10 years)
• Limited range of learning modalities and delivery modes	• Virtual, blended learning: Anywhere, anytime, anyhow, anyone	• Predominantly residential, prescribed courses offered over and over within set periods
• Impact is usually known	• Impact can be developed with some effect	• Impact may never be known
• Individual, internal employees	• Intact teams/ communities of practices/sets of stakeholders	• Individual student
• Individual technical skills	• Core organizational competencies	• Generic knowledge/expertise/ skills
• HR as owner of learning and development	• Business as owner of learning/teaching	• Academic institution owns education

Adapted from Veldsman, 2005

to the concept of a corporate university and follow the characteristics outlined in the table, they choose not to use the name "university." For these organizations, the relabeling only creates confusion and detracts from their original and intended strategic roles. Others make it such a departure that it should be renamed. Thus, the term corporate university will rarely be used in this book. We prefer the term *learning and development function* or department, although many of the examples presented are from organizations that refer to these functions as a *corporate university*.

Strategic Roles

The CLO is poised to assume several roles in developing and supporting organizational strategy. In some organizations, only one or two roles are developed, while in world-class learning and development organizations, as many as five roles are defined to build a strong linkage with strategy.

Strategic Planning. The first important role for the CLO is to develop a strategic plan for learning and development. This brings strategy to the department and functional level. Beginning with a mission statement or business objective, this plan contains specific strategies that the learning and development staff members can understand and implement while staying connected to the organization.

Strategy Formulation. The learning and development department, is often involved in developing the strategic plan for the organization. In this role, the CLO has a "seat at the table" where strategy is developed and provides important input, raises critical issues, voices necessary concerns, and offers suggestions and solutions to shape the direction of the learning function. This is perhaps the most critical role of learning and development in its linkage to strategy.

Strategy Implementation. As different parts of the organization implement strategic plans, the CLO is often involved in the implementation with specific programs, services, and processes. Almost every strategy implementation will include the need for learning and development programs and services because learning and application are essential to achieve the strategic objectives.

Strategic Results. When learning and development programs and services are successful, business results are produced—usually linked to strategic objectives. Thus, the learning and development function is operating strategically as it drives the important operating and business performance measures.

Figure 2-1. Thinking strategically.

Training on Strategy. A final role assumed by some learning and development functions is to teach the strategic planning and implementation process to others in the organization. A successful organization requires an adequate level of knowledge and skills with strategic planning and implementation processes. Every employee should understand some level of the processes, requirements, tasks, and outcomes of strategic planning. Through consulting services and learning programs, the learning and development department can build the appropriate expertise.

Developing the Role. Several operational frameworks are used to develop a strategic role for the learning and development organization. A strategic role requires a major shift for learning and development where there is more focus on purpose and direction. As depicted in Figure 2-1, the early focus of the training department was on products or programs. The staff developed as many products or programs as possible, bundled them together in a variety of combinations, and published the choices in a catalog format. There was little concern about whether the program was needed or actually worked. The goal was to have as many products or programs as possible used by as many groups and individuals as possible.

The shift to a service-focused learning and development function was an improvement, where the focus was on ensuring that products and services met the actual needs of the organization. The client concept entered the process, and customer service became extremely important. With various customers identified, the staff focused on ensuring that customers were pleased with the products and services delivered.

The learning and development function is now strategically focused, implementing products and services and meeting organizational needs that are linked to strategic objectives. The focus goes beyond client satisfaction, ensuring that the products and services are closely linked to important strategies in the organization and achieving desired results. This mindset helps ensure that the learning and development function is adding value to the organization and becoming an important business partner with the management team.

STRATEGIC PLANNING MODEL

Several models are available that reflect the varied stages, processes, and steps of developing a strategic plan and process for the organization. From the perspective of creating value, the model shown in Figure 2-2 is the most useful and practical model. Each step in the model is briefly described in the following pages.

Develop Vision for Value

An important part of developing the strategic direction of the learning and development department is to develop the appropriate vision that reflects strategy and other shifts in the learning and development function. At times, vision starts with the value the organization places on its people. Although top executives *claim* that people are the most important issue, sometimes it needs to be more specific.

For example, at SABMiller, one of the world's largest brewing companies with operations in over 40 countries and beer brands in the world's top 50 (more than any other brewery), the efforts of the training institute is reflected in its initial value. According to SAB,

> Unquestionably, SABMiller believes in the value of people as a core element of business success. Today, SABMiller competes successfully in the global beer industry and is proud to acknowledge that one of our key points of differentiation is our Human Resource Proposition. Whilst virtually all our competitors leverage a brand-led or capital resource–led expansion strategy, our international expansion has been led by our people proposition. This proposition has established our reputation for attracting the most talented individuals. A corporate university allows not only world-class skills development, but an opportunity to instill in employees the corporate culture, corporate ethics and the soul of the company. Leadership by examples is SAB's corporate brand essence and this is woven into the culture the corporate university imparts to all delegates (Surridge, 2005).

The following vision comes from a large health care chain and reflects the connection to the strategy as the organization shifts from the traditional education and training to a learning and performance-consulting role:

We will exceed the expectations of our business partners by providing world-class learning and performance development processes,

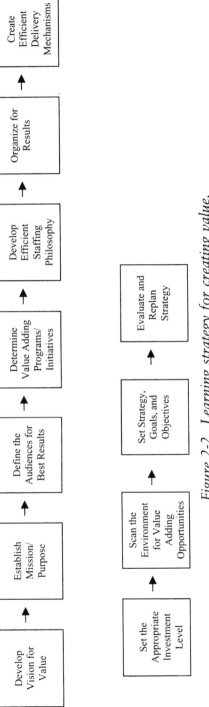

Figure 2-2. Learning strategy for creating value.

expertise, and tools driving superior performance. We will achieve this vision by:

- Consulting with our business partners to assess performance gaps, recommend improvement strategies, and shepherd ongoing performance improvement;
- Designing, developing, and delivering learning/performance improvement programs for work processes and employees— new and old; and
- Evaluating the impact of learning/performance improvement programs focused on the organization's strategic imperatives of achieving superior customer satisfaction, dominating market share, maximizing profitability, and promoting a culture of winning with highly motivated, well-informed, diverse associates.

Establish Mission/Purpose

The next step of the model is to develop the specific mission or purpose for the organization, whether it is a learning and development position in a major department, division, unit, subsidiary, or the entire company. The mission statement describes why the learning and development organization exists. It is usually simple, sometimes one sentence, and serves as the reason for being. For example, the mission of Motorola University was as follows:

To be a major catalyst for change and continuous improvement in support of the corporation's business objectives, we will provide for our clients the best value, leading edge training, and education solutions and systems in order to be their preferred partner in developing a Best-in-Class work force.

General Motors also has a learning mission. It is the world's largest vehicle manufacturer, claiming 15 percent of the world market. The CLO for General Motors has the title of President, General Motors University (GMU). GMU was established in 1997 and operates with 14 functional colleges offering 2,200 courses. Over 1.5 million total hours of learning are attained by 455,000 learners. GMU's mission is to provide leading edge learning resources for developing personal and professional excellence, resulting in technical and business leadership.

Sometimes the mission statement is quite simple and very specific. QUALCOMM is a leading developer in supplying digital wireless communication products and services and is the innovator of code division multiple access (CDMA), a technology that has become the world standard for the wireless communications industry. It is truly one of the most successful wireless communications and technology companies today. QUALCOMM's learning center's mission statement is: "We are committed to expand employee knowledge by providing learning opportunities linking overall business goals and professional development needs."

Part of the mission is defining the overall purpose of the learning and development function. Traditionally, the learning and development function has been shifting from an activity-based process to a results-based process. This is a slow process for some and a much quicker one for others. A learning and development function focusing on results with a desire to create value for the organization will quickly move to a results-based process. Figure 2-3 shows the shift that has been occurring for some time. The focus on results is more than just measuring success; it is creating value throughout the process from beginning to end. Programs and solutions are developed with the end in mind described by very specific business needs. Performance issues and objectives are developed beyond learning to include expected behavior and business impact. Results and expectations are communicated to a variety of audiences with the focus on learners. An environment is prepared to support the transfer of learning. Partnerships are developed with all key managers and clients, and metrics are utilized, including a healthy dose of ROI. More important, the planning and reporting is based on output, not input, as measured by the number of programs, hours, employees, and processes. This, in essence, is the focus of much of this book; to show organizations how the CLO is adding value along all of these dimensions—and others—as the shift to value is occurring.

Sometimes the mission and purpose defines the key strategies for learning as well as a competitive advantage. The following are QUALCOMM's key strategies for employee development:

1. A centralized and highly focused training organization;
2. Utilization of experts across the world to provide relevant, timely, and current content;
3. Multiple delivery methods to accommodate all learning styles, including access to distance education and online courses; and

Paradigm Shift in Learning

Activity Based	Results Based
• No business need for the learning programs/solutions	• Programs/solutions linked to specific business needs
• No assessment of performance issues	• Assessment of performance effectiveness
• No specific measurable objectives	• Specific objectives for behavior and business impact
• No effort to prepare participants to achieve results	• Results expectations communicated to participants
• No effort to prepare the work environment to support transfer	• Environment prepared to support transfer
• No efforts to build partnerships with key managers	• Partnerships established with key managers and clients
• No measurement of results or benefit/cost analysis	• Measurement of results and benefit/cost analysis
• Planning and reporting is input focused	• Planning and reporting is output focused

Figure 2-3. Shifting to results.

4. Opportunities for employees to align their professional development needs with the division or corporate group's objectives through individual development plans.

This definition of purpose also includes the competitive advantage, as shown in Figure 2-4.

Define the Audiences for Best Results

In many organizations, the "clients" of the learning and development function are predetermined by a manager or executive and may not be adjusted easily; however, sometimes there is some flexibility.

Our Competitive Advantage

- Outsourcing model which provides the highest quality of training from content experts

- Progressive/aggressive online learning model that focuses on providing learning opportunities to all employees anytime and anywhere

- Highly flexible organization with internal staff expertise in consulting, needs assessment, and instructional design

- Utilization of individual and organizational needs assessment to create customized learning opportunities

- Division-specific business needs aligned with individual employee development

- Strong focus and investment in engineering and management development

- An award winning learning organization enabling high employee satisfaction and retention

---

Figure 2-4. QUALCOMM Learning Center's competitive advantage.

In most organizations, there are a variety of audiences that can be served by the CLO. Figure 2-5 shows the variety of audiences in a typical multiple purpose organization.

Although a CLO may be part of a division or a subsidiary or even a business unit within a major organization, the same issues may be developed.

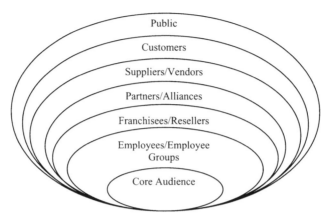

Figure 2-5. Target audiences.

The employees (or employee groups served) are at the core of any learning and development function. This key target group has several subdivisions ranging from professional staff to sales staff, to manufacturing, to technical support, to research and development, and many others. The CLO should focus on all employee groups and levels as this is the fundamental target for creating results.

The next logical progression is the one involving those groups closely aligned with the employee network. These are the franchisee owners or resellers, individuals who are charged with selling the product or services. This is an excellent audience for leveraging results. Most of the learning and development opportunities will focus on value adding processes that are easily measured and should translate into sales growth and market share enhancement. A notable example of franchisee training is Hamburger University, the learning center for McDonald's. Franchisees and their employees develop a variety of skills for job performance, providing a tremendous opportunity for improving sales, increasing profits, decreasing customer complaints, and preventing excessive employee turnover.

The next logical audience is the partners or alliances. These groups or organizations may represent joint ventures, alliances, or partnerships, both formal and informal. From the learning and development perspective, there is value in helping partners develop skills, knowledge, and capabilities, although the payoff may not be as direct as with employees, franchisees, and resellers.

Another prospective audience is made up of suppliers and vendors. For some, it may seem unusual for a supplier or vendor network to participate in the formal learning process. However, because of the need to have consistency in processes and focus on quality and standardization, some organizations provide learning opportunities for the supplier network. For example, the learning and development functions at Saturn Corporation, Honda, Microsoft, Cisco Systems, and Motorola provide a variety of training and development programs for their suppliers.

Another interesting audience group is the actual customers. While this group is not appropriate for every organization, some organizations provide learning and development opportunities for their customer base with the goal of enhancing the use and implementation of their products and services. For example, the learning center at Home Depot provides customer clinics, demonstrating how to use tools and processes to successfully complete home improvement projects. Microsoft Learning, through a variety of learning centers, provides all types of training and certification on the proper use of Microsoft products. Verizon Communications provides a similar service.

A final target audience is the public; companies target this audience by offering a variety of learning and development opportunities for anyone interested in improving skills and competencies. These are usually developed after a learning and development function has established a reputation for being successful in communicating their innovative approaches and ideas. Several notable organizations have developed these types of programs. In the '70s and '80s, Xerox developed a tremendous number of learning opportunities externally and ultimately sold this division as an external company. DuPont and Motorola have offered a variety of programs to the public. The Walt Disney Company designed the Disney Institute to provide customer service training to a variety of organizations. These programs represent a great opportunity to generate results as these learning components are usually operated at profit centers, sometimes driving a significant amount of revenue for the organization while enhancing the corporate image.

If there is flexibility, audiences should be selected for maximum results. Some audiences, such as those dealing directly with the customers, the public, franchisees, and employees, represent some of the best opportunities for driving results. Usually those connected closely to the customer provide the best opportunities for adding value.

Determine Value Adding Programs/Initiatives

The types of programs, solutions, projects, and initiatives sometimes affect a particular learning center. In many situations, the types of programs are set. However, sometimes there are options in terms of which programs are offered or delivered to the audiences.

Groups

The greatest opportunity for creating value is to deliver programs designed for and by the executives of an organization. Executive and leadership development can have tremendous payoff because behavior change and executive commitment is leveraged throughout the organization. Successful executive development can have a multiplicative effect in the business unit directed by the leader. With increased focus on succession planning and talent management, greater opportunities to develop leaders are being created. This may be the most crucial value-added type of development for a particular audience.

The next most critical area would be the middle managers and first-level team leaders. These individuals often need a lot of development, training, and skill building to be successful. The first level leaders are in a particularly vulnerable position, often caught between the management group seeking results and accountability and an employee work team seeking leadership and direction. At times, a team leader may have been promoted out of the group and often has more loyalty to the team than to the organization. A great opportunity exists to leverage results through development programs for this important group.

Another place to add value is to offer technical or engineering training. This is often specialized, requiring internal facilitators or external specialists, and, many times, is coordinated or organized within specific technical work groups.

Product and sales development is another area where skill building can add tremendous value, particularly to the relationship managers, client partners, and other frontline sales teams. Skill building and development programs can translate into direct sales increases, improvements in market share, and new product launches.

Orientation and onboarding are always an important part of the learning and development process. It is critical to bring employees into the organization quickly, efficiently, and successfully. This increases time to productivity and generates faster business results. Making sure that the employees are aware of the organization and its mission, vision, values, and culture is critical in the early stage. Many companies are spending significant time and money on extensive onboarding programs for senior leaders. This involves communicating job expectations, facilitating important connections, valuable relationships, and introductions to key stakeholder partners. A critical element of learning and development adding value is to reduce turnover costs through effective onboarding programs.

Need

Another important consideration when deciding on which types of programs to implement is how it will meet the obligations and needs of the organization. However, determining needs can be an elusive area because there are often more needs than the organization can or is willing to address. Some of the needs are personal and unrelated to the needs of the organization.

An effective approach to consider needs and priorities is to group them into two major categories: proactive versus reactive and renewal versus maintenance (Veldsman, 2005). As shown in Figure 2-6, there should be an appropriate balance between reactive (attempting to solve an immediate problem with a quick fix or to address a crisis situation) and proactive programs (scheduled skills, upgrades, and routine projects along with identifying opportunities for improvement). The other category is maintenance (those routine processes that are dissipated or serviced directly) and renewal (new material or renewed efforts from existing content). Strategies should examine these two areas to decide where the corporate balance should be for the learning and development center.

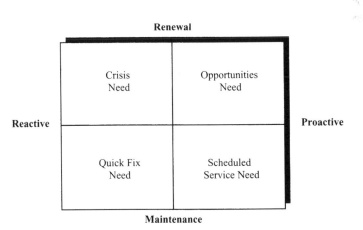

Figure 2-6. Different learning and development needs. (Adapted from Veldsman, 2005)

	Focus	Costs per Employee	Time for Payback	Risk for Payback
Training	Job-related skills	Low	Short	Low
Education	Preparation for the next job	Moderate	Medium	Moderate
Development	Cultural change and continuous learning	High	Long	High

Figure 2-7. Human resources development issues.

Value

A final issue is to make sure that the program selected can add value in a reasonable time frame. It is helpful to examine the nature of human resource development and distinguish between training, education, and development as depicted in Figure 2-7. Specific training is often job related, developing skills that are needed on a current job. The costs are relatively low, and the time for payback is short, leaving a low risk situation. Education is preparation for a job that an individual does not have at the present time. The costs are greater, the time for payback is in a medium range, and the risk is more moderate. Examples of developmental activities are cultural change and continuous learning, where the costs are often very high and the payback is long with a higher risk scenario. This does not suggest that all funding be applied to training—that would be a very short-term view. There must be an appropriate blend of these three issues—developing current jobs, preparing for future jobs, and bringing continuous culture change in the organization.

Michael Lee, the executive vice president for Human Resources for LG Corporation, puts it this way, "This is like the half-life of learning. Some types of learning activities such as training (how to make that widget) will have a very short half-life, whereas education (how to be an effective leader) has a longer half-life and development an even longer one." Investing in education can have a longer benefit than investing in training. That's because new technology, processes, and products constantly change and people need more training relatively quickly. Education, such as leadership development or decision making, does not change as quickly, so it delivers longer term benefits. The challenge is to be aware of the relevant time frames while examining the risks and rewards.

	All Internal	Partial Outsourcing	Complete Outsourcing	Insourcing
Analysis/ Assessment	X			
Design/ Development		X		
Delivery/ Implementation				X
Evaluation/ Reporting			X	
Management/ Coordination	X			

Figure 2-8. Staffing philosophy matrix.

Develop an Efficient Staffing Philosophy

Staffing levels reflect the philosophy of who should perform the work. Figure 2-8 shows the range of possibilities for specific learning and development functions for a particular large organization. The first issue is deciding which particular functions are to be performed by the internal staff or by others outside the organization. The figure shows the typical breakdown of functions. Analysis and assessment include the up-front costs of consulting, performance analysis, and needs assessment. Design and development are needed for new or revised programs and initiatives. Delivery and implementation include facilitation and delivery through a combination of methods. Evaluation includes reporting results by program and scorecard for the total learning and development function. Management and coordination involve providing the leadership and coordination of each program.

One of the options is to have all the duties performed internally. Some organizations prefer to do this because the work is unique and a specially trained staff is needed. This can be quite expensive, bureaucratic, and is usually not the most efficient method. Client services may suffer. In this example, the CLO wanted complete control of analysis/assessment (to ensure that the solutions were correct) and management/coordination.

Partial outsourcing may be the ideal solution when certain parts of the process will be outsourced. Because of the magnitude of the costs, some organizations prefer to outsource all delivery and implementation. This is the biggest financial expense of the learning and development organization. When this is the case, analysis, assessment, and evaluation are usually managed or performed internally. In this example, a portion of design/development is outsourced to cover peak workloads.

Complete outsourcing is another alternative, and for some, this may be the most efficient and economical way to deliver the needed services. In the example, evaluation is totally outsourced to maintain an objective view of results. Insourcing is a way to use internal resources that are part of an outsource provider. The external provider essentially "takes over" the function, sometimes using the previous staff. In this case, the delivery/implementation is insourced to keep costs under control.

The important issue is to staff the learning and development function in the most efficient way to deliver what is needed and to create a function that works for the organization. External resources can sometimes be more responsive, efficient, and much cheaper. Inefficiencies can develop when processes are duplicated and staffs become bureaucratic and inefficient in their operation.

Organizing for Results

When focusing on results, organizational structures are very important for the CLO. Structure can sometimes make the difference between an inefficient, bureaucratic, and unresponsive learning organization and an efficient, productive, and effective process. The first issue involves the actual reporting relationship of the CLO. Figure 2-9 shows the potential reporting relationships. Where the CLO is positioned in the organization often reflects the senior executives' view of learning. Ideally, the CLO should report directly to the CEO. This placement ensures the proper support and direction from top management and sends a strong message throughout the organization: Learning is important. However, in large organizations

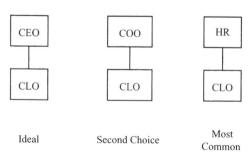

Figure 2-9. Potential reporting relationships.

with so many issues, functions, and priorities, the CLO reports to other executives.

A second choice is reporting to the chief operating officer (COO) or the equivalent role. Because most of learning supports the operations of the organization, this choice provides a direct link to the leader of that function. A growing trend is for CLOs to report directly to operating units to ensure support, commitment, and direction from the customers are most often served. One disadvantage is that the service to nonoperating units may suffer on the priority list. Another disadvantage is corporate oversight of the function and alignment with the CEO and their direct staff.

A common approach is to have the CLO reporting to the top human resources executive. There are pros and cons for this relationship. Because of the focus on human capital and intellectual capital, the learning component is an important element and fits naturally into the human resources and human capital arena. Many of their programs are complementary and highly integrated, particularly when involving performance improvement, organizational development, and talent management. A disadvantage for this relationship is that it removes the CLO from the top executive. In unionized industries, labor relations command much of the attention of the top HR officer, as in the case of most automobile manufacturers and service delivery companies such as UPS. With issues such as compensation, benefits, employee relations, health/safety and compliance taking precious time from the HR executive, the CLO may be left without the necessary support. Learning programs and initiatives need support from the top—visibly as well as emotionally—and a stretched HR executive may not be able to provide that support.

When organizing the function for results, the next issue is the actual organizational structure of the learning organization. While there can be many different structures, four basic approaches are used. Most organizations will either follow these approaches or have a blend of the four. Figure 2-10 shows the approaches, ranging from functional to global.

A functional approach structures the learning center into functional units of analysis and assessment, design and development, delivery and implementation, and evaluation and reporting. A structure based on programs builds on the specialties within learning delivery, ranging from sales and marketing to professional, technical, leadership, and manufacturing, supporting all business units and other functions.

The business unit approach ensures that the learning organization is aligned with the business units and providing staffing support. A

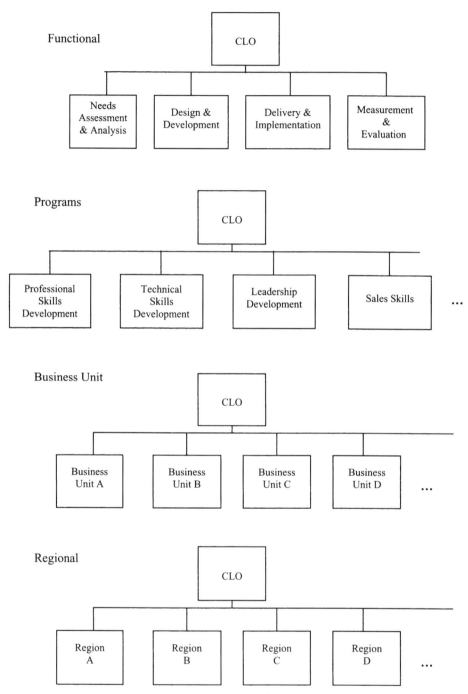

Figure 2-10. Potential structures.

variation of this would be to have support for the different functional units of manufacturing, sales, finance, research and development, and so on.

The regional approach is to break the organization down into different regions and provide learning support in a particular geographic area. The global approach is broader and has the learning manager for each country reporting to the CLO.

Whatever approach, the following issues must be considered when creating the proper organizational structure:

1. Position the learning function as closely as possible to where learning takes place.
2. Ensure that the learning function is as responsive as possible to changing business needs.
3. Avoid overlap and duplication across the organization.
4. Build the functional expertise within the learning organization to be expert providers of services.

These factors can affect not only responsiveness and efficiency but the overall effectiveness and value added to the organization.

Create an Efficient Delivery System

Delivering learning to a diverse audience requires a variety of learning delivery approaches. The first issue to consider is whether delivery will be on or off the job. The reality facing the learning community is that the vast majority of learning occurs on the job. Some estimate that 10 percent of the learning occurs in structured courses, 20 percent comes directly from others, and 70 percent is obtained through challenging work assignments. With this reality, it is important that delivery systems include both organized, structured courses and convenient, on-the-job learning opportunities using a variety of formats. One of the most notable shifts—an important issue in setting strategy—is the approach to e-learning. The use of e-learning has grown so significantly over the years that it has joined instructor-led learning as one of the preferred delivery methods.

Blended learning—a combination of e-learning, instructor-led, and other learning mechanisms—is a more appropriate approach for some. It may be helpful to review how General Motors University (GMU) tackles this issue. These are the specific learning challenges facing GM:

Learning Strategy

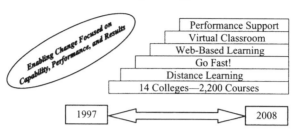

Figure 2-11. *Learning delivery at GMU.*

1. Budgets are declining;
2. Expectations are rising;
3. Time for training and learning is diminishing;
4. Competitive pressure is increasing; and
5. Everyone wants it faster!

Consequently, e-learning and on-the-job support are big parts of the solution. Subsequently, GMU has shifted from primarily instructor-led courses to a variety of closer-to-the-job formats. Figure 2-11 shows the learning delivery systems at GMU, which are transforming dramatically. Each step in the process has improved effectiveness, speed, and cost efficiencies through reduction in fragmentation, redundancies, and misalignment.

Another delivery issue is centralized versus local delivery. Currently, there is a gradual shift to making learning available locally. Gone are the days of having a centralized learning facility where people travel great distances to attend programs. This shift requires corporate universities and complex learning and development centers to become decentralized in the delivery of much of the learning. A closer-to-the-source delivery usually means that the learning specialist can be more responsive to needs, provide more efficient delivery, and drive increased results. The downside is that there can be duplication of products, processes, staff, technology, and expertise.

Another issue is condensing programs into small, digestible modules accessible through wireless technology (mobile learning or m-learning). The trend is toward fast paced learning and learning on demand as individuals need new skills or knowledge quickly and in short bursts. This often requires the use of learning where participants can remotely access a program as needed. This delivery is radically transforming the way learning is typically provided in organizations and will continue to grow as technology improves, more content is available, and fast paced and instant access continues to be critical.

A final topic to address in this section is the issue of learning solution versus performance improvement solution. Although this is discussed in another chapter, this is part of the delivery strategy—to decide if the processes provided go beyond the traditional learning and involve nonlearning solutions. For example:

1. To what extent can the learning organization confront and address nonlearning needs presented to them?
2. Should the learning organization provide limited performance improvement initiatives-such as reward systems, job aids, electronic performance support, and limited job redesign?
3. Are there handoff mechanisms to get others involved when nonlearning solutions are needed from other groups?

The important challenge for this part of the strategy model in creating an efficient delivery mechanism is to focus on both efficiency and effectiveness. Efficiency will add value by providing low-cost deliveries, requiring a shift into more e-learning and blended learning. Effectiveness creates more results and adds value through increased productivity, enhanced quality, reduced cycle times, and improved satisfaction. Delivery systems that are very close to the job, highly integrated into the job, and less disruptive in the workplace can make a difference in adding value. Because this issue is critical, it is fully explored in a later chapter.

Set the Appropriate Investment Level

Setting the investment level—the actual monetary amount invested in learning in the organization—is a critical issue for creating value, perhaps the most important issue in setting the strategy. Five approaches are typically used to set the investment level in the organization. An important consideration in strategy development is to decide which strategy fits the organization best and review it regularly. In some cases, a combination of strategies may be appropriate. Because of its importance, the next chapter is devoted entirely to these different strategies, including the advantages and disadvantages of each.

Scan the Environment for Value Adding Opportunities

Scanning the external environment for critical issues that will affect the strategic direction of learning in the organization is important. For learning, this may involve examining the quality of the workforce being recruited, which can have a huge impact on the scope and amount of training that will be required. The availability of resources for preparing new employees for jobs must be considered as well as the degree to which resources are available for potential outsourcing of analysis, design, development, and delivery.

Technology developments continue to play an important part in learning delivery. Even the legal and regulatory developments in the industry and in local areas can have an effect on the learning process. This would require the CLO and other key staff members to be constantly aware of the external environment, developing partnerships when appropriate, creating alliances to assist and share information, and joining major benchmarking groups to compare data when they are collected.

Appropriate resources should be used to develop the learning and development staff. As staff members develop skills, knowledge, and competencies of employees, they must also take care of their own development. Local resources and opportunities should be made available, encouraged, and supported by the CLO.

Finally, it can be helpful to brand the learning organization to create an awareness of the formal learning structure in the organization and to stress the importance of learning. Branding is not limited to audiences inside the organization but often extended outwardly, particularly if learning opportunities are offered to customers and suppliers. In some cases, company advertisements in the marketplace include external branding of the corporate university.

Collectively, all of these issues must be scanned, monitored, and evaluated. A mechanism must be provided to continuously update the learning and development processes, position, and team.

Set Strategy, Goals, and Objectives

These strategic considerations are closely related to creating value, and they form the basis from which to develop a strategic plan. This strategic plan is usually a formal document with some specific goals and timetables. The plan can be simple and straightforward or quite complex. For example, the operating strategy for GMU is straightforward:

1. Align to GM's global function.
2. Link learning to business results.
3. Improve global leverage and access.
4. Improve quality, productivity, and financial performance.
5. Increase e-learning and blended learning.
6. Focus on leadership curriculum and Performance Management Process (PMP).
7. Enable key cultural change.

These strategic objectives clearly position the CLO at GMU to create value for the organization. Strategy is delivered through a complex structure. Figure 2-12 shows how the alignment and key strategies are delivered.

GMU Structure

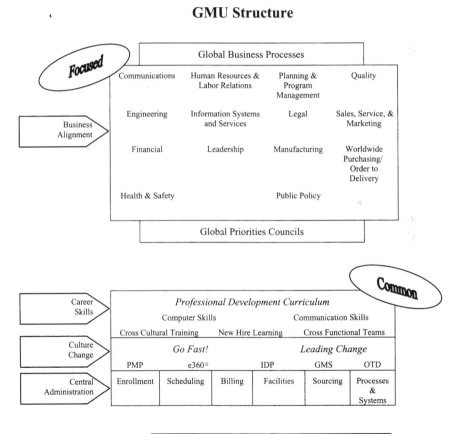

Figure 2-12. Structure of GMU.

PROCESS STEPS

LINKS TO STRATEGY

*Figure 2-13. Connecting training and development with strategy,
step by step.*

When developing the strategy, it is sometimes important to make sure the strategy affects different parts of the learning and development process. Figure 2-13 shows how the strategy is linked to different parts of the learning cycle. It is important for the connection to the strategy to be routine and ongoing throughout the organization.

Evaluate and Replan Strategy

A final part of the model is to evaluate and replan strategy. No strategy should be set in stone. It is important to review how the different components are working and make adjustments, as needed, to be more efficient and effective in the delivery processes. Also, as the environment changes, the learning function must change. And more important, as the organization continues to change and evolve, the learning function must adjust for that as well.

Perhaps the best illustration of continuous improvement and evolution of the learning and development function can be found in the SABMiller Training Institute—a corporate university in one of the

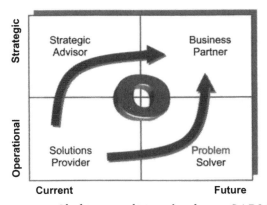

Figure 2-14. Shifting traditional roles at SABMiller.

world's largest breweries. The Training Institute began in February 1992 and initially focused on technology training. Training was dominated by classroom-based lecturing with no alignment strategy or vehicle for addressing future needs. Today, the Training Institute is vastly different. It covers the entire value chain for sales, distribution, marketing, HR, finance, IT, and leadership and executive development. The learning methodologies are much more sophisticated in their outcomes. The evaluation is more comprehensive and thorough, even demonstrating ROIs. Also, the increase in the use of blended learning techniques and multiple methods in their approach provides a more versatile institute meeting today's challenges. Finally, SABMiller has partnerships with external institutions locally and internationally, and they are aligned with national and international standards. Still, SABMiller sees their role continuing to shift. As shown in Figure 2-14, the shift is moving from a solutions provider to a business partner. This is consistent with many new development functions where there is a shift from a traditional role of simply providing learning solutions to being instrumental in driving and improving the business in a variety of ways and ultimately becoming a true business partner.

FINAL THOUGHTS

This chapter has explored the very basic beginning of the formal learning process linking learning to strategy. Although most organizations have an ongoing learning function, it may be helpful to review the current approach to learning and assess the degree to which learning is connected to strategy. A variety of issues and approaches are described, all focusing on how the CLO can create value for the organization. This focus on accountability, results, and creating value is critical to the success of the CLO and the learning process.

> *CLOs should be business planning people and build alliances with senior business planning people. They need to have interaction with strategic leaders in an organization and assist in removing roadblocks for the learning staff below them.*
>
> Kevin Wilde, Vice President and
> Chief Learning Officer, General Mills

REFERENCES

Allen, Mark. *The Corporate University Handbook.* New York, NY: Amacom, 2002.

Meister, Jeanne. "The Growth of Corporate Universities," *Training and Development.* November 1998.

Moore, Jim. "The New Corporate University," *Corporate University Review.* March–April 2001.

Surridge, Tanya. "Building the Business Case for Corporate Universities." Presentation at the Skills Africa Summit IRR. May 2005.

Veldsman, Theo H. "The A to Z of Corporate Universities." Presentation at the Skills Africa Summit IRR. May 2005.

CHAPTER 3

Setting the Investment Level

It's important to measure the cost of ignorance—it exceeds the investment in people by 10 times. All people should get access to education and training to keep them productive in the work environment.

Bill Wiggenhorn, Former President, Motorola University and Vice Chairman of Global Ed-Tech Management Group

One of the most critical strategic issues facing the CLO is determining the appropriate investment level for learning and development. While some use benchmarking only—and maybe to a fault—other strategies may be successful. This chapter details five specific strategies for determining the investment level:

1. Let Others Do It (Avoid the investment altogether.)
2. Invest the Minimum (Invest only what is absolutely necessary.)
3. Invest with the Rest (Use benchmarking to guide the appropriate investment.)
4. Invest Until It Hurts (Spend too much on learning and development either intentionally or unintentionally.)
5. Invest as Long as There's a Payoff (Use a measurement system to understand the value of learning and development compared with the investment.)

The majority, if not all, of organizations use one or more of these strategies. This chapter provides details, examples, and information to help guide CLOs to determine which strategy will best fit their situation. Although the investment levels may be set initially, this is an issue that should be reviewed periodically (Brennan, 2004).

LET OTHERS DO IT

Some executives prefer to take a passive role when investing in employees, attempting to minimize the investment altogether. While somewhat dysfunctional, this approach has proven to be effective for some organizations, depending on their strategic focus. This section explores the strategy of avoiding the investment in learning and development in detail, the forces behind it, and the consequences— both positive and negative—of implementing it.

This strategy is implemented using one or more of two different approaches. The first approach is to use contract and temporary employees in place of permanent employees. This arrangement allows the organization to add and remove employees with little or no commitment, thus reducing the expense connected to employee acquisition, training, development, and termination. The second approach is to use outsourcing to get the job done, often at lower cost. Taken to the extreme, employers can outsource most of the functions that would be performed by regular employees in the organization.

Several factors motivate executives to pursue one or more of these approaches:

- The cost of learning and developing employees. Some executives cannot—or will not—build the infrastructure to support learning and development.
- The need to bring stability to the organization, particularly as expansion and decline occurs in cyclical or seasonal industries. Letting others make the investment in learning enables them to balance employment levels, address particular needs, and control costs at the same time.
- Expertise may be unavailable in the organization. It may not be practical to develop the experience needed, so executives will take advantage of external expertise.
- Some executives pursue this strategy for survival. They cannot afford to invest in human capital, at least not to the extent needed to build a successful team.

Most CLOs realize that employee acquisition and maintenance is expensive. Table 3-1 shows the cost categories for acquiring and maintaining competent staff. The CLO is directly involved in all of

Table 3-1
Total Cost of Developing and Maintaining Competent Employees

- Recruiting
- Selection
- Orientation/Onboarding
- Socialization
- Initial Training
- Continuous Development
- Career Management
- Competitive Pay and Benefits
- Reward Systems/Motivation
- Maintenance/Discipline
- Exit Costs

these areas with the exception of pay, benefits, and legal and compliance issues. Because of the magnitude of these expenses, executives have a desire to avoid them. Recruiting trained employees reduces the cost of orientation, socialization, initial training, development, and on-the-job training. Although the salary and benefits may be higher than that of less skilled employees, other costs are reduced. Ultimately, this approach will cost more money because new employees will need to be hired as skills are no longer desired. The cost of hiring is typically more expensive than training current employees. Lost time in productivity is also a critical factor.

Executives hire contract employees in an attempt to avoid all of these costs, particularly the cost of benefits, the exit costs, and some of the acquisition costs. Contract employees should be ready to work and make an immediate contribution. Executives also outsource major functions to lower their total cost of human capital. Most outsource providers offer services at lower cost; however, their cost premiums can sometimes outweigh the savings of outsourcing.

Employing Temporary and Contract Workers

Because of the high cost of attracting and retaining employees, particularly in cyclical industries, some firms employ contract workers. This practice is based on the belief that the nature of the employment cycle can create unnecessary expense when employees are being acquired and removed. Table 3-2 shows all the cost categories related to turnover. In recent years, departing costs have become significant as employers spend large amounts on severance packages and services to enable employees to find other jobs. Some experts say the cost of turnover is up to 3x a person's salary. Coupled

Table 3-2
Turnover Cost Categories

Orientation/Training Costs	Departure/Exit Costs
Preemployment training	Exit interview costs
Development	Administration time
Delivery	Management time
Materials	Benefits termination/continuation
Facilities	Pay continuation/severance
Travel (if applicable)	Unemployment tax
Overhead (administration)	Legal expenses (if applicable)
Orientation program	Outplacement (if applicable)
Development	
Delivery	**Replacement Costs**
Materials	Recruitment/advertising
Facilities	Recruitment expenses
Travel (if applicable)	Recruitment fees
Overhead (administration)	Sign-up bonuses
Initial training	Selection interviews
Development	Testing/preemployment examinations
Delivery	Travel expenses
Materials	Moving expenses
Facilities	Administrative time (not covered above)
Time off the job	Management time (not covered above)
Travel (if applicable)	
Overhead (administration)	**Consequences of Turnover**
Formal on-the-job training	Work disruption
Development	Lost productivity (or replacement costs)
Job aids	Quality problems
Delivery	Customer dissatisfaction
Management time	Management time
Overhead (administration)	Loss of expertise/knowledge

with the high cost of attracting and developing employees, some organizations conclude that a highly capable contract employee is the best option.

Many organizations manage performance fluctuations by reducing the number of employees, often through a "last-in-first-out" process, which is frequently used by unionized organizations. This leaves the most senior and highest paid, but not necessarily the most productive, employees on the payroll (Nalbantian *et al.*, 2004). To avoid lowering employee morale by placing pay and jobs at risk, temporary and contract workers are hired.

Outsourcing

Recognizing the high cost of maintaining employees, particularly on a long-term basis, some organizations have resorted to outsourcing to keep their employee head count to a minimum. For other companies this is a strategy that enables a highly flexible, adaptive organization. Outsourcing can benefit a learning organization that is using external experts to deliver leading edge learning programs. This approach essentially creates a small number of employees and a tremendous network of subcontractors who provide services that regular employees provide in other firms or that regular employees previously performed. Outsourcing usually costs less and can bring in much needed expertise and specialization.

INVEST THE MINIMUM

While the previous section examined organizations that let others do the investing in learning, this one examines those that invest only the minimum. A few organizations adopt this strategy by choice; others do it out of economic necessity. Either way, this is a viable option for many organizations. This section explores the issues involved in selecting and using the strategy of minimum human capital investment and examines its challenges, consequences, and advantages. This strategy also has several hidden land mines that can be detrimental in the long term if not recognized and addressed.

Basic Strategy

This strategy involves investing the very minimum in learning and development, providing training only at the job skills level with almost no development and preparation for future jobs. Organizations adopting this philosophy operate in a culture that is sometimes reflective of the industry and the competitive forces in the industry. These organizations experience high turnover and usually adjust processes and systems to take into account the constant churning of employees.

This strategy should not be confused with efficient resource allocation. Obviously, efficiency is gained by keeping costs at a minimum. The strategy presented here is a deliberate effort to dispense only the minimum investment. This strategy is about facing the inevitable in some situations, or making a deliberate attempt to invest as little as possible in employees.

Forces Driving the Strategy

The primary forces driving this strategy can be put into three words—cost, cost, and cost. Some organizations work in such a low-cost, low-margin environment that a minimal human capital investment appears to be the only option. Low margin businesses, such as Wal-Mart, operate on volume to make significant profits. Competition forces this issue in many cases, and it is inherent in some industries such as retail stores and restaurants.

In some cases, the minimum investment strategy is adopted out of the need to survive—the organization must invest as little as possible to make it, particularly in the short term. These organizations are often managed by executives who see little value in their employees and view them only as a necessary cost to deliver the service. They consider employees to be dispensable, easily recruited, and quickly discharged if they are not performing appropriately.

The Cost of Turnover

Organizations investing only the minimum amount in learning usually do not understand the true cost of turnover. They see the direct cost of recruiting, selection, and initial training, but do not take the time to understand the other impacts. Both the direct and indirect cost of turnover must be taken into consideration. Since many CLOs have the responsibility for retention management, the cost of turnover is a critical issue.

The total cost of turnover includes both the direct and indirect costs. This total cost is rarely calculated in organizations investing minimally in their human capital. When cost is estimated, it is often underestimated. More important, estimations of the total cost are not communicated throughout the organization, leaving the management team unaware of the potential costs. Earlier, Table 3-1 listed the costs in the sequence in which they occur. This table suggested that there are many different costs, some of which are never known with certainty but can be estimated if enough attention is directed to the issue. When the total costs are calculated, they are often expressed as a percentage of annual pay for a particular job group.

Table 3-3 shows the cost of turnover expressed as a percentage of annual pay for selected job groups. As shown in this table, these costs, arranged in a hierarchy of jobs, are significant. The data for this table were obtained from a variety of research studies, journals, academic publications, industry publications, private databases, and professional associations. Collectively, these external studies provide a basis for understanding the total cost of this important issue and understanding that the impact of turnover is the first step toward tackling it.

When the phrase *fully loaded cost* is used, it is important to consider what goes into those costs. The turnover costs in Table 3-3

Table 3-3
Turnover Costs for Selected Job Groups

Job Type/Category	Turnover Cost Ranges (Percentage of Annual Wage/Salary)*
Entry level—hourly, unskilled (e.g., fast food worker)	30–50
Service/production workers—hourly (e.g., courier)	40–70
Skilled hourly (e.g., machinist)	75–100
Clerical/administrative (e.g., scheduler)	50–80
Professional (e.g., sales representative, nurse, accountant)	75–125
Technical (e.g., computer technician)	100–150
Engineers (e.g., chemical engineer)	200–300
Specialists (e.g., computer software designer)	200–400
Supervisors/team leaders (e.g., section supervisor)	100–150
Middle managers (e.g., department manager)	125–200

*Percentages are rounded to reflect the general range of costs from studies. Costs are fully loaded to include all of the costs of replacing an employee and bringing him/her to the level of productivity and efficiency of the former employee.

Table 3-4
Turnover Cost Components

Exit cost of previous employee	Lost productivity
Recruiting cost	Quality problems
Employee cost	Customer dissatisfaction
Orientation cost	Loss of expertise/knowledge
Training cost	Supervisor's time for turnover
Wages and salaries while training	Temporary replacement costs

contain both direct and indirect cost components. A complete list of the cost components is included in Table 3-4. This table contains a list of cost items that can be derived directly from cost statements and others that have to be estimated. Essentially, those on the left side of the table can easily be derived while those on the right side typically have to be estimated. When considered in total, excessive turnover is expensive and very disruptive.

Advantages and Disadvantages

There are many advantages to this strategy. The first and most obvious is low direct costs. Executives taking this approach strive to be the low-cost provider of goods or services. In doing so, they must invest at minimum levels. Another advantage is that this strategy requires simplistic jobs, tasks, and processes. These job elements make recruiting, training, and compensation relatively easy. Finally, this may be the best strategy for survival, particularly on a short-term basis. By the nature of the business, some organizations must operate with minimum commitment to employees.

Despite the advantages, investing the minimum in learning and development can result in negative consequences for organizations. First, a minimum investment strategy must be considered only in the context of simple, lower level jobs. Automation is desired if the jobs can be eliminated. If not, they must be broken down into simple steps. Second, organizations using this strategy must be able to cope with a high turnover rate. With little investment, employees will move on to another organization with just a slight increase in pay. Executives must ensure that hiring costs are minimal and initial training costs are extremely low. For example, McDonald's keeps the jobs simple and the training very efficient, resulting in a low cost to build job capability. With these costs at a minimum, McDonald's executives expect high turnover and are willing to live with and adjust for it. Third, this approach can have a long-term negative impact as the turnover costs cause the efficiency of the organization, the quality of service, and the ultimate impact on indirect costs to deteriorate. This is not a major issue in a fast food chain where jobs can be broken down into small parts and can be administered efficiently. However, for a manufacturing organization or a large customer call center, it may be difficult to deal with the high turnover inherent with this strategy on a long-term basis. CLOs in these companies are typically trying to increase the investments in learning and development. This is a difficult road to travel; however, with the right internal champions, changes can be made. Using benchmarks, demonstrating value-added contributions, and aligning to business goals will assist in increasing investment in learning and development.

INVEST WITH THE REST

Some organizations prefer to invest in human capital at the same level that others invest. Investing with the rest involves collecting data from a variety of comparable organizations, those that are often perceived as implementing best practices to determine the extent to which those organizations invest in learning. The benchmarking data are used to drive improvement or changes, if necessary, to achieve the benchmark level. In essence, this strategy aligns the organization to a level of investment that the benchmarked organizations achieve.

Forces Driving the Strategy

There has been a phenomenal growth in benchmarking in the last two decades. Virtually every function in an organization has been involved in some type of benchmarking to evaluate activities, practices, structure, and results. Because of its popularity and effectiveness, many CLOs use benchmarking to show the value of, and investment level for, learning and development. In many cases, the benchmarking process develops standards of excellence from "best practice" organizations. The cost of connecting to existing benchmarking projects is often very low, especially when the available data are considered. However, when a customized benchmarking project is needed, the costs are significant. Organizations such as the American Society of Training and Development (ASTD) have a benchmarking forum that uses a standardized tool for evaluating learning and development practices and compares them by industry, company size, and geographic location. Other helpful benchmarks come from articles in *Training, Chief Learning Officer,* and *T&D* magazines. These sources provide excellent opportunities to understand and validate investments in learning.

An important force driving the invest-with-the-rest strategy is that it is a safe approach. Benchmarking has been accepted as a standard management tool, often required and suggested by top executives. It is a low risk strategy. The decisions made as a result of benchmarking, when proven to be ineffective, can easily be blamed on faulty sources or faulty processes, not the individuals who initiated or secured the data.

Benchmarking is a strategy that can be used in conjunction with other approaches. With its low cost approach, benchmarking can provide another view of the learning and development function and the investment required for it.

Benchmark Measures

Investment benchmarks are captured in a variety of benchmarking studies focused on a few measures. The most dominant measure is the learning and development expenditure as a percent of the total employee payroll. The investment percent has become a standard in professional societies such as ASTD. In ASTD's 2005 benchmarking study, an average of 2.25 percent was reported. Best practice organizations showed 3.16 percent (Sugrue and Rivera, 2005). When smaller organizations are included, this number will probably decrease.

Other measures can be quite beneficial. For example, it may be helpful to understand the total learning and development expenditure for an employee in order to understand how much is invested annually or quarterly for a particular employee category or group. In the ASTD survey, $955 was invested per year per employee; best practice was $1,554 per year. Globally, the investment as a percent of payroll is usually higher in Europe and Asia (Shackleton, 2005). Another helpful measure is the total investment of learning and development as a percent of revenue. This is particularly helpful in the knowledge industry where the individual employee is generating revenue in many cases—in large consulting firms, for example. This shows how much is being invested in the learning and development of those individuals who are actually driving the revenue. The ASTD study reported 0.66 percent of revenue; best practice was 0.8 percent.

A measure used less often—but one that may be helpful in some situations—is to consider learning and development as a percent of operating costs. This measure recognizes that most of learning and development supports the operational issues in an organization and compares its costs with other operational expenditures.

The total investment, as described earlier, can be divided into different job groups, categorized by department, division, regions, or units. Still other ways to continue to analyze investment are by functional categories such as the following: analysis and assessment, design and development, implementation and delivery, coordination and management, and measurement and evaluation.

The investment number must represent a meaningful value for the organization, particularly when it comes from organizations representing a best practice.

Concerns

Several issues that often inhibit the benchmarking process should be addressed. The sources for benchmarking involve two challenges. The first is to understand the sources that currently exist for benchmarking studies. Here, the principal organizations are needed for benchmarking studies involving credible data. Table 3-5 shows some of the benchmarking sources that attempt to offer data across most of the United States as well as some limited international data. It is even more difficult to benchmark at the international level. A replication process is necessary for benchmarking in each country. When there are differ-

Table 3-5
Current Benchmarking Studies

Benchmarking Sources

- *Training* magazine
- American Society for Training and Development (ASTD)
- Saratoga Institute/PWC
- American Productivity and Quality Center
- Society of Human Resource Management
- Conference Board
- Corporate Executive Board
- *Chief Learning Officer* magazine

ences in the practices of the countries, making comparisons to organizations located in another country becomes fruitless.

The second concern is the organizations in the benchmark report. The measure must be meaningful, respected, and comparable. Many benchmark reports contain data that are not easily replicated or easily obtained in organizations. It must come from organizations representing best practice and those that compare well to other organizations. Not all benchmarking sources represent best practices. Often, they reflect organizations willing to pay the price to participate. Businesses use "competitive intelligence" to drive business decisions based on comparative and competitive data. It is important for a CLO to determine the right metrics for their own organization and management. Once a CLO shares a metric within an organization, they need to be prepared to share the same metric every year. Metrics should be replicable and easily obtained. CLOs need to be prepared to demonstrate consistency in their metrics.

Creating a Custom Benchmarking Project

The concerns about benchmarking may leave the CLO with little choice but to develop a customized benchmarking project. Although this appears unnecessary as well as expensive, it may be the only way to match the organization's interests and needs to those organizations pursuing the comparison. Incidentally, if more organizations developed their own benchmarking studies, there would be more available data from the various partners. Figure 3-1 shows a seven-phase benchmarking process that can be used to develop the custom-designed benchmarking project. Other sources provide more detail on the phases of benchmarking (Phillips, 2005).

Advantages and Disadvantages

Benchmarking satisfies a variety of needs and is used in several important applications. It is extremely helpful in the strategic planning for the learning function and in determining the desired investment level. Information and measures derived from the process can enable CLOs to meet strategic objectives. Benchmarking is also useful in identifying trends and critical issues for learning and development management. Measures from benchmarking can become the standard of excellence for an activity, function, system, practice, program, or a specific initiative. It has become an important measurement tool, as well as a routine management tool.

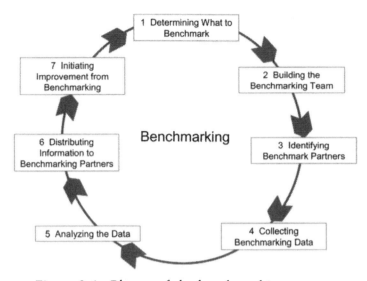

Figure 3-1. Phases of the benchmarking process.

The benchmarking process is not without its share of problems, consequences, and issues. Benchmarking must be viewed as a learning process, not necessarily as a process to replicate what others have accomplished. Each organization is different; what is needed in one organization may not be the same as in another. Also, developing a custom-designed benchmarking project is time consuming. It requires discipline to keep the project on schedule, within budget, and on track to drive continuous process improvement. Determining what the best practices are is an elusive goal; benchmarking can create the illusion that average data, taken from a group willing to participate in a study, represents best practices. Gathering national and international data is a difficult issue that often limits benchmarking as a global tool. Finally, benchmarking is not a quick fix; it is a long-term improvement process, and one that needs to be continually replicated to be valuable and taken seriously.

Invest Until It Hurts

While some organizations invest at the same level as other organizations, many operate under the premise that more is better. They over invest in learning. The results of such an approach can be both disappointing and disastrous. A few CLOs do this intentionally; others do it unknowingly. Either way, this is a strategy that deserves serious attention. With this strategy, CLOs invest in learning beyond what is needed to meet the goals and mission of the organization. Executives implement almost every learning program they see and teach every new idea that comes over the horizon.

Rationale for the Strategy

Some advocates suggest that overinvesting in employees is not an important issue—after all, they think, the more you invest, the more successful the organization. However, others will argue that overinvesting occurs regularly and is unnecessarily burdening organizations with excessive operating costs. Overinvesting puts pressure on others to follow suit, thus creating an artificial new benchmark. Investing until it hurts is often not a deliberate strategy. Executives are unaware that the increase in spending is not adding value.

Signs of Overinvesting

Many signs indicate that companies are overinvesting in learning and development. For example, consider the comments of the CEO of Sears, Roebuck & Co. when announcing disappointing financial performance. In an interview with a major publication, the CEO indicated that the company's poor performance was due, in part, to the excessive amount of training. Employees enjoy training, want to take any course that is offered, and store managers support the training. The result: There is not enough staff to serve the customers, causing customer dissatisfaction and ultimately loss in revenue.

Some companies make a deliberate attempt to invest a certain number of hours or days in training. Consider, for example, Saturn Corporation, once the shining star at GM. Saturn made a commitment to have each employee in the plant spend over one hundred hours each year in training. Manager bonuses were attached to this goal and trimmed significantly if targets were not met. As expected, employees attended all types of training. Some employees complained that they were attending unnecessary training programs—often unrelated to their work—simply to meet their training goals. What was once designed to show a commitment to learning and development turned into an expensive practice and, in some cases, a major turnoff in the eyes of employees.

The signs of overinvesting appear in an excessive number of programs. When Les Hayman took over SAP's Human Resources department, he revamped much of the curriculum at SAP University, the company's internal training organization. "They were spending more time worrying about generic training courses, such as negotiation training and time management," he says. "You can hire outside people to do that." Instead, he and the institute's director devised new courses that focused on specific tasks that SAP managers handled in their jobs, such as giving performance reviews. Drawing from his own career experience, Hayman also reduced the role of training in staff development. "You learn best by doing," he says. "So we build 10 percent of development around training, and another 20 percent around coaching. The other 70 percent comes from on-the-job training" (Kiger, 2004).

Forces Driving This Strategy

Several forces come together to cause overinvesting. Some of these are realistic challenges; others are mythical. Either way, they cause firms to routinely overinvest. During the 1990s, retention became the main battle cry. The labor market was tight, skilled employees were scarce, and organizations would do almost anything to keep employees or attract new ones. This often led to investing excessively in learning and development, well beyond what would be necessary or acceptable in many situations. It may be concluded that offering all types of learning opportunities helps keep turnover low and is necessary for business survival. However, many organizations—even industries—were able to maintain low turnover without having to resort to this strategy.

Some executives overinvest to remain competitive in the market. They must attract and maintain highly capable employees and are willing to invest in them. They sometimes offer all types of programs, which can cost the company too much. The talent becomes an important part of competitive strategy.

Some executives have an appetite for new fads. They never met one they did not like, so they adopt new fads at every turn, adding additional costs. The landscape is littered with programs such as Open-Book Management, The 7 Habits of Highly Effective People, Empowerment, Fish, and dozens of leadership solutions. Once a fad is in place, it is hard to remove, adding layers of programs and going beyond what is necessary or economically viable.

Overinvestment in learning can occur because organizations are unwilling or unable to conduct the proper initial analysis to see if learning is needed. Analysis will indicate if learning and development is the right solution to a particular problem or concern. Without the analysis, programs are conducted when they are not needed, wasting money.

Some organizations overinvest because they can afford to do so. They are very profitable, enjoying high margins and ample growth, and want to share the wealth with employees. During the 1990s, many high tech companies made tremendous amounts of money. A number of them overinvested because they felt they could afford it. When the economy turned, the companies could not sustain some of these expenditures.

Concerns

Obviously, overinvesting is not a recommended strategy. There are many problems depicted in this section that are the byproducts of overinvesting, not only for the company but also for the industry. The most significant disadvantage of overinvestment is the less-than-optimal financial performance. By definition, overinvesting is investing more than necessary to meet the objectives of the organization. The relationship between investing in learning and financial performance is depicted in Figure 3-2. As the figure shows, a certain level of investment yields additional financial results, but there is evidence of a point of diminishing return, where the added benefits peak then drop as investments continue. As indicated, the "overinvesting" area reflects no increased financial performance for additional investments. Then, there is a point reached where the actual performance goes down. This is excessive investing, which can eventually erode performance in the organization, particularly in industries where the human capital expense is an extraordinarily high percentage of the total operating cost. The knowledge industry is a good example.

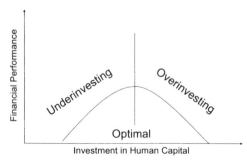

Figure 3-2. The relationship between investing and human capital.

The company overinvests in human capital and the impact on the bottom line is severe.

INVEST AS LONG AS THERE IS A PAYOFF

Some organizations prefer to invest in learning when there is evidence that the investment is providing benefits. They often compare monetary benefits of learning programs with the costs of learning. This strategy is becoming more popular following the increased interest in accountability, particularly with the use of ROI as a business evaluation tool. With this strategy, all learning programs are evaluated, and a few key programs are evaluated at the ROI level—that is, they are calculated the same way as the ROI is calculated for an investment in buildings or equipment.

The ROI Strategy

This ROI strategy focuses on implementing a comprehensive measurement and evaluation process for expenditures in an organization. This involves the possibility of capturing up to seven types of data in the learning value chain, as shown in Figure 3-3 (Phillips and Phillips, 2005).

Using this philosophy, only a small number of programs are taken to ROI, whereas every program is evaluated with reaction and satisfaction data. Also, when business impact and ROI are developed for a program, one or more techniques are utilized to isolate the impact of the program on the business data.

Wachovia Corporation is the fourth largest banking organization in the United States, with $464 billion in assets, 14 million customers, and 3,100 branches in 15 states. Wachovia takes a very comprehensive approach to evaluating learning initiatives. Data are collected for each program implemented by the learning and development function. All programs are evaluated for employee reaction: 60 percent of the programs are evaluated for learning; 30 percent of the programs are evaluated for application (behavior change); 10 percent are measured for their impact on business; and 5 percent are evaluated at the ROI level, where the actual monetary value is compared to the cost of the program. Table 3-6 shows the breakdown in terms of percentages of programs developed at each level.

IBM spends approximately $1 billion per year on learning. Given the sums involved, top management asked learning and development to determine whether this investment was aligned with the

The Chain of Impact of an HR Program

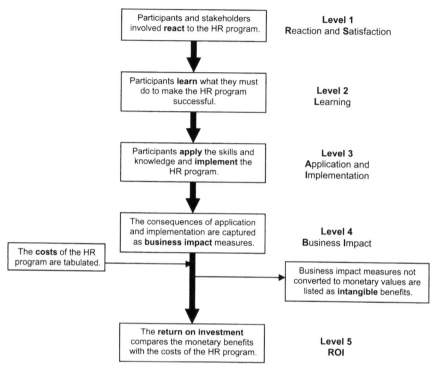

Figure 3-3. Business impact and ROI from an HR program.

Table 3-6
Evaluation Targets for Wachovia Bank

Level of Evaluation	Percent of HR Programs Evaluated at This Level
Level 1—Reaction	100%
Level 2—Learning	50%
Level 3—Application	30%
Level 4—Business Impact	10%
Level 5—ROI	5%

company's strategic goals and delivered an adequate ROI. In order to answer these questions, learning and development launched a measurement initiative to prove that learning is delivered in a cost-effective manner, reinforces the importance of human capital as a key differentiator for IBM, and ensures that the learning investment supports IBM's business priority of attracting, motivating, and retaining the best talent (Bates, 2003).

Forces Driving Change

Although the trend toward additional accountability has been increasing over the last decade, there are several reasons why this strategy is critical at this time. In the last few years, CLOs have had to demonstrate the value their programs and departments add to the organization. They have also had to develop the skill to communicate with other managers—in the language of business—the learning contribution to the financial bottom line. In a world in which financial results are measured, a failure to measure learning policy and practice implementation dooms this function to second-class status, oversight, neglect, and potential failure. It has become apparent that the CLO needs to be able to evaluate, in financial terms, the costs and benefits of different strategies and individual practices.

The increasing cost of learning is another driving force. As has been discussed throughout this book, investment in learning is quite large and growing. As budgets continue to grow—often outpacing other parts of the organization—the costs alone are requiring some executives to question the value. Consequently, these executives are often requesting or suggesting that the impact of learning be determined or forecasted. In some cases, the ROI is required at budget review time. A production manager, for example, proposes investing in new technology and incorporates into the proposal projected increases in productivity and resultant decreases in unit production cost. With this in mind, learning professionals must compete for scarce organizational resources in the same language as their colleagues and present credible information on the relative costs and benefits of interventions.

A special research report from *CFO* magazine provided input on ROI from the perspective of the CFO:

> There is an argument to be made for trying to calculate the ROI. Taken as a whole, . . . human capital is an unavoidable cost of business. When considered as a collection of smaller investments, though, there are clearly choices to be made. Which training programs are worth investing in? If managers can gain some sense of the return on these different options, then they can ensure that money is being put to the best use. This may

not mean putting a dollar value on the different choices, but perhaps understanding their effect on key non-financial indicators, such as customer or employee retention. (Durfree, 2003)

More CLOs are managing the learning and development function as a business. These executives have operational experience and, in some cases, financial experience. They recognize that learning should add value to the organization and, consequently, these executives are implementing a variety of measurement tools, even in the hard-to-measure areas. These tools have gradually become more quantitative and less qualitative. ROI is now being applied in learning just as it is in technology, quality, and product development. A decade ago it was almost unheard of to use ROI in this area. Now, business-minded executives are attempting to show value in ways that top executives want to see. Top executives who are asking about the value of the investment, including ROI, are viewing learning and development differently than they have in previous years and are no longer willing to accept the programs, projects, and initiatives on faith. This is not to suggest that they do not have a commitment to learning, but now they see that measurement is possible—and ROI is feasible—and they want to see more value.

The Value of the Investment (VOI) Methodology

Rather than focusing on the "return," some companies focus on the "value" of learning and development. Assessing the value involves looking at how much it would cost the company if they did not execute in a certain area. For example, how much would it cost if they didn't provide good customer service or if the company did not meet product schedules? Hence, providing learning and development is important. For executive teams that value education and development of employees, the VOI is important. In organizations where continuous development and education are a primary company value, metrics around the value, of the investment are ideal.

Common criteria used to assess the VOI in learning and development are as follows:

- Business change: learning that supports products, processes, or services
- Information sharing: increased information flow across the organization
- Effectiveness of learners: how people apply their learning

- Speed of decision making: reduction in the time it takes to make decisions
- Employee retention: acceleration of learning and growth
- Costs of not learning: wasting time, market delays, mistakes, and product failure

VOI usually does not involve a calculation of actual costs avoided and may not be ideal in all organizations or with all executives. The ROI methodology described next takes into consideration the costs avoided.

The ROI Methodology

To develop a credible approach for calculating the ROI in learning and development, several components must be developed and integrated as depicted in Figure 3-4. This strategy comprises five important elements:

1. An evaluation framework is needed to define the various levels of evaluation and types of data, as well as how data are captured.
2. A process model must be created to provide a step-by-step procedure for developing the ROI calculation. Part of this process is the isolation of the effects of a program from other factors in order to show its monetary payoff.
3. A set of operating standards with a conservative philosophy is required. These "guiding principles" keep the process on track to ensure successful replication. The operating standards also build credibility with key stakeholders in the organization.

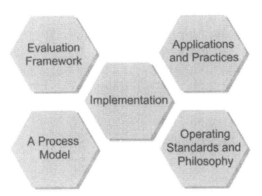

Figure 3-4. The key elements of the ROI process.

4. Resources should be devoted to implementation to ensure that the ROI methodology becomes operational and routine in the organization. Implementation addresses issues such as responsibilities, policies, procedures, guidelines, goals, and internal skill building.
5. Successful applications are critical to show how ROI works with different types of programs and projects.

Together, these elements are necessary to develop a comprehensive evaluation system that contains a balanced set of measures, has credibility with the various stakeholders involved, and can be easily replicated. Because of the importance of and interest in this ROI strategy, the remainder of this chapter is devoted to taking a closer look at these five essential pieces.

Chapter 8 focuses directly on the measures that are used—including the actual ROI—showing how they can be collected, not only on an individual program basis, but in an overall format for a learning and development scorecard.

Advantages and Disadvantages

The ROI methodology has several important advantages. With it, the learning and development staff and the client will know the specific contribution of a program in a language the client understands. Measuring the ROI is one of the most convincing ways to earn the respect and support of the senior management team—not only for a particular program, but for the learning and development function as well. The client, who requests and authorizes a learning program or project will have a complete set of data to show the overall success of the process.

Because a variety of feedback data are collected during the program implementation, the comprehensive analysis provides data to drive changes in processes and make adjustments during implementation. Throughout the cycle of program design, development, and implementation, the entire team of stakeholders focuses on results. If a program is not effective, and the results are not materializing, the ROI methodology will prompt modifications. On rare occasions, the program may have to be halted if it is not adding the appropriate value.

This methodology is not suitable for every organization and certainly not for every program. It has some very important barriers to success. The ROI methodology adds additional costs and time to the learning budget, but not a significant amount—probably no more than 3 to 5 percent of the total direct learning and development budget. The additional investment in ROI should be offset by the results achieved from implementation. However, this barrier often stops many ROI implementations early in the process. Many staff members may not have the basic skills necessary to apply the ROI methodology within their scope of responsibilities. The typical learning program does not focus on results, but on qualitative feedback data. It is necessary to shift learning and development policy and practice from an activity-based approach to a results-based approach. Some staff members do not pursue ROI because they perceive the methodology as an individual performance evaluation process instead of a process improvement tool.

FINAL THOUGHTS

This chapter has explored the five different strategies that are being used to set the investment level in learning and development. While some strategies appear to be dysfunctional, there are often logical reasons for using any one of them. Letting Others Do It is a strategy to avoid investing altogether. For some, this fits the overall mission of the organization and may be an appropriate method to achieve a corporate strategy. Investing Only the Minimum may be a requirement for survival for many organizations, although it often leads to serious turnover issues. Investing with the Rest is a very popular approach that uses benchmarking, although the data may not truly represent best practice organizations. Invest Until It Hurts can be a dysfunctional approach that is harmful to both the organization and the profession. Finally, Investing When There Is a Payoff is an emerging strategy to show the organization the return on the learning and development investment. This process is explored in more detail in Chapter 8.

To look at this from an ROI perspective, culture building has more return on value than competency since the information retained is used longer and doesn't get outdated as quickly.
Michael Lee, Executive Vice President of
Human Resources, LG Corp.

REFERENCES

Bates, Stephen. *Linking People Measures to Strategy.* Research Report R-1342-03RR. New York, NY: The Conference Board, 2003.

Brennan, Michael. "The Chief Learning Officer's Investment Portfolio," *Chief Learning Officer.* July 2004, 54–56.

Durfree, Don. *Human Capital Management: The CFO's Perspective.* Boston, MA: CFO Publishing Corp., 2003.

Kiger, Patrick J. "Les Hayman's Excellent Adventure," *Workforce Management.* August 2004, 43.

Nalbantain, Haig R., *et al. Play to Your Strengths: Managing Your Internal Labor Markets for Lasting Competitive Advantage.* New York, NY: McGraw-Hill, 2004.

Phillips, Jack J. *Investing in Your Company's Human Capital: Strategies to Avoid Spending Too Much or Too Little.* New York, NY: Amacom, 2005.

Phillips, Jack J., and Patricia P. Phillips. *Proving the Value of HR.* Alexandria, VA: Society for Human Resource Management, 2005.

Shackleton, J.R. "The Impact of Economic Circumstances of Training Spending: How Was It for You?" *Reflections on the 2005 Training Development Survey.* CIPD, 2005, 22–24.

Sugrue, Brenda, and Ray J. Rivera. *State of the Industry.* Alexandria, VA: ASTD, 2005, 6–7.

CHAPTER 4

Align the Learning Enterprise with Business Needs

> *To create an effective learning strategy CLOs should start by understanding what senior leadership is trying to achieve and aligning with their business goals.*
> Frank Anderson, President, Defense Acquisition University

IT IS ABOUT THE BUSINESS

CLOs are committing more resources—both time and money—for needs assessment and analysis to ensure that learning and development programs are necessary and are linked to individual and organizational performance. Several methods are being used to identify precise organizational and individual performance needs, learning needs, and non-learning solutions. The result is a more focused learning strategy and delivery—creating additional value for the organization.

Number One Problem

The ROI Institute conducted a review of over 800 impact studies of learning and development programs. In this review, the goal was to understand what caused the learning and development program to fall short of its potential. Some of the programs were outright failures and the studies uncovered the causes. In others, there was success, but additional success could have been achieved, and this review uncovered the barriers to additional success. This review identified 11 key categories that led to lack of success. The number one cause was lack of alignment to the business. In many of these studies, there was insufficient evidence, if any, that the learning solution was actually connected to the business. In some studies, there was no alignment with any business issue, yet several stakeholders wanted to have this alignment; they wanted the programs to connect to the business in some way. These disappointing results underscore the tremendous challenge facing learning and development professionals to ensure that a proper needs assessment is conducted and, in some cases, provide evidence of linkage to business measure.

THE CHALLENGE

A Growing Trend

Companies today demand innovative senior leaders who inspire confidence, middle managers who can translate the corporate vision for their functional or geographic area, and front-line managers who can get the job done. Directly or indirectly, these challenges rely heavily on learning and development, whether provided by internal corporate departments or external partners. Yet, discussions about linking strategy to learning are often dysfunctional. Perhaps some managers think that learning should be independent of corporate strategy because they've had too many top executives whose idea of strategy was a flavor-of-the-month. Fortunately, this is changing (Houde, 2005).

Organizations are now focusing increased attention on evaluation, which often leads to a more detailed and accurate needs assessment process. It is critical for learning and development professionals to conduct thorough needs assessments so they can achieve appropriate evaluation metrics. Thinking about how to evaluate a program or initiative first can result in a better needs assessment on the front end. Studies that have shown an increased use of evaluations have also revealed additional emphasis on the needs assessment process.

The increased emphasis on the bottom-line contribution and return on investment (ROI) in learning and development is driving increased emphasis on needs assessment and analysis. As organizations attempt to evaluate programs at this level, deficiencies in the needs assessment process are often revealed, leading to added attention and more resources developed, and trained in, needs assessment and analysis.

One of the foundations of the performance consulting process is bringing more attention to the front-end analysis to determine specific business needs. Several studies have indicated an increase in the needs assessment process as the performance analysis process has been implemented.

Because of the vital role that needs assessment plays in the learning and development process, failure to address this process properly can lead to ineffective or failed training efforts. Organizations are now placing more emphasis on the needs assessment process as an integral and routine part of the analysis. One of the key areas of focus is on development of the learning and development staff to ensure that they are trained to conduct effective needs assessment. Programs like those offered by the ROI Institute (certification), CPI/performance consulting, performance consulting (Robinson) and impact mapping (Brinkerhoff) are good developmental opportunities for staff interested in expanding their knowledge in needs assessment and evaluation. It is critical for learning professionals to become experts at understanding business and individual needs.

The learning and development process is mature in most organizations, and this maturity is obvious as learning and development staff has carved out a legitimate place in the organization. As it matures, more attention is placed on improving the basic elements of the process. Needs assessment is one of the key elements accepted as a necessary and important part of the process. Unfortunately, in the early evolution of the learning and development function, needs assessment was sometimes omitted. As the process matured, more resources were devoted to it.

In many organizations, the payoff of the needs assessment is beginning to be realized. Consequently, additional resources for needs assessment are allocated. In some situations, the needs assessment benefits are documented and compared to investment in the process. For example, when the needs assessment and analysis process results in a lower cost solution, the net value is documented and becomes an item of the total savings generated by needs assessment and analysis. The actual and potential payoff is causing some CLOs to invest more in needs assessment and analysis.

Finding the Business Need

Although proper analysis should begin with a business need, sometimes the challenge is to identify a particular business issue or

need in the organization. Today, the CLO must have a solid comprehension of the business and the challenges surrounding the business. When requests for learning programs are made, the CLO must
have some understanding of the potential business connection even
before an analysis is conducted. To be engaged in organizational
issues and tuned into business needs, the CLO must focus on several
important areas:

- *Operational issues and an understanding of the methods,
  processes, and the concerns of the organization.* More important, they must understand the operational flow of the organization, which often defines learning needs.
- *The key metrics across the organization in all areas.* What are
  the important measures in each function? What are the top three
  or four? These are often issues that spawn learning program
  requests when the metric is not doing so well.
- *Serious problems and challenges facing the organization.*
  Serious problems may involve quality, customer service, talent
  shortage, or high absenteeism. These problems lead to bottle-
  necks, which lead to disruptions, inefficiency, and poor service.
  Most of all, they have a negative impact on the organization
  and create learning needs.
- *The strategic plans: where the organization is going and how
  particular programs or projects fit into those plans.* Ideally, this
  is part of the strategic planning process and projects are considered at the time the strategic plans are developed. An ongoing assessment of overall strategic plans and even strategic
  plans in different functional areas of the organization will help
  the CLO stay abreast of important issues. Figure 4-1 shows the
  strategy—learning relationships at Old Mutual, a large insurance and financial services company based in Europe (Pillay,
  2005).
- *The tactical plans with operating and performance goals.* These
  plans often translate directly into training and learning requests.
  Being aware of these performance goals throughout the organization can help the CLO relate training needs and requests to
  those areas.
- *Opportunities for improvement.* Throughout the organization,
  individuals and groups are discussing, reviewing, identifying, or
  suggesting opportunities for improvements. Often, the learning
  and development group is key to seizing these opportunities and
  turning them into payoff situations. For example, new product

Strategy—Learning Interaction

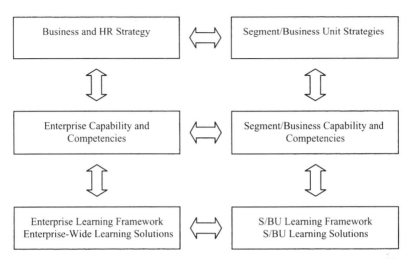

Figure 4-1. Strategy—learning interaction at Old Mutual.

development, the use of technology, and service delivery improvements represent important opportunities.

- *Industry.* Every industry segment has one or more specific areas that often create challenges, and the CLO must be aware of them. For example, in the restaurant and retail store industries, employee turnover is almost always an issue; in heavy manufacturing and mining, safety is a critical issue; in the financial services industry, consolidation is a major issue; and in technology, innovation is a critical issue. Being aware of these issues might create opportunities for initiatives or programs aimed at tackling these problems.

- *Market and Industry.* The CLO must understand the market in which the organization serves and how the products and services fit into those markets. Understanding the market and industry helps the learning function respond to requests for new talent and new skills to meet these challenges.

These are just a few of the many areas that the CLO must understand, and be constantly aligned with, to be a genuine business partner. In addition, it is an essential first step for needs assessment.

Dilemma of Analysis

The analysis portion of needs assessment is often misplaced, mis-understood, and misrepresented. Additional analysis conjures up images of complex problems, confusing models, and a plethora of data with complicated statistical techniques. In reality, needs analysis does not have to be so complicated—simple techniques may uncover the appropriate learning needs.

Analysis is not often pursued in the necessary detail for several major reasons:

- *Learning needs appear to point to a solution.* When analysis is conducted at the skill level, results sometimes indicate a solution that may not be linked to a particular business need. Thus, in some major initiatives or programs, additional analysis must be conducted to connect the learning need with the business need to ensure that they are aligned. This underscores the weaknesses of self assessments for learning needs. Employees may indicate a particular need or skill gap that may or may not be related to improving job performance or a particular business initiative.

- *Learning solutions appear to be obvious.* Some learning solutions appear obvious when examining certain types of data. For example, where there is a high employee turnover and employees are suggesting in exit interviews that their supervisors are not treating them with respect and dignity, there appears to be a learning need. The managers need to learn how to demonstrate care and compassion for the employees. In reality, the supervisors may know how to do that, but they are not encouraged or required to do so. Thus, a seemingly obvious solution may not be the correct solution. Additional analyses can reveal this.

- *Managers often have an opinion about the "learning solution."* Sometimes, managers think that any deficiency in a business measure is automatically linked to a lack of knowledge. When employees do not perform satisfactorily, managers assume it is because they do not know how to perform. For example, if employees are not delivering consistent and helpful customer service, it is assumed that they do not know how to do this. In reality, they may know how, but are not required, encouraged, or otherwise rewarded for providing excellent service.

- *Analysis takes too much time.* A proper needs assessment will take time and consume resources. However, the consequences of no needs assessment or an inadequate needs assessment can be more expensive. If learning solutions are implemented without determining specific needs, time and resources may be wasted—the results can be more damaging than doing nothing at all. If incorrect solutions are implemented, the consequences can be more devastating. The problem still exists, but the resources have been wasted in other learning programs. When planned properly and pursued professionally, a needs assessment and analysis can be completed within the organization's budget and time constraints. The key is to focus on efficient tools and processes for the situation.
- *Analysis appears confusing.* Determining the causes of performance problems and the link to business needs may appear to be complex and confusing. However, some analyses are simple, straightforward, and achieve excellent results. The process does not have to be so sophisticated, confusing, and statistically precise.

With these misconceptions about needs assessment and analysis, the difficulty to use more analysis becomes apparent. This is a critical issue that cannot be omitted; otherwise, the learning cycle is flawed from the beginning.

Deflecting a Request for a Learning Program

One of the most challenging issues facing the learning function, and sometimes the CLO, is how to deflect a request for a new learning program to more analysis—especially when the requestor is an executive and wants no additional analysis. In some cases, the requests are accompanied with instructions to conduct no analyses; the executive has determined that the problem is a learning issue and implementation by the CLO is expected. These executives are not interested in additional analysis because they have made their decision. What should the CLO do? More specifically, what should the learning and development staff do as these requests are routinely brought to the learning and development function? Here are a few strategies that have proven effective for some learning and development organizations:

1. *Ask pertinent questions.* "What will change on your perform-ance goals, scorecard, dashboard, or operating report if this learning need is achieved?" Based on that response, several follow-up questions should be asked. If the measures are iden-tified, the obvious question is, "How did you determine that this solution is connected to that measure?" If the executive cannot clearly identify what will change, the issue at hand is obvious. If there is no business connection, the question must be raised as to whether this program or initiative should be implemented. Several other follow-up questions can uncover flaws in the analysis, if they exist. In some cases, the executive may retreat or request analysis to uncover the answers to the questions.

2. *Remind the requestor of the possible consequences of imple-menting this program without additional analysis.* In essence, if this program is not the proper solution, the need that pre-cipitated this request will still exist and the organization will have expended valuable resources addressing the wrong issues. Essentially, the problem is made worse, time and money have been wasted, the correct solution has been delayed, and the image of the learning and development process has been tar-nished. With this reminder, the executive may allow additional analysis, at least on a limited basis.

3. *Conduct a low-profile analysis.* Almost every learning solution request will require some time for implementation as the content is finalized, programs are purchased, and logistics are organized. During this time, a low-profile analysis may be con-ducted concurrently to see if the learning need will address the problem that led to the request. If this analysis reveals inconsistencies with the original conclusion, the data may be presented to the requestor with the comment, "As we were working with subject matter experts to implement the program, we uncovered these particular concerns, which indi-cate that this may not be the correct solution." Additional analysis may be allowed.

4. *If the preceding arguments are not effective, show the requestor how much the project will cost.* In this case, the fully loaded cost profile may have more impact. Ask the question, "Are we willing to spend this amount of money ($500,000, for example) to implement a program when we're not sure that it is the right solution?" This may cause the executive to rethink the situa-tion. Because this expenditure will ultimately be charged or allocated to his or her function, more analysis may be allowed.

5. *Consider adopting a policy or practice with the approval of the management team.* This policy would require that any request over a certain monetary limit would require at least a brief needs assessment. Most executives would agree that expensive projects need analysis before they are implemented. It is best to adopt this policy before a specific request is on the table. Remind the executives that there is a policy—approved by the executive team—requiring some analysis. Although this may not be the desired approach, it brings consistency for analysis.

6. *If all else fails, learn from this situation.* When the executive cannot be persuaded to pursue further analysis, agree to implement the program with the promise to conduct an impact study to determine if it was the proper solution. The impact study data will clearly indicate if it was the correct solution. This is an opportunity for both the CLO and the requesting executive to learn a lesson that might pay off in situations when future requests are made.

Collectively, these strategies, combined with the creativity of the staff in exploring other ways to deflect a request for learning programs into more analysis, can result in avoiding the number one problem plaguing the learning and development field: lack of business alignment.

The Role of Objectives

An earlier section demonstrated the importance of having objectives for programs beyond learning objectives to include application, impact, value, and occasionally, ROI. For the evaluator, the need for higher levels of objectives becomes quite obvious. This is the first place the evaluator will explore when trying to understand the impact of a specific learning program. What were the application objectives; what were the impact objectives? How does this add value? Shifting the concept of developing objectives beyond learning to include the application and impact is a major paradigm shift for many individuals involved in the learning and development cycle.

For too many years, the entire function has been anchored exclusively to using learning objectives. When this is the case, evaluation is restricted to capturing learning measures for a credible analysis. Evaluation at application and impact levels are difficult to obtain when only learning objectives are available. Thus, the tremendous paradigm shift that must take place with the staff involved in the learning and development process is to develop objectives beyond the learning level to include application and impact. These objectives provide much value to members of the organization beyond those attempting to evaluate the success of learning. All key stakeholders in the learning cycle need these higher levels of objectives. Consider the perspective of key stakeholders:

1. *Designers and developers* need clear and precise application (Level 3) and impact (Level 4) objectives to provide the focus needed with the learning programs. This often translates into scenarios, examples, skill practices, exercises, and problems that reflect job-related environment and ultimate consequences of applying the learning (application and impact).

2. For *facilitators and instructors*, higher levels of objectives (Levels 3 and 4) translate into guidance for teaching a program. Facilitators clearly describe on-the-job situations and applications and communicate to participants what they can, should, and must do to be successful and solve problems and issues. Consequently, facilitators may drive the impact measure as desired. This approach is needed to provide the focus for ultimate application and success.

3. With these objectives, *participants* have a clearer direction of where the program is going. The mystery of how this learning program will affect the organization is removed. No longer would participants leave a learning program wondering how it will affect the organization. They clearly see what is in it for them as they apply and secure results, often raising their interest in the application and ultimate success of the program.

4. With this approach, *sponsors or stakeholders*—key clients who fund or request the learning program—have measures or issues that are very important to them. They see more value in the ultimate business impact and less value in satisfying a participant's individual learning need.

Thus, with these important objectives, an immediate question surfaces: "Why aren't the four levels of objectives developed for every program?" The answer is based on resources and feasibility. Forcing objectives for all four levels means that the analysis would have to be conducted at the four levels described earlier. This is not feasible or desirable in most organizations.

Table 4-1
Measuring Reaction and Satisfaction with the Learning Programs

Developing Reaction and Satisfaction Objectives

Reaction objectives are critical in this measurement chain because they:
- Describe expected immediate and long term satisfaction
- Describe issues that are important to the success of the program
- Provide a basis for evaluating the beginning of the measurement chain of impact
- Place emphasis on planned action, if feasible

The best reaction objectives:
- Identify issues that are important and measurable
- Are attitude-based, clearly worded, and specific
- Explain how the participant has changed in thinking or perception as a result of the program
- Underscore the linkage between attitude and the success of the program
- Represent a satisfaction index from key stakeholders
- Have the capability to predict program success

Key questions are:
- How relevant is this program?
- How important is this program?
- Are the facilitators effective?
- How appropriate is this program?
- Is this new information?
- Is this program rewarding?
- Will you implement this program?
- Will you use the concepts/advice?
- What would keep you from implementing objectives from this program?
- Would you recommend the program to others?

When the objectives are needed, it is helpful to make sure that these objectives are developed in a proper way and worded as precisely as possible. Tables 4-1 through 4-4 show the key issues involved in developing the different levels of objectives.

Table 4-1 addresses the central rationale for developing reaction objectives. These are usually understood, but not listed. Sometimes

Table 4-2
Measuring Skills and Knowledge Enhancement

Developing Learning Objectives

Learning objectives are critical to measuring learning because they:
- Communicate expected outcomes from facilitation
- Describe competent performance that should be the result of learning
- Provide a basis for evaluating learning
- Focus on learning for participants

The best learning objectives:
- Describe behaviors that are observable and measurable
- Are outcome-based, clearly worded, and specific
- Specify what the learner must do as a result of the learning
- Have three components:
  1. Performance—what the learner will be able to do at the end of the program
  2. Condition—circumstances under which the learner will perform the task
  3. Criteria—degree or level of proficiency that is necessary to perform the job

Three types of learning objectives are:
1. Awareness—Familiarity with terms, concepts, processes
2. Knowledge—General understanding of concepts, processes, etc.
3. Performance—Able to demonstrate the skill (at least at a basic level)

it is helpful to detail these objectives so that the program can focus on important reaction areas. Reaction measures will always be included in an overall scorecard or business measurement.

Table 4-2 has the classic elements of developing learning objectives advocated by many of the pioneers in the field of measurement and evaluation. They are classic and documented adequately in most organizations.

Table 4-3 extends the objectives to on-the-job application and provides the stakeholders with invaluable information, as described earlier. This is an important trend in organizations.

Table 4-4 details the characteristics of impact objectives, the ultimate objectives, showing the connection to the business needs. These impact measures are powerful and are detailed as much as is feasible.

Table 4-3
Measuring On-the-Job Application of Knowledge and Skills

Developing Application Objectives

Application objectives are critical to measuring application of skills and knowledge because they:
- Describe expected intermediate outcomes
- Describe competent performance that should be the result of the learning program
- Provide a basis for evaluation of on-the-job performance changes
- Place emphasis on applying what was learned

The best application objectives:
- Identify behaviors that are observable and measurable
- Are outcome-based, clearly worded, and specific
- Specify what the participant will change, or has changed, as a result of the program
- May have three components:
  1. Performance—what the participant has changed/accomplished at a specified follow-up time after training
  2. Condition—circumstances under which the participant performed the task
  3. Criteria—degree or level of proficiency under which the task or job was performed

Two types of application objectives are:
- Knowledge based—general use of concepts, processes, etc.
- Behavior based—able to demonstrate the use of the skill (at least at a basic level)

Key questions:
- What new or improved *knowledge* was applied on the job?
- What new or improved *skill* was applied on the job?
- What is the *frequency of skill* application?
- What new *tasks* will be performed?
- What new *steps* will be implemented?
- What new *action items* will be implemented?
- What new *procedures* will be implemented or changed?
- What new *guidelines* will be implemented or changed?
- What new *processes* will be implemented or changed?

Table 4-4
Measuring Business Impact from Application

Developing Impact Objectives

Impact objectives are critical to measuring business performance because they:
- Describe expected outcomes
- Describe business unit performance that should be the result of a workplace learning and performance program
- Provide a basis for measuring the consequences of skills and knowledge application
- Place emphasis on achieving bottom line results

The best impact objectives:
- Must contain measures that are linked to the skills and knowledge in the program
- Describe measures that are easily collected
- Are results-based, clearly worded, and specific
- Specify what the participant has accomplished in the business unit as a result of the program

Four types of impact objectives involving hard data are:
- Output focused
- Quality focused
- Cost focused
- Time focused

Three common types of impact objectives involving soft data are:
- Customer service focused
- Work climate focused
- Work habits focused

Collectively, these objectives create the direction needed for the learning enterprise and become the cornerstone of results-based learning and development.

STATUS OF NEEDS ASSESSMENT

Although there has been increased emphasis and additional use of needs assessment and analysis, there is still much confusion concerning the steps, techniques, methods, and strategies involved in the process. Assessment is so crucial that some would argue that if there is no legitimate need for a learning and development program, then there will be no economic benefit derived from it. Needs assessment has earned its place in the learning and development process. Almost every training, learning, and development model will include needs assessment as an initial step. However, because of pressure to develop a program quickly, a lack of resources to conduct the analysis, a lack of understanding as to why it is needed, or a lack of learning and development staff trained in it, the needs assessment and analysis process is sometimes omitted. The challenge is to overcome the realistic barriers to its use.

Initiating a Needs Assessment

It is helpful to begin the description of this process by defining four important terms. A *need* is a gap or deficiency existing between the current state and the desired state. The *needs assessment* is the identification of the need and a determination of its importance and cost to satisfy. *Needs analysis* uncovers the cause of the gap that has been identified. A *solution* is a feasible process, program, or initiative that will remove the gap or correct the problem.

Several events or situations can initiate a needs assessment.

- New employees enter the organization and need specific training.
- New equipment, processes, and procedures are implemented.
- New jobs are created or new responsibilities are developed for current jobs.
- New products are developed or new processes are implemented.
- Major change programs are undertaken.
- Management may request a needs assessment or a program that leads to a needs assessment.
- Skills are upgraded, improved, or planned for improvement.
- A regulation or compliance requirement is put in place.
- A significant opportunity exists for performance improvement.
- An annual budget process is undertaken.
- Annual learning and development planning is undertaken.
- A performance problem has been identified.

A needs assessment can actually serve several purposes. It can uncover the current level of skills, knowledge, attitudes, and performance and compare them to an ideal state. This process essentially identifies the gap. The analysis uncovers the causes of the gap and identifies solutions to overcome or remove discrepancies between current and optimal skills, knowledge, attitudes, and performance. A needs assessment also identifies potential future problems along with solutions.

Sometimes, needs assessments are grouped into different types based on the scope and comprehensiveness of the approach. A job/function needs assessment identifies skill gaps and specific needs for a job, a job family, or a functional unit. For example, a needs assessment conducted for new, first-level managers might identify the need for training on policies and goal setting.

A second type of needs assessment is a performance/problem analysis where a problem is identified, causes are developed, and solutions are recommended. For example, if excessive staff turnover is a problem, a performance/problem analysis can often uncover inadequacies with management's recognition or communication and find ways to improve it. Finally, a macro-level needs assessment identifies needs for the total organization or a large segment of the organization. Changing job requirements create new demands for knowledge and skills. For example, a needs assessment on technology identifies how the implementation of new software could assist the entire workforce while increasing productivity.

Steps for Needs Assessment and Analysis

A comprehensive needs assessment and analysis process involves at least 14 distinct steps, as follows:

1. Determine the specific purpose and type of needs assessment.
2. Identify and select the sources for information for the needs assessment.
3. Involve key management in the process and gain necessary commitment.
4. Begin with the end in mind, with specific business impact measures (needs).
5. Use multiple sources of input and a variety of data.
6. Select the data collection methods appropriate for the situation, culture, and resources available.
7. Collect data according to a predetermined data collection plan.
8. Link business needs to job performance needs, including tasks, behavior, and environment.

9. Identify the barriers to successful implementation of the solution.
10. Determine specific skills and knowledge deficiencies, if applicable.
11. Integrate and analyze all of the data.
12. Prioritize specific needs in terms of importance and cost to resolve.
13. Provide recommendations for specific solutions.
14. Communicate results of the needs assessment and analysis to appropriate target audiences.

Using all of these steps represents a comprehensive approach; some may be omitted when a simple process is needed or when the stakes are not so high. A shortened version of this process is presented in Figure 4-2.

It describes a basic performance assessment and analysis process, which is a basic four-level needs assessment and analysis process that focuses on the business and job performance issues in addition to learning needs. The four levels in this model relate to the evaluation levels shown in Figure 4-3.

The levels of evaluation are described in Chapter 8. Information needed to determine the success of a program at each level is derived from specific objectives for the program. For example, the business impact from a learning program is developed from measures contained in the impact objectives. The application of learning on the job is derived from application objectives. Learning is measured based on learning objectives. Some programs have reaction or satisfaction objectives, which measure the participant reaction to the program.

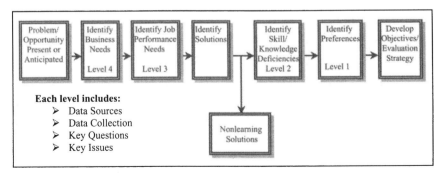

Figure 4-2. Performance assessment and analysis process.

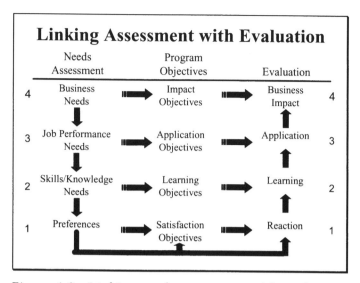

Figure 4-3. Linking needs assessment with evaluation.

Program objectives at all four levels are derived from the needs assessment process. For example, specific business needs uncovered in the needs assessment process will drive impact objectives and identify the business impact. Also, the job performance needs assessment will uncover changes in tasks, behavior, and procedures needed in the job environment. This will determine the specific application objectives for the program. The skill, knowledge, and attitude needs will determine specific learning gaps, which will appear as learning objectives in the program. Finally, preferences for learning delivery (i.e., type of program, length, location, facilitator, media, and timing) will drive these issues and appear as satisfaction objectives. Thus, needs assessment is clearly linked to program objectives and evaluation and are often referred to as levels of needs assessment, objectives, and evaluation.

An example of this process is shown in Figure 4-4, where an absenteeism problem in a call center has been linked to specific supervisory skills and knowledge deficiencies and a program has been developed to overcome them. The absenteeism problem was verified by comparing the current absenteeism rate with those of other call centers in the same organization, other call centers in the same geographical area, previous performance, and the current year's goals for absenteeism. This confirmed a business need.

A variety of problem solving and performance analysis techniques were used to uncover the cause of the absenteeism. While there were

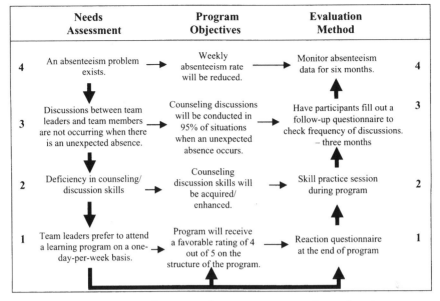

Figure 4-4. Linking needs assessment with evaluation (an example).

many possible causes (most of them nonlearning issues), the organization uncovered the fact that the supervisors/team leaders were not conducting counseling and performance discussions when an employee was unexpectedly absent. Without these discussions, there was no behavior change; thus, a job performance need was revealed. Essentially, the supervisors/team leaders were not doing something they should be doing, thus influencing the business need.

Next, the knowledge and skill needs were uncovered when the skill levels of supervisors were examined. If the supervisors could conduct the discussions, there was no learning need; if they could not, a learning need was evident. In this situation, the supervisors were uncomfortable performing this task. Consequently, the need for a learning solution was determined.

The final part of this process was to determine the preference of the solution, addressing issues such as the length of the program, who conducts it, and when, how, and where it is conducted. To define the preferences, information was sought from the supervisors/team leaders as well as the call center manager and other key stakeholders.

In this example, the needs assessment and analysis levels clearly drive program objectives, and an appropriate evaluation method

Business Needs	• What business-level problems or opportunities exist that need to be improved? • What business measures reflect this need? • Where are they located? • What are the historical values?
Job Performance Needs	• What is preventing the business measures from improving? • What is not being performed on the job as desired or as needed? • What behaviors are needed? • What tasks should be performed? • What actions are needed? • What resources are required?
Skills/Knowledge Needs	• What skills and knowledge levels are needed? • What gaps exist in skills and knowledge? • How can skills and knowledge be acquired or enhanced?
Preference Needs	• Which learning activities are preferred? • Which delivery mechanisms are desired? • What is the appropriate timing? • What is the appropriate setting? • Where is the best location?

Figure 4-5. Key questions for needs assessment and analysis.

would be used to collect data to satisfy the requirements for the particular evaluation level.

To develop this process effectively, several key questions need to be asked for each needs assessment level, as shown in Figure 4-5. These questions are very powerful in uncovering the validity of the learning program request. When used diplomatically and consistently, these questions have a lasting effect with the initial requestor.

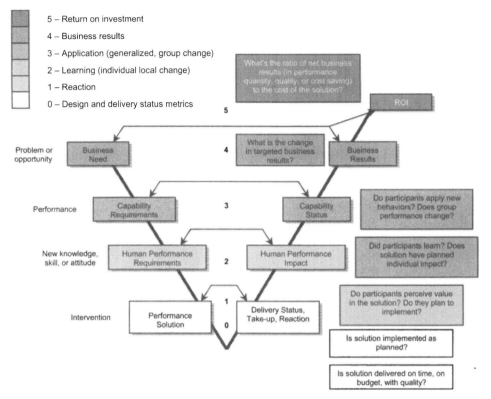

5 – Return on investment

4 – Business results

3 – Application (generalized, group change)

2 – Learning (individual local change)

1 – Reaction

0 – Design and delivery status metrics

Figure 4-6. Accenture's adaptation of the linkage model.

In the future, the requestor may consider these questions, thus avoiding the need for an additional program.

Figure 4-6 shows Accenture's adaptation of the linkage model. Accenture, a very large, successful consulting firm, uses this model with their learning solutions. As the model reflects, the four levels of needs assessment are addressed and the solution is measured at the five levels, including the actual ROI. Other organizations have adapted this model to show the linkage between needs assessment, objectives, and evaluation. When this linkage is understood by all stakeholders, the result is extremely powerful.

NEEDS ASSESSMENT TACTICS

A Sensible Approach

Not every needs assessment should be conducted at all levels. The value of the information obtained is greater at the business needs level. Frequency of use is reversed. Preferences are a very common type of needs assessment. For example, a catalog of learning programs is distributed to a target audience, asking them to select the programs they would be interested in attending in the next six months. This is a level of needs assessment based on preference. Ideally, this should be based on management's assessment that these are appropriate courses for the individual. However, participants may attend a program based on their preference for location, duration, or facilitator. Ultimately, needs assessment should occur before attending any program. Managers, individuals, and the organization (as in high potential program identification) are all sources of good needs assessment.

On the other end of the scale, the analysis of business needs and the connection to job performance is conducted infrequently, primarily because it is very difficult and time consuming. In reality, only a few types of programs should be taken to the level four and three assessment (e.g., programs where the scope is large and the impact or costs are great). The criteria for pursuing a higher level of needs assessment often hinge on the following:

- The anticipated impact of the proposed program in terms of cost savings or profit generation
- The life cycle of the proposed program (one time vs. forever)
- The importance of the proposed program in meeting operational goals or solving an operational problem
- The linkage of the proposed program with strategic objectives
- The cost of the proposed program (expensive vs inexpensive)
- The expected visibility of the program (perhaps even controversial)
- The size of the target audience for the proposed program

Strategy Mapping

Business alignment is sometimes achieved with strategy maps. A strategy map is a one-page picture of an organization's strategy that articulates the strategic objectives from four perspectives: financial, customer value proposition, internal processes, and learning and growth. These four areas are the traditional categories of measures in the balanced scorecard. A strategy map becomes an anchor for creating performance measures with which an organization can manage and motivate its employees (Frangos, 2004).

A strategy map can explain the cause-and-effect relationships between a learning objective, and the internal processes can link learning to the organization's customer value proposition and to a financial outcome. Using the strategy map, shown in Figure 4-7, the CLO works jointly with business executives to clarify the enterprise strategy in powerful new ways. A "shared model" of strategy is often the missing link between learning and the enterprise. Once developed, the CLO has a point of reference for defining the impact of learning on the strategy and tailoring his or her developmental and learning programs based on strategic priorities.

Needs Assessment Methods

A variety of methods are available to collect data for needs assessment and analysis. The data collection method revolves around the assessment instrument. The most common types of instruments are the following:

- Questionnaires, which are versatile and collect a variety of data
- Surveys, which typically collect opinion and attitude data
- A variety of tests to measure skills or knowledge
- One-on-one interviews
- Focus groups
- Observations
- Performance records in the organization
- Executive talent reviews

The source of data for the needs assessment is critical to the process. A variety of sources are available and include participants, supervisors of participants, subordinates of participants, peer groups, subject matter experts, organizational performance records, and the learning and development staff.

Other sources may be appropriate for the specific type of situation and different level of needs assessment. For example, at the business needs level, sources include industry data, benchmarking data, strategic and operational plans, annual reports, business performance data, human resource records, and performance appraisals. At the job performance level, sources may include job descriptions, performance appraisals, policies and procedures, job tasks, and subject matter experts. At the skills and knowledge level, sources may include tests, simulations, performance reviews, and job descriptions.

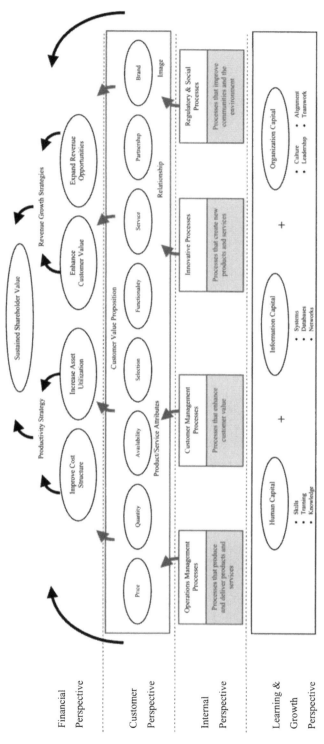

Figure 4-7. Strategy map. (Source: Frangos, 2004. Used with permission.)

Selecting a specific method for data collection is a very important task. The issues that determine the appropriate method often involve items such as:

- Cost of data collection
- Participant time required
- Training and development staff time required
- Amount of disruption of normal work activities
- Cultural preferences
- Accuracy
- Type of data

In summary, the data collection method for a needs assessment is the most visible and time-consuming process. The method must be selected recognizing the issues and concerns just mentioned.

Communicating Needs Assessment

The results of the needs assessment can usually be presented in several ways. Data can be reported about the current state of affairs, including challenges and opportunities and specific actions that are needed. More often than not, the needs assessment will present needs by priority—the most critical listed first with the least critical listed last. The prioritization is based on either the cost of satisfying the need or the critical importance of the need to the organization's success. This provides a framework to tackle the issues in a logical way.

Needs assessment results are also categorized by the recommended solutions based on the analysis. Both learning and nonlearning solutions are addressed. (This issue is covered in the next chapter.)

The results are usually presented to key stakeholders and the individuals who supplied the information. To obtain support for the process, management must understand the need for a particular solution and realize the factors that have influenced it. This can perhaps shape the implementation of the solution as well as determine its success.

Consequences for the CLO

A more comprehensive needs assessment process may not be embraced by some stakeholders. It takes time, adds cost, and often delays the implementation of requested programs. Learning and development staff members may not have the appropriate expertise to conduct a proper needs assessment. Some staff members may even have the opinion that needs assessments may not be necessary and are a waste of time. Also, when management requests a program, some learning staff members are reluctant to challenge the request, preferring to implement the program without a needs assessment. These are all legitimate barriers to success. The inability to overcome these barriers will make it difficult to invest more in the needs assessment process.

Each barrier must be overcome for the process to grow and be successful. Perhaps one of the most difficult challenges is to deflect requests for new learning programs to an appropriate needs assessment and analysis. Also, the management team needs to understand the purpose of needs assessment and their role in making it successful.

The potential payoff of additional investment is very high. When linked to evaluation, it becomes quite clear that, without the proper needs assessment and analysis, the success of a program is in jeopardy. An effective needs assessment process may prevent unnecessary programs or result in a radically redesigned program with cost savings. A tally of savings can be generated, which can ultimately be very impressive, offsetting the additional investment.

It appears that this trend will continue. Positive results with needs assessment will continue to influence additional investment in learning and development. While there are legitimate barriers to making the process more effective, implementation is essential. As an integral part of the shift to performance analysis, additional emphasis will be needed. This is definitely a win-win trend, but it may require some work for it to be effective.

Final Thoughts

Overall, the needs assessment process involves a variety of steps and many key areas that must be addressed throughout the process. It requires careful planning, data collection from a variety of sources, careful analyses, and thoughtful conclusions to provide the appropriate recommendation. While the needs assessment and analysis process requires resources that some learning and development staff may be reluctant to provide, additional investment should result in improved learning programs and may prevent unnecessary programs from being implemented. The payoff is in adding value to the organization, the CLO's primary role.

CLOs need to deeply understand and be aligned with their company and line of businesses' strategy. The most effective CLOs are able to "translate business strategy into individual and organization enablers."

Susan Burnett, Senior Vice President of People & Organization Effectiveness, The Gap

REFERENCES

Frangos, Cassandra A. "Aligning Learning with Strategy," *Chief Learning Officer.* September 2004, 32–37.

Houde, Leah. "Aligning Education with Business Strategies," *Chief Learning Officer.* September 2005, 26–31.

Pillay, Dev. "Aligning Learning in Your Organization to Your Corporate Strategic Objectives," *Skills Africa Summit IIR.* May 2005.

CHAPTER 5

Shifting to Performance Improvement: Learning Is Not Always the Answer

> *Learning should demonstrate efficiency and effectiveness, and in order to do so, it's important to have an effective design at the highest level of productivity. CLOs should focus on providing learning at critical points in peoples' careers through an integrated talent strategy.*
>
> Ted Hoff, Vice President of Learning, IBM

Some CLOs are gradually shifting the learning and development function to a function that focuses on performance improvement. Because many performance problems cannot be solved with learning solutions, the learning and development department is offering a variety of learning and nonlearning solutions to improve performance in the organization. There is a movement toward not only individual performance improvement, but also organizational improvement. Linking individual performance to business performance is critical in today's business environment. Perhaps no issue on the CLO landscape has been more pronounced and publicized than this shift to performance improvement. Books, articles, studies, and conferences have been developed on this topic, describing in detail how this process must be tackled.

This paradigm shift represents a major change in the way the learning and development function has traditionally been organized and has delivered services. When the shift occurs, the roles, skills, and deliverables are different, and the learning and development function is transformed into a group of competent performance improvement specialists. The shift is not for every learning and development department or for every CLO. This chapter explores these issues.

MAJOR INFLUENCES

Several influences have created the shift to a performance improvement role. The pressures of competition in business and the emphasis on efficiency and cost control in all organizations require more efforts to improve employee and organizational performance. Learning and development leaders are being asked to become involved in a variety of performance initiatives to enhance employee and organizational performance.

The failure of many learning programs is traced to this issue. A learning solution is implemented when a nonlearning solution is actually needed to correct a problem or increase performance. Consequently, the learning staff is forced to address these issues with more comprehensive performance assessment and analysis. In most situations, where there is a performance issue, training or learning is not the solution needed.

Studies continue to show that a tremendous amount of learning is not being transferred to the job. Several factors in the work environment must be altered, modified, removed, or minimized for learning to be applied effectively. A performance improvement role requires more attention to the work environment, sometimes with changes focusing directly on modifications of the workplace, the environment, and support mechanisms to ensure that the learning is transferred to the job. As a result, the CLO must reach beyond the traditional role of developing programs to remove performance inhibitors and for large-scale opportunities for change (Broad, 2005).

The concept of performance improvement often communicates that the emphasis is on improving organizational and departmental performance, something that managers have desired for many years. Too often, the learning function has overlooked the role they plan in impacting the systematic performance of the company.

The requirement for measurement and evaluation, often causes organizations to focus more attention on the need for analysis to sort out the various causes of performance gaps. The implementation of a performance improvement mindset represents the integration of a variety of different processes, techniques, and elements to bring about needed changes in the organization. To meet the challenge, the CLO must address all the elements in the complete system of performance improvement beginning with analysis of the problem.

This shift creates an awkward situation for most CLOs. When nonlearning solutions are needed to correct a problem, but the only services in the learning and development charter is programs, it becomes difficult to resolve problems and meet needs. Ultimately, the need must be handed off to a different part of the organization, leaving the client frustrated and unfulfilled. To address this dilemma, some learning and development leaders have broadened the range of learning services to include both learning and nonlearning solutions or, in some cases, to replace learning solutions. Oftentimes, a significant issue for CLOs is that the learning function has been traditionally perceived as a place to go for programs. CLOs have gradually broken the traditional model and are responsible for expanded solutions including organization development, talent management, performance management, succession planning, change management, and organization design. The skill set for CLOs and their staffs has grown to include expertise in these areas, which enable the learning function to more fully meet the overall learning and performance needs of the organization.

PERFORMANCE IMPROVEMENT ISSUES

The broadening of skill sets beyond traditional learning and development has set the stage for the next step: embracing performance improvement.

Models

The first step in analyzing this trends is to examine a performance improvement model. In an American Society of Training and Development (ASTD) study, several important models were examined to arrive at what was ultimately labeled the ASTD Human Performance Improvement Process model (Rothwell, 1996). Figure 5-1 shows the model developed in the study. This is a simplified process representing six critical steps in the performance improvement process. In the first step, the performance problem, or opportunity, is thoroughly analyzed to identify a particular performance gap. This involves a comparison of present performance to desired performance. This comparison includes analysis of the environment and the individu-

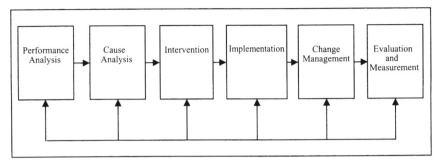

Figure 5-1. ASTD Human Performance Improvement
Process model. Used with permission.

als who are influenced by the performance gap. The impact of this gap is analyzed as well as the cost of continuing with the problem (Piskurich, 2002).

In the second step, the cause of the gap is addressed. A variety of potential causes are examined including rewards, information flow, capability, motivation, compensation, support, culture, systems, procedures, and practices. Using a variety of analysis tools, the specific cause or causes are identified.

The third step is to select the appropriate intervention. Fortunately there are many solutions to resolve business issues, depending on the specific cause. Job design, work flow, policy changes, compensation, rewards, performance, support, technology, and staffing changes may be appropriate, along with learning and development. The challenge is to select the right solution without taking on too many or too few.

In the fourth step, the solution is implemented with these individuals involved in the performance gap. When changing practices and policies, implementation may take very little time; changing systems or installing new technology may take weeks or months. Implementation is carefully scheduled with the appropriate resources identified.

Managing the change is the fifth step. Sometimes, the individuals involved take on new roles, tasks, or assignments as they resist the change. The implementation is monitored and steps are taken to ensure that the appropriate individuals receive information and are involved in the process. Information and involvement can reduce resistance. Building support and buy-in and keeping the process on schedule are critical issues.

The last step, evaluation and measurement, provides a variety of methods to collect data to determine the extent to which the performance improvement process has been successful. Various types of data are collected involving qualitative and quantitative categories to determine the extent to which the performance improvement process has been successful in its implementation, ultimately changing job performance and driving a positive business impact. The measurement and evaluation process is planned in advance, and the data are collected after the process has been implemented. The results are presented to key stakeholders.

Perhaps the most important model in shifting traditional learning and development to performance improvement comes from the work of Jim and Dana Robinson. Figure 5-2 shows the performance improvement process based on their almost two decades of practice (Robinson and Robinson, 1995). In this model, the performance improvement process is divided into three phases. The partnership phase takes about 10 to 20 percent of the time and focuses on the client relationship. This involves responding to requests and having dialogue around particular issues, problems, or opportunities. The next phase is the assessment, which is the most difficult for many learning and development professionals. Here, a variety of performance improvement assessment methods are used to determine the cause of the problem, identify performance gaps, and determine the degree of the desired performance levels. Some of the tools presented in the previous chapter can be helpful for this performance assessment issue. The third phase, and perhaps the most time consuming, is implementation. This involves the traditional work within the client group to ensure that the particular solution has been implemented and the results are reported.

Paradigm Shift

The shift to the performance improvement role represents a change in paradigm for all those involved in the traditional learning and development function. Table 5-1 shows important paradigm shifts that are typical when an organization makes this transformation. These paradigm shifts represent major changes in processes, practices, duties, and procedures and are briefly described here in categories.

Performance Analysis. As described in both models, there must be a focus on performance. Business needs must be identified as well as the job performance issues. Not only are the gaps identified, but the causes are also detailed. This is perhaps one of the most important elements in performance improvement. The result is a

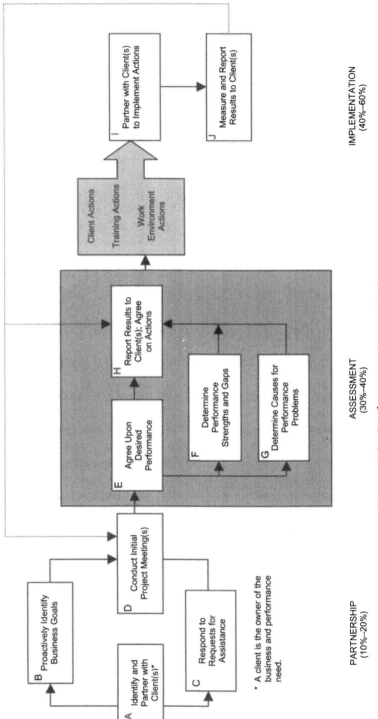

Figure 5-2. Performance improvement process.

Table 5-1
Paradigm Shift to Performance Improvement

Traditional Learning function Characterized by	Performance Improvement function Characterized by
• Business need rarely drives the learning program.	• Solution linked to specific business needs.
• Very little assessment of performance issues.	• Routine assessment of performance issues and causes.
• Most problems have learning solutions.	• Nonlearning solutions are common.
• Services organized around design and delivery structure.	• Full range of services to improve performance.
• Specific objectives focus on learning.	• Specific objectives focus on application, business impact, and ROI.
• Little effort to prepare program participants to achieve results.	• Results expectations are regularly communicated to participants, clients, and stakeholders.
• Little effort to prepare the work environment to support transfer of learning.	• Environment is prepared to support performance solution.
• Typical job title includes Designer or Trainer.	• Typical job title includes Performance Consultant or Performance Technologist.
• Work activities focus on preparation and teaching.	• Work activities focus on collaboration and consulting.
• Few client relationships are established.	• Process revolves around client relationships.
• Contacts outside the learning and development center are limited.	• Contacts outside the performance improvement center are frequent and necessary.
• No efforts to build partnerships with key managers.	• Partnerships established with key managers and clients.
• Skills and competencies of team members are narrowly focused.	• Skills and competencies of team members are broadly focused.
• Center has a training or learning label, usually reporting to a Human Resources executive.	• Center has a performance improvement label, usually reporting to an Operations executive.
• Very little measurement of results or cost benefit analysis.	• Frequent measurement of results and cost benefit analysis.
• Reporting on progress is input-focused or activity-based.	• Reporting on progress is output-focused or results-based.

Table 5-2
Performance Analysis Outcomes

- Agree Upon Desired Performance

  Outcomes:
  - Describe successful performance required to achieve business goals (using competency or performance language).
  - Clarify future performance needs and skill sets.
  - Describe work environment that supports performance.
  - Reach agreement with clients on the performance or competency model.

- Determine Performance Strengths and Gaps

  Outcomes:
  - Describe current performance.
  - Identify gap between SHOULD and CURRENT.
  - Clarify implications of performance gap.

- Determine Causes for Performance Problems

  Outcomes:
  - Identify causes of performance gaps.
  - Identify skill and knowledge needs.
  - Identify work environment factors.
  - Clarify implications of performance gap.

- Report Results to Client(s); Agree on Actions

  Outcomes:
  - Report and discuss conclusions and implications of performance assessment.
  - Contract for implementation.
  - Define roles of Performance Consultant, clients, and other team members.
  - Determine how intervention will be measured.

Source: Robinson, Dana Gaines, and James C. Robinson, *Performance Consulting: Moving Beyond Training*, San Francisco, CA: Berrett-Koehler Publishers, 1995.

clear understanding of the business impact of the opportunity, the specific performance gaps that exist, and the causes of those gaps.

Table 5-2 shows the outcomes of the performance and assessment process advocated by the Robinsons. Defining specific outcomes of each step is important so that stakeholders know when success has

Table 5-3
Typical Performance Improvement Solutions

• Benchmarking	• Job/work design
• Change management	• Performance management system
• Coaching	• Work flow changes
• Compensation	• Reward systems
• Documentation	• Recruiting
• Reengineering/reinventing	• Succession planning
• Electronic performance support	• Team building
• Health/wellness	• Talent management
• Job aides	

occurred. In addition, the performance analysis may use some of the techniques presented in Chapter 4.

Solutions and services. Because the learning and development function may be required to offer a variety of nonlearning solutions, the service mix is expanding—from the traditional array of services with structured learning experiences to a full range of performance improvement possibilities (Sugrue and Fuller, 1999). The categories for potential solutions and services can be quite broad, as suggested in Table 5-3. These solutions may be beyond the capabilities of the staff—both present and planned. Because of this, the range of services is often limited in organizations in the early stages of the performance improvement shift.

Preparation and expectation. Another important paradigm shift is the focus on preparation for the solution, whether it is a learning or nonlearning issue. The challenge comes from the specific objectives developed to focus on application and business impact. These levels of objectives go beyond the traditional learning objectives—clearly defining the changes that must be made (application) and the corresponding improvement (impact). Objectives are communicated to participants as well as clients and other stakeholders directly involved in the process. In addition, the job environment is prepared to support the transfer of performance to the job, whatever the solution. This preparation focuses on strategies in two categories: 1) removing barriers and obstacles, and 2) implementing or reinforcing enablers and enhancers. This will ensure that the job environment accepts, supports, and nurtures the solution so that the desired success will be ultimately realized.

Work activities and roles. Traditional work roles and duties are modified with this paradigm shift. Typically, work activities focus on conducting a needs assessment, developing and designing materials for a learning experience, and delivering them to a defined audience. The new role focuses more on collaboration and consulting. Consequently, job titles have been changed to reflect performance consultant or performance technologist, instead of designer or trainer. Table 5-4 shows a comprehensive listing of the competencies in the ASTD Human Performance Improvement Process model (Rothwell, 1996). Thirty-eight competencies are listed with the first fifteen associated with the core competencies involving all human performance improvements. The remainder are grouped into four key roles that have been identified. These roles—analyst, intervention specialist, change manager, and evaluator—are very different from the traditional learning and development roles and titles.

Relationships. Shifting to a performance improvement role translates into increased focus on building relationships. The most obvious and critical is the relationship with the client. The client/consultant relationship is established early and continues throughout the process. Other stakeholders, who have an important concern for, or interest in process, are often routinely involved in communications, information sharing, and problem solving activities. Consultants in performance improvement roles must build and nurture relationships to solve problems, provide feedback, and effectively implement solutions. Since the new roles are involved with new processes, it is critical that key stakeholders understand what performance improvement means and their role in the success of the process. For example, in the transformation to performance improvement at Rohm and Haas, it was critical to communicate key messages to target audiences. Figure 5-3 shows the four target audiences and the key message for each audience (Phillips, 1999).

Structure. The structure of the learning and development function shifts as the performance improvement role is undertaken. The structure of a traditional learning and development department is shown in Figure 5-4. The learning and development function will have specialists involved in needs assessment and evaluation, designers and developers producing structured learning programs or purchasing the programs, facilitators conducting the programs, and managers keeping the programs organized.

Table 5-4
Core Competencies Associated with Performance Improvement Work

---

Core Competencies Associated with Human Performance Improvements

1. Industry awareness	Understanding the vision, strategy, goals, and culture of an industry; linking human performance improvement interventions to organizational goals
2. Leadership skills	Knowing how to lead or influence others positively to achieve desired work results
3. Interpersonal relationship skills	Working effectively with others to achieve common goals and exercising effective interpersonal influence
4. Technological awareness and understanding	Using existing or new technology and different types of software and hardware; understanding performance support systems and applying them as appropriate
5. Problem-solving skills	Detecting performance gaps and helping other people discover ways to close the performance gaps in the present and future; closing performance gaps between actual and ideal performance
6. Systems thinking and understanding	Identifying inputs, throughputs, and outputs of a subsystem, system, or suprasystem and applying that information to improve human performance; realizing the implications of interventions on many parts of an organization, process, or individual; taking steps to address any side effects of human performance improvement interventions
7. Performance understanding	Distinguishing between activities and results; recognizing implications, outcomes, and consequences
8. Knowledge of interventions	Demonstrating an understanding of the many ways that human performance can be improved in organizational settings; showing how to apply specific human performance improvement interventions to close existing or anticipated performance gaps
9. Business understanding	Demonstrating awareness of the inner workings of business functions and how business decisions affect financial or nonfinancial work results
10. Organization understanding	Seeing organizations as dynamic, political, economic, and social systems that have multiple goals; using this larger perspective as a framework for understanding and influencing events and change

Table 5-4 *Continued*

11. Negotiating/ contracting skills	Organizing, preparing, overseeing, and evaluating work performed by vendors, contingent workers, or outsourcing agents
12. Buy-in/advocacy skills	Building ownership or support for change among affected individuals, groups, and other stakeholders
13. Coping skills	Knowing how to deal with ambiguity and how to handle the stress resulting from change and from multiple meanings or possibilities
14. Ability to see "big picture"	Looking beyond details to see overarching goals and results
15. Consulting skills	Understanding the results that stakeholders desire from a process and providing insight into how efficiently and effectively those results can be achieved

Competencies Associated with Specific Roles

There are also specific competencies associated with each role played by those involved in human performance improvement work.

Role 1: Analyst

16. Performance analysis skills (front-end analysis)	The process of comparing actual with ideal performance in order to identify performance gaps or opportunities
17. Needs analysis survey design and development skills (open-ended and structured)	Preparing written (mail), or oral (phone), or electronic (e-mail) surveys using open-ended (essay) and closed (scaled) questions in order to identify human performance improvement needs
18. Competency identification skills	Identifying the knowledge and skill requirements of teams, jobs, tasks, roles, and work
19. Questioning skills	Gathering pertinent information to stimulate insight in individuals and groups through use of interviews and other probing methods
20. Analytical skills (synthesis)	Breaking down the components of a larger whole and reassembling them to achieve improved human performance
21. Work environment analytical skills	Examining work environments for issues or characteristics affecting human performance

Table 5-4 *Continued*

Role 2: Intervention Specialist

22. Performance information interpretation skills	Finding useful meaning from the results of performance analysis and helping performers, performers' managers, process owners, and other stakeholders to do so
23. Intervention selection skills	Selecting human performance improvement interventions that address the root cause(s) of performance gaps rather than symptoms or side effects
24. Performance change interpretation skills	Forecasting and analyzing the effects of interventions and their consequences
25. Ability to assess relationships among interventions	Examining the effects of multiple human performance improvement interventions on parts of an organization, as well as the effects on the organization's interactions with customers, suppliers, distributors, and workers
26. Ability to identify critical business issues and changes	Determining key business issues and applying that information during the implementation of a human performance improvement intervention
27. Goal implementation skills	Ensuring that goals are converted effectively into actions to close existing or pending performance gaps; getting results despite conflicting priorities, lack of resources, or ambiguity

Role 3: Change Manage

28. Change skills	Determining what the organization should do to address the cause(s) of a human performance gap at present and in the future
29. Communication channel, informal network, and alliance understanding	Knowing how communication moves through an organization by various channels, networks, and alliances; building such channels, networks, and alliances to achieve improvements in productivity and performance
30. Group dynamics understanding	Understanding how groups function; influencing people so that group, work, and individual needs are addressed
31. Process consultation skills	Observing individuals and groups for their interactions and the effects of their interactions with others

Table 5-4 *Continued*

32. Facilitation skills	Helping performers, performers' managers, process owners, and stakeholders discover new insights

Role 4: Evaluator

33. Performance gap evaluation skills	Measuring or helping others measure the difference between actual and ideal performance
34. Ability to evaluate results against organizational goals	Assessing how well the results of a human performance improvement intervention match intentions
35. Standard setting skills	Measuring desired results of organizations, processes, or individuals; helping others establish and measure work expectations
36. Ability to assess impact on culture	Examining the effects of human performance gaps and human performance improvement interventions on shared beliefs and assumptions about "right" and "wrong" ways of behaving and acting in one organizational setting
37. Human performance improvement skills	Finding ways to evaluate and continuously improve human performance improvement interventions before and during implementation
38. Feedback skills	Collecting information about performance and feeding it back clearly, specifically, and on a timely basis to affected individuals or groups

In the performance improvement model depicted in Figure 5-5, the roles are different. The performance analysis and design group analyzes the problem, determines the causes, and designs or develops the appropriate intervention. Performance consultants and facilitators implement the solution and coordinators keep the process on track throughout the implementation. The evaluation is separate, with an independent and objective evaluation team.

Evaluation. Evaluation in a performance improvement function is similar to the evaluation role in learning and development. The primary difference is that the evaluation will usually occur at the business impact and application level when using a five-level evaluation framework, discussed in Chapter 8. Evaluators are tracking

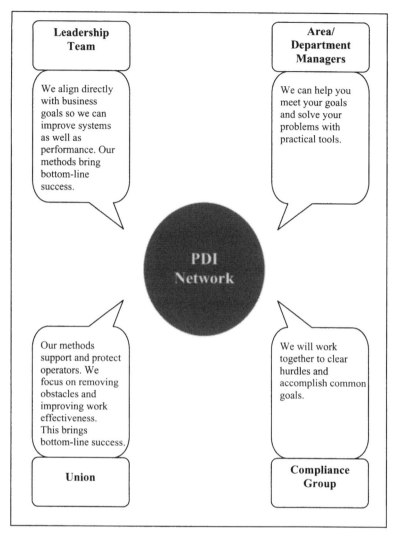

Figure 5-3. Target audiences and key messages.

business impact measures, application and implementation measures, learning measures, and reaction measures to provide a full
range of evaluation information. They are also reporting data to a
variety of target audiences.

PLAN OF ACTION

The shift can be slow to develop in some organizations and may
be resisted by some CLOs, creating quite a dilemma. An important

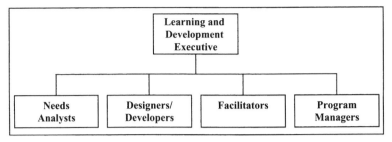

Figure 5-4. A structure for a traditional learning and development center.

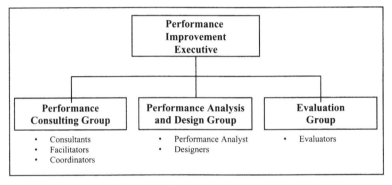

Figure 5-5. A structure for a performance support center.

issue is to decide if the learning and development function *wants* to be in the performance improvement business and if that is the right model for the organization. Ultimately, the function and the structure need to reflect the business. Most companies are making the shift to expand the learning role to a performance role. In some cases, the learning and development function may have no desire to be involved in performance improvement processes; its charter is to provide learning and development solutions, and it would prefer to continue to perform in that capacity. If that is the case, this shift would not be an issue; the learning and development function would be best to remain a learning program. However, it is helpful for the CLO to be aware of this trend and to be able to make adjustments to meet the pressures that caused this trend to develop in the first place.

On a positive note, this shift allows the CLO to expand the range of services to gradually include a variety of nonlearning solutions and to work in different roles with key managers in the organization. However, the CLO may not have the resources to develop performance improvement solutions. Many of the learning team members are not equipped for these new roles and are unable to offer some of the nonlearning solutions.

Building Skills

The most significant impact on the function is that new skills must be acquired. A casual review of the competencies outlined in the ASTD model reveals the skills and knowledge needed to be successful in this role. This will require substantial preparation for the staff and, in some cases, may require extensive development or employing new staff possessing the required skills.

Above all, the learning specialists must become performance technologists. For example, while the typical learning and development background may require someone with an education or psychology major, the performance improvement background may include engineering and business. Also, individuals with research and statistics degrees may be a part of the team. Recently, the human performance field has made great strides in improving the capability in this area. A variety of certification programs are offered, including two from leading performance improvement organizations in the United States: the International Society for Performance Improvement (ISPI) and the American Society of Training and Development (ASTD). Recently CLO Magazine created the CLO Academy to also provide development in this area. In addition, some degree programs are available to help prepare people for this important field.

Handoff Approaches

Many organizations cannot develop the full capability to provide performance solutions (or even any additional capability beyond typical training); therefore, they must rely on some type of handoff mechanism. When problems arise that are considered nonlearning, they can be handed off to qualified individuals. Three handoff approaches are possible. One approach is to offer a few solutions that are closely related to learning and development, such as coaching, mentoring, problem solving, or organization development. Any requests beyond these areas are directed to another part of the organization with little coordination and follow-up.

A second approach is to detail specific procedures for handing off to other parts of the organization. This handoff is carefully tracked to ensure that the ball does not get dropped and that the issue is addressed by the appropriate group.

The third approach is to partner with other solution providers specializing in a particular area. These may be within the human resources or human capital area, but they also include technology, systems, and organization design. The partner is pulled into the analysis, and the handoff is seamless to the client.

Overcoming Staff Resistance

For some staff members, these new roles are a radical departure from existing (and comfortable) roles. For them, every problem is a learning problem, and they will continue to teach, even when non-learning solutions are needed. Because of this resistance, the transition is often very slow. To expedite the process, the CLO will have to provide clear communications and expectations, as well as staff development.

Table 5-5 shows the typical reactions to this change. These reactions are typical as individuals become emotionally attached to previous work and reluctant to shift their skill base and operating framework to performance improvement. These negative reactions are nothing more than resistance to change and, in such cases, a

Table 5-5
Typical Objections to the Performance
Improvement Shift

Open Resistance

1. It costs too much.
2. It takes too much time.
3. Who is asking for this?
4. It is not in my job duties.
5. I did not have input on this.
6. I do not understand this.
7. We don't have a charter for this.
8. How can we be consistent with this?
9. The process is too complicated.
10. Our managers will not support this.
11. This is not practical.
12. This is a change.

Figure 5-6. Building blocks for overcoming resistance.

change management process might be needed. In some cases, there will be significant staff turnover; in other cases, significant employee growth will occur.

Figure 5-6 shows the building blocks necessary for overcoming the resistance. An important initial challenge is to assess the current climate to see if the staff is ready, capable, and willing. Next, the specific roles and responsibilities are defined and adjusted as this process evolves. Goals and plans are established with the involvement of the entire team. Policies, procedures, and practices need to be developed, and the staff must be prepared for them. Ideally, they should be developed with input from the staff. In some cases, resources may be required beyond the current staff capability. Quick wins are important. Initiating some projects for nonlearning solutions and learning from the experiences is very valuable. Then the management team (mid-level managers) can be prepared based on these successes. The management team is usually prepared through workshops. Impediments, obstacles, and barriers to this shift must be identified and minimized, removed, or sometimes, eliminated altogether. Finally, there must be constant monitoring of progress, including improving processes and communicating data.

Language of Business

As part of the focus on performance improvement, the learning staff members must learn about the organization, its challenges, its opportunities, and its performance issues. They must learn the language of operating managers and be able to converse regularly with this group. They need to know strategies, organizational goals, and the current status of major initiatives in the organization. They need to understand the key principles of human performance and how various solutions can be implemented. They must know the systems, processes, and products of the organization. One of the most comprehensive approaches to understanding the business, and the important language of business, is presented in Table 5-6. This table shows the different categories essential not only for the CLO, but for the entire learning and development staff. For the organization, each staff member must understand the inputs, conditions, processes, outputs, consequences, and feedback (Langdon, 1995).

Letting the Organization Know

The CLO must communicate the new performance shift to a variety of stakeholders, particularly the key managers, clients, and organization. All stakeholders need to understand the new approach and framework and what it means to them. Without adequate explanations, understanding, and demonstrations, the managers may become skeptical about the transformation and view it as a new fad floating through the organization. Because the shift represents a major change in delivery, some managers and even participants may resist the process. When a manager requests a particular learning program and the response is an analysis that leads to a nonlearning solution, frustration may surface among the managers, particularly if they do not understand the process. The key is to communicate completely so that resistance is minimized.

The success of communication begins with the reputation of the learning and development function. Unless the reputation is excellent, it may be difficult to make this transition. As one telecom executive stated, "How can a learning and development function, which struggles to connect to the organization now, suddenly be in the business of improving performance? If they are not successful where they are, how can they handle additional responsibility?" While this assessment may seem harsh, it is a reality for some. In this situation, a performance shift will probably not achieve the desired results. Some performance improvement shifts have failed when the only action is changing the name. For example, some corporate Training functions changed their name to Performance Improvement in an attempt to address more solutions. It takes more than rewording the

Table 5-6
The Lexicon of the Language of Work

The New Language of Work

Element	Typical Sources	Definition
Inputs	• People (human capital) • Ideas (knowledge) • Equipment/technology • Facilities • Funds (financial capital) • Information • Requests/demands	The resources and requests available or needed to produce outputs. What must be present for something (the output) to happen.
Conditions	• Rules • Policies • Environment • Attitudes	Existing factors that influence the use of inputs and processes used to produce an output.
Process	• Designing/developing • Manufacturing/producing • Testing/evaluating • Selling/marketing • Servicing/supporting	The actions necessary for using the inputs to produce outputs, performed by someone or something under certain conditions.
Outputs	• Services • Products • Facts • Knowledge	That which is produced as a result (product/service/knowledge) of using inputs under certain conditions and through a process.
Consequences	• Customer satisfaction • Needs met • Problem solved • Opportunity realized	The effects that an output has on a person, product, service, or situation.
Feedback	• Client reactions • Information needs • Reinforcements	That which completes the work cycle; response to outputs that confirms success or indicates adjustment is needed. Also, response to processing.

Adapted from Langdon, 1995

label to make this work; it takes all the processes described in this chapter.

Success of this shift will be grounded in projects connected to the business. As projects are developed, success stories must be communicated, not in a boastful, egotistical way, but using very subtle communication. When sending a message, and it is important for others to understand it; it must be succinct and credible. If this occurs, managers will request other solutions because they see evidence of success and understand what is being accomplished, and they recognize the great opportunity.

Molson Coors, a large global brewery, is shifting from traditional learning to performance improvement when appropriate. One of their projects is the start-up of a new brewery. The project extends beyond developing skills and start-up capabilities and involves many other solutions that would normally be assigned to other functions. Essentially, it is a combination of a learning and development effort that comes from brewery operation learning and development (BOLD) and involves process design, work flow, job aids, technology support, and reward systems. All of these solutions are coordinated by the BOLD team based on key questions that were asked at the beginning of the project, including "What are the measures of success of the start-up itself?" "What is the success of the brewery in terms of quality, quantity, efficiency, and costs?" and "How will data be used to improve the project?" This project clearly involves a variety of performance solutions.

Outlook

It appears that this trend will continue over the next several years as organizations explore new ways to improve productivity and competitiveness. Not only will the drivers continue to influence the shift, but the benefits derived from implementing a performance improvement process are also significant. In many situations, this is a more efficient process that avoids unnecessary programs when learning is not the solution. Since the selected performance improvement solution focuses directly on business problems, the results are usually significant, desired, and welcomed by the key managers in the organization. Because the true causes of performance problems will be identified, the chances of improving or reducing the performance gap are greatly enhanced.

This process also aligns the learning and development function more closely with the strategic initiatives of the organization and the key operating executives. This often helps create success for new efforts and initiatives. With the additional benefits, coupled with the drivers for the shift, it appears performance improvement is here to stay.

FINAL THOUGHTS

This chapter explored a changing issue: moving from traditional learning and development to providing performance improvement solutions. Many CLOs are challenged to ultimately transform learning and development into an overall performance improvement function. Many forces and processes are driving this trend. Too often, nonlearning solutions are ignored or improperly addressed by the learning and development function. Serious problems can develop if the needed solution is not a learning issue. When a nonlearning issue *is* uncovered, it is important to have a mechanism to address the issue, either through the learning and development function or with some type of handoff mechanism. Some experts in the field advocate that all learning and development functions must move into this process to add efficiency and productivity to the organizations. Others see this as a huge challenge, arguing that many CLOs do not have a charter to offer these kinds of solutions. Whatever the position, the CLO must confront this issue in a productive way.

The strategic CLO is adequately prepared to transition his or her learning function into a place where performance of individuals and the organization can be significantly addressed and improved. Focusing on training solutions is not fully effective for meeting today's business challenges. CLOs are required to move beyond traditional methodologies and systems to enhance the businesses they serve. Many CLOs have expanded their roles to include recruitment and staffing, employee communications, workforce planning, organizational development, and organizational effectiveness. The growth of the CLO role enables more alignment with the business strategy, executive involvement, and increased value add. The role will continue to evolve into areas that have the largest business impact.

> *Talent discussions are centered around business impact and results. . . . We develop leaders and provide coaching so that they attain great results through people.*
>
> Rick O'Leary, Director, Human Resources &
> Diversity, Corning

REFERENCES

Broad, Mary L. *Beyond Transfer of Training: Engaging Systems to Improve Performance.* San Francisco, CA: Pfeiffer, 2005.

Langdon, Denny. *The New Language of Work.* Amherst, MA: HRD Press, 1995.

Phillips, Jack J. *HRD Trends Worldwide: Shared Solutions in a Global Economy.* Woburn, MA: Elsevier, 1999.

Piskurich, George M., ed. *HPI Essentials.* Alexandria, VA: ASTD, 2002.

Robinson, Dana Gaines, and James C. Robinson. *Performance Consulting: Moving Beyond Training.* San Francisco, CA: Berrett-Koehler Publishers, 1995.

Rothwell, William J. *Model for Human PI: Roles, Competencies, and Output.* Alexandria, VA: ASTD, 1996, 18–19.

Sugrue, Brenda, and Jim Fuller, eds. *Performance Interventions: Selecting, Implementing, and Evaluating the Results.* Alexandria, VA: ASTD, 1999.

CHAPTER 6

Creating Value-Based Delivery

> *People's learning styles have been, and will continue to be, expanded by technology at the speed we all need to learn to "survive and thrive." CLOs can accelerate and enable this change by building "bite sized" e-learning modules and "powerful" job aids rather than five day classroom programs.*
> Donnee Ramelli, President, General Motors University

The delivery of learning and development to varied audiences is changing rapidly across organizations. Traditional instructor-led learning is declining, replaced by a variety of technology and media methods to deliver more effective learning. These methods, which are gaining additional emphasis, include coaching and mentoring, structured on-the-job training, just-in-time learning, action learning, job aids, performance support tools, team training and peer teaching, and a variety of technology-assisted delivery techniques. Learning technology incorporates presentation as well as delivery methods, using interactive multimedia, video conferencing, virtual reality, GroupWare, M-learning and electronic performance support systems. Internet/intranet, CD-ROM, satellite, e-mail, and voicemail are common examples of technology used for learning applications.

The picture of the dramatic change in the environment for learning can be summarized as follows:

- The focus of learning activities is shifting away from isolated skillbuilding and information transfer to performance improvement and support, often near the job site.

134

- The focus on learning models and methods is shifting from the perspective of the teacher or facilitator to that of the learner or participant.
- More learning is occurring just in time and directly in the context of the job or task.
- Bite-sized learning modules are available on mobile phones as employees need reminders, information, and reinforcement.
- Self-directed learning and team learning are increasing dramatically in their use and success.
- Group training events are being used less to transfer information or to teach skills and more to motivate and bond groups to clarify direction and purpose.
- The use of coaching is the fastest growing development process, often replacing classroom teaching.
- Learning is more likely to occur with the help of some form of technology. E-learning is growing rapidly, in many cases replacing instructor-led learning altogether.

These important developments underscore the primary issues discussed in this chapter. The chapter discusses two broad categories: technology and alternative delivery.

WHY THE SHIFT?

Although the shift away from instructor-led learning has been occurring incrementally for many years, it has exploded recently with the use of technology, coupled with additional information about blended learning, e-learning, and learning transfer, and the need to scale learning for a global audience.

Alternative Delivery

The inefficient learning that occurs in traditional learning and development programs has caused some organizations to focus more efforts on new ways of learning. In a traditional environment, lecture and discussion have been the principal methods. Many studies have shown that this approach is not effective for acquiring skills and knowledge. Other techniques are much more effective, even in diverse cultures. Thus, as organizations have examined different ways of learning, the shift to other innovative and more efficient techniques has occurred.

The cost of providing traditional learning and development continues to grow. Classroom facilities are becoming more expensive. Travel and participants' time continue to escalate. The days of traveling a long distance, taking weeks away from the job, and sitting all day in a classroom environment are disappearing. More organizations are realizing that to be more cost effective, the participant's time away from the job must be minimized; travel costs must be eliminated where possible; and facilities need to be relocated for better efficiency. Furthermore, there is a rise in the mobile workforce, which has driven learning professionals to create alternative delivery methods to meet those business demands. Consequently, much of traditional delivery has been replaced with alternative processes.

The transfer of learning to the job is sometimes diminished through the traditional learning processes. The Research Institute of America has found that 33 minutes after completion of a course, students retain only 58 percent of the material covered. By the second day, 33 percent is retained, and three weeks after the course, only 15 percent of the knowledge delivered is retained (Snipes, 2005).

Because the participants are physically removed from the job—sometimes by great distances—there are many opportunities for a disconnect between what has been learned and what is used on the job. Support mechanisms are absent and the transfer process is often woefully inadequate. Therefore, to improve the effectiveness of learning in terms of driving specific outcome measures, traditional processes are being supplemented or replaced by a variety of alternative delivery methods.

When learning is delivered near the workplace, preferably integrated with the actual work to be done, several important benefits are derived.

- Learning is more likely to be transferred directly to the job since it is near or at the site.
- Learning is usually more relevant because it is directly related to the work being done.
- Adjustments in the learning process can quickly be made as problems are uncovered and solutions are identified.
- Workplace learning often involves the manager or the supervisor of the learner. This involvement adds value in terms of reinforcement and support.

Finally, shifting the responsibility for learning and development to the management team is altering the way it is delivered. As presented in Chapter 10, managers and participants are assuming a greater role in the responsibility of learning in their divisions or work units. When managers accept the responsibility for learning, they are more actively involved and will push for methods that bring it closer to the job, make it more relevant, and take the participants away from their work a minimal amount of time. When participants assume their responsibility, they will become more involved in self-directed learning, self-study, and just-in-time learning activities.

Collectively, these influences shift learning from the traditional delivery to a variety of alternative methods.

Technology

Although learning technology has been available for some years, it is now feasible for most organizations to shift the delivery mechanisms through some technology media. Even organizations with relatively modest learning and development budgets are using technology to deliver learning. In addition, learning can be delivered effectively in remote locations through new technology. This was not possible a few years ago. Time savings for those involved in the process is captured in two ways: by reducing the time required to travel to a learning facility—whether it is 15 steps or 200 kilometers away—and by reducing the time spent learning. For example, technology-based learning can reap savings by reducing the time required to reach certain levels of knowledge and skills. Typically, technology-based learning projects require a much shorter timeframe to accomplish the same learning objectives as facilitator-led instruction (Levy, 2004).

Two critical factors in the use of technology are global dissemination of information and the growing mobility of employees. Cost for learning has also been a tremendous factor in the development of technology. As the demand for learning continues to grow, some organizations cannot afford classroom space. Also, travel expenses can be eliminated as technology is utilized to deliver learning. Although the cost to develop e-learning is greater than that of traditional facilitator-led development, savings are found in its long-term use. Table 6-1 compares the cost of facilitator-led learning and web-based learning. Assuming all technical equipment and systems are in place, the initial cost to develop web-based learning is significant. However, travel expenses, materials, and the facilitator's salary have been virtually eliminated. In addition, the variable cost of additional participants is eliminated when employees learn on the web. When the cost of the time for participants to be off the job is considered, the cost savings are even more dramatic.

Table 6-1
Cost Comparison: Facilitator-Led Versus Web-Based Training

	Facilitator-Led Training Costs	Web-Based Training Costs
Course development	$50,000	$150,000
Travel and expenses per offsite learner	1,000	0
Training materials per learner	50	0
Facilitator per session	4,000	0
Total for one learner	55,050	150,000
Cost to Train		
1 Group—20 learners	$75,000	$150,000
2 Groups—40 learners	100,000	
3 Groups—60 learners	125,000	
4 Groups—80 learners	150,000	
25 Groups—500 learners	675,000	
50 Groups—1,000 learners	1,300,000	150,000

Work itself is becoming increasingly computer intensive. A significantly larger percentage of the workforce is using a computer; in many organizations, every employee is networked via a PC, laptop, or wireless device. The availability of computing has created an appropriate setting to deliver learning at the work site. Thus, e-learning and m-learning (mobile learning) are natural applications for these employees.

Two important trends related to technology development are merging: cost and computer capability. The cost of technology is decreasing significantly, making learning applications more viable. An online program can be developed more quickly and with less money than was possible just a few years ago. At the same time, the trend of increasing the capacity and capability of computers has made the process much more adaptable to learning situations. The growth of software applications has also helped. Some predict that in the future, all learning will be available in a computer-generated format. This is evident today as almost every type of environment is simulated. High-performance computers, high-bandwidth communications, and intelligent software create complex business scenarios. Even personal skills can be developed in online learning applications.

The need for just-in-time learning has driven the advancement of technology. Employees must learn quickly, acquiring skills as they are needed on the job. This leaves traditional classroom learning inefficient where an individual may have to wait until adequate numbers are available to attend a program. With technology-based learning, only those employees who need it will participate in the program and at a time that is convenient for all.

Busy employees are often glued to their work. Prying them away to attend a formal learning session is becoming increasingly difficult and in many cases, not necessary. This situation often drives the development of technology, necessitating that more learning be delivered at or near the employee, often in small increments to minimize the amount of disruption.

Finally, technology-based applications are sometimes the only, or the most efficient, way to accomplish certain types of learning. In situations involving safety and compliance, computerized simulation is the only realistic method for providing real-life training opportunities. For example, the Panama Canal Authority uses a very high-tech electronic simulator for training pilots on how to maneuver ships through the canal. Obviously, it would be too unsafe and costly to train on the job using real ships. In other situations, e-learning is necessary because of the sheer number of people who need the learning programs. For example, Banco Popular, a large Puerto Rican–based company, needed to train all of its 8,000 employees on a new software tool. To make matters more complicated, these employees were scattered throughout several countries and the training had to be completed in three weeks. The only way to accomplish this was through e-learning.

Traditionally, the term *e-learning* has been used narrowly to refer to online training (change in skills) or online education (change in knowledge). A more specific definition refers to e-learning as Internet-enabled learning targeted at achieving business goals. This includes different forms or solutions, such as online training, collaboration, electronic performance, knowledge management, and online learning management (Van Dam, 2005). All of these forms or solutions use the Internet for learning purposes to create a rich, blended learning solution. The overall goal of learning should be to enhance human performance, and each of these Internet-enabled solutions should have an ultimate impact on business performance. Figure 6-1 captures the relationship between training, education and learning, and the different learning solutions that make up e-learning.

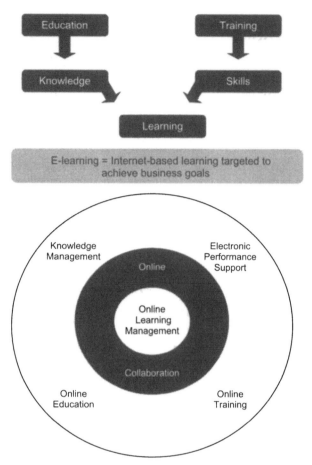

Figure 6-1. A blended approach to e-learning.

USE OF TECHNOLOGY

Although this book has described the tremendous amount of change that has taken place in learning and development, the speed of change in the domain of information technology makes other changes look like a gradual evolution. Computers are becoming a necessity in work and in our lives, and there has been an exponential growth in their power and speed. A parallel phenomenon has been the major improvements in the design and development of software; this began in the 1970s and continues at an extraordinary pace. Not surprisingly, technology-based learning has reflected the same dramatic changes, although the application has been slower than the actual development of hardware and software.

Table 6-2
Technology Delivery: Frequency of Use

Media	Never Used	Seldom Used	Often Used	Always Used
Audiocassettes	54%	41%	5%	0%
CD-ROM	9%	53%	35%	2%
DVD/diskettes	29%	48%	22%	1%
Internet/intranet/extranet	11%	35%	47%	7%
Satellite/broadcast TV	61%	31%	8%	0%
Teleconferencing	34%	42%	24%	1%
Videoconferencing	48%	32%	18%	1%
Videotapes	12%	32%	50%	6%

Source: *Training*, October, 2004

Technology allows flexibility in learning locations as well as delivery methods. Learners are able to choose a convenient time and place to learn. This learning includes the use of the Internet and intranets, CD-ROMs, DVDs, e-mail, satellite TV, instant messaging, short message service (SMS), webinars, and other methods of distribution. Key issues driving technology-based learning include effectiveness, efficiency, and cost. Table 6-2 shows the breakdown of frequency of use of various technology approaches (Dolezalek, 2004).

The challenge for the CLO is to address the technology issue on a rational and logical basis. Some of the key actions needed are the following:

- Deciding if and when to use a specific technology application
- Using technology to meet learner-specific needs
- Using technology to meet the organization's needs
- Selecting an appropriate supplier to provide the technology
- Securing the appropriate learning and development staff to support the technology
- Applying basic design principles involved in technology applications
- Preparing program designers to utilize authoring tools

Fortunately, there are many excellent references to guide professionals through this maze. This section attempts to capture a brief glimpse of some of the technology applications to build an appreciation for the almost endless possibilities that exist for the learning and development field (Allen, 2003).

The Technology-Enhanced Classroom

Perhaps one of the most important starting points in the examination of technology is to explore its use in today's classroom. While technology-based learning is particularly useful on the job, it is also having a dramatic effect in the classroom. One learning facility at a Houston-based organization includes four classrooms, a teleconferencing room, and a multimedia development lab with the latest, state-of-the-art equipment. The learning center uses a broad range of advanced resources, including the following:

- Each classroom has over three dozen high-performance PCs that are continually upgraded.
- Three cameras in each classroom capture the instructor's image as well as those of the students. Remote controllers turn the camera to focus on a facilitator or a learner and project the image to in-room monitors or to offsite classrooms.
- Facilitators use a flexible control system to adjust audio, room lighting and camera views, and to start a video presentation.
- Three 32-inch color monitors in each classroom can display images from the facilitator's or any learner's PC.
- Eighteen ceiling microphones help learners communicate in each room. The microphones are voice activated, not when someone coughs or whispers.
- An image-projection system allows the facilitators to view student screens and has the ability to take control of a student's PC to demonstrate a feature.
- Three servers power the network: one houses instructional software for the classrooms; another handles faculty and staff e-mail; and a third performs file- and printer-sharing chores. Servers are connected via a fiber-optic network running throughout the building.
- A compressed video network connects the learning center rooms with classrooms offsite. Video connections travel via two T-1 lines.
- The heart of the network and A/V systems, the main distribution facility, contains a high-performance PC, the codec, and the network hub.

- Learners use the multimedia lab for burning CD-ROMs and editing videos. The lab is equipped with a nonlinear broadcast video editing system, 17-inch monitors, a camcorder, studio-class speakers, and digital video effects software.

This facility underscores the tremendous complexity and possibilities available to the classroom.

Web-Enabled Learning

The Internet makes it possible to communicate quickly, easily, and inexpensively anywhere in the world. A program can be broadcast simultaneously over the web in Brussels, Sydney, Hong Kong, and Toronto with virtually no cost attached. The web brings users a range and quantity of information that would be impossible to find through any other source. Billions of pages of text, graphics, sounds, video simulations, animations, and computer programs are available. All of this can be downloaded onto a personal computer with a simple click, and can now be downloaded to PDAs and cell phones as well.

The Internet can also be used as a way to share information and communicate, coproduce, and interact with a vast number of users. It provides real-time information and its distribution is immediate. From a learning perspective, the Internet has almost limitless potential to provide lectures, forums, bulletin boards, publications, online help, simulations, file transfer, and even role plays.

Most large organizations have their own intranet, a private, secure version of the Internet. The intranet offers the advantages of privacy within an internal network. One difference between the Internet and the intranet is the speed of delivery. The Internet is slower in delivery of information and learning programs, while intranets are much faster since they are not tied to one supplier's standard and the company can determine its needed power and speed. The intranet market outperforms the Internet due to its ability to streamline communication within the organization and operate with less cost.

Deciding if a program is appropriate for placement on the web requires serious consideration. Issues such as audience location, content, security, duration of program, and learner skill level should all be examined.

CD-ROMs and DVDs

While CD-ROMs and DVDs are used often, they have both disadvantages and advantages. Employees cannot update CD-ROMs or DVDs, and compatible hardware must be installed in order to receive the learning program. However, CD-ROMs and DVDs have vast storage capacity, which allows reduced cost per unit of information and increases information management potential. A single DVD with supporting materials equates to several hours of learning instruction.

Interactive Communication

Interactive communication includes e-mail, interactive TV, collaboration tools and teleconferencing. Through these vehicles, instructors, participants, and subject matter experts (SMEs) have the ability to communicate with each other sometimes simultaneously. E-mail and collaboration tools are especially effective when communicating with others in different time zones around the world. The greater the interactivity, the more effective the learning.

Video teleconferencing uses standard video equipment and uplinks to a satellite with participation from various locations. While video teleconferencing can be used individually, it is usually utilized by groups of learners. The development of video teleconferencing programs is a minor issue in organized learning. Usually, development includes maximum use of video camera capabilities, telephone, fax, and computer.

Web conferencing, however, is geared to individual users in any location. Learners link with the host computer, and the instructor begins the topic. Learners comment on the issues and can also create side discussions to elaborate on particular issues. In standard classroom training and video teleconferencing, learners can participate passively; with web conferencing, learners must actively participate.

Networks

Networks provide several desktop platforms to interface with a single source of information. Network technology includes the internet, intranet, local area networks (LANs), wide area networks (WANs), and WiFi. Organizations utilizing networks to deliver learning show reduced costs. Development of learning programs via network technology requires little complex authoring software.

Word processing software, in combination with the Internet, allows users to not only have immediate access to learning program information, but to create learning.

Multimedia

Interactive multimedia is a cost-effective and efficient way to deliver training. It is computer-based learning with two important components. First, the programming allows learners to obtain desired information when they want it. Programming also allows information to be obtained in the format specified by the learner. The second feature is the audio and video component. Because of the advances in computing capability, multimedia programs are now available on cell phones, assisting employees who travel and need to learn on the road.

Blended learning shows much promise as an integrated approach to improve learning. Figure 6-2 shows an example of blended learning being used to teach project management to professionals at Unilever and to prepare them to take the certified project management exam. The program involves an instructor-led, three-day workshop, three e-learning modules, workbooks, virtual sessions, and the project management exam.

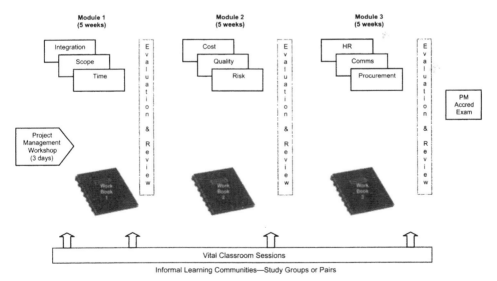

Figure 6-2. A blended learning example at Unilever. (Adapted from Beck, 2005)

Electronic Performance Support Systems (EPSS)

One of the most useful trends in technology is the growing acceptance, application, and continued interest in electronic performance support systems (EPSS). EPSS is a rapidly changing process, and sometimes it is difficult to define. Early in its application, EPSS was defined as the use of technology to provide on-demand access to integrated information, guidance, advice, assistance, learning, and tools to enable high-level job performance with minimum support from other people. Shifting from its primary purpose earlier in its development, EPSS now has the goal of improving performance instead of providing information and access to information.

A more current definition of EPSS from a system's viewpoint is that it is the electronic infrastructure that captures, stores, and distributes individual and corporate knowledge assets through an organization, enabling individuals to achieve acquired levels of performance in the fastest amount of time with minimum support. This definition is broader than prior definitions. Thus, an EPSS encompasses all of the software needed to support the work of individuals, not just one or two specific software applications. The EPSS integrates knowledge assets into the interface of the software tools rather than separating them as add-on components. For example, company policy information may be presented in a dialogue box message rather than as a separate, online document. EPSS examines the complete cycle, including the capture process and the distribution process, and it includes the management of electronic as well as nonelectronic assets.

EPSS has improved in its application and use; it is more than a passing fad. A well-designed EPSS application delivers what expert systems were supposed to, but never did. An EPSS is more than an electronic page turner or multimedia document. It incorporates the decision-making support of expert systems. With the information accessibility of electronic text retrieval systems and the individualized instructional capabilities of computer-based training, a well-designed EPSS provides the intended results. It simplifies tasks and empowers employees to perform work competently and productively. In short, EPSS encompasses the use of components of technology and information to deliver on-the-job performance. It holds much promise and is making much headway.

ALTERNATIVE DELIVERY SYSTEMS

The second major focus of this chapter is the growth of alternative delivery methods (non-technology oriented). These close-to-the-job processes have continued to expand, adding value along the way.

Job Rotation

Some organizations use a formal job rotation program to develop employees in current assignments and prepare them for future roles. A common type of job rotation has two or more people exchanging places, with each taking on new responsibilities. For example, in the quality section of one manufacturing firm, quality team leaders work at different stages in the manufacturing process. Team leaders rotate systematically to gain a clear understanding of the different quality control issues and problems. Sometimes job rotation is a part of a formal learning and development program. For example, in one financial services firm, management trainees rotate through all major departments, remaining in each department for one month. Job rotation is often included as a major part of succession planning programs. Specific development assignments are identified and included as part of the succession plan.

A part-time or temporary job rotation allows two people to provide instruction in each other's job duties. For example, one organization temporarily assigns district sales representatives to work in marketing at corporate headquarters when corporate staff members are on vacation. This provides additional learning for district sales representatives while it improves the cooperation and working relationships between field and headquarters staff.

Finally, if budget and organizational settings permit, an extra employee can be allocated to a learning slot. The individual learns as many jobs as possible, usually in preparation for the next opening, or they can be cross trained and used to fill in for other individuals. One manufacturer keeps an extra production supervisor in each major department—usually a newly promoted supervisor—who fills in when someone is on vacation or away on a short leave of absence.

Job rotation has advantages for both the organization and the managers who initiate it. A manager may have more flexibility in assigning work when more than one person can fill the position. The operation continues to run smoothly while the company prepares employees to assume other jobs and advance their careers. Job rotation prepares replacements for positions that eventually have to be filled. It even allows an employee to develop a replacement for his or her own job, eliminating the anguish of having a promotion deferred because a prepared successor is not available. Job rotation also helps the organization objectively identify those who have the ability and skills to be promoted.

In addition to the advantages for the organization, job rotation provides benefits for the individual. It prevents stagnation on the job and lets employees learn more about other jobs along with other aspects of the organization. Because different experiences teach different lessons, employees may develop skills and abilities not required for current assignments. Overall, job rotation can raise self-esteem, increase skills, and enhance careers.

Structured On-the-Job Learning

Although job rotation is an important type of on-the-job learning, other types of learning activities also occur on the job. Because on-the-job learning should be planned, it is sometimes referred to as structured, on-the-job learning. In practice, most learning occurs on the job—most early efforts to teach employees occur on the job, sometimes under the direction of an immediate supervisor. Establishing on-the-job learning involves several key elements:

1. First, individual learning needs must be uncovered to determine if structured, on-the-job learning is appropriate, feasible, and desired.
2. Both the learner and the trainer must be prepared for their assignments. Trainers may be employed on a full- or part-time basis.
3. Ideally, a specific plan needs to be developed, outlining what activity should occur at what time. The sequencing, timing, and expectations of each step should be clearly detailed. Specific measurable goals should be set so that the completion of each step can be observed and verified.
4. Job duties and tasks are examined to see how on-the-job learning can fit into the current work assignments. It should be as nondisruptive as possible and, at the same time, connected and supporting the current job task.
5. As the plan is followed, progress reports should be required in some way to measure the success and adjust the strategy, if possible.

6. The process should be evaluated to see how much learning has occurred and the extent to which it has been transferred into routine job assignments.

Self-Directed Learning

Self-directed learning is an important alternative delivery mechanism. For this approach to be successful, the employee must be motivated to learn new skills, technology, and methods. Many organizations recognize their obligation to make learning opportunities available and stimulate interest in those opportunities. At the same time, they emphasize self-directed learning. Highly motivated employees, eager to learn more, will take advantage of this approach to learning. Others will follow if encouraged, or required, to do so.

Organizations use several approaches for providing self-directed learning. Some provide a suggested reading list and others develop a prescribed program with assignments and follow-up meetings. This reading material must be related to the job and developed for easy comprehension. This approach works best if top managers set the example and develop their own reading schedule.

Technology is often the best and most appropriate way to take advantage of self-directed learning. Employees can select the modules or courses they need and study at a time that is most convenient for them, often within the comfort of their own homes.

Self-directed learning allows the learner to proceed at his or her own pace, learning one topic before going to the next. Reinforcement and repetition are used to ensure that the employee fully understands the material. Self teaching has two major advantages:

- It requires the active involvement of the employee. He or she responds to a question-stimulus after the presentation of small amounts of information.
- It provides immediate feedback about the quality of the participant's response. Participants are immediately provided with correct answers and can compare their responses with the preferred answers.

Local evening courses and part-time degree programs are another approach to self-study. Available at local colleges and universities, these programs help employees sharpen skills as well as build expertise in a variety of topics.

Individual Development Plans

Since much of the employee's development depends on his or her nature, learning and development can be efficiently accomplished through effective planning. One such approach involves the use of individual development plans (IDPs). These plans are developed around what the employee needs to know to perform more effectively, to enhance skills, and/or to prepare for movement to other jobs. IDPs may be developed for all employees or restricted to selected groups. One organization, for example, limits this approach to those employees it considers to have high potential for advancement; in this case, high potential is defined as the ability to advance two job levels in five years.

Individual development plans outline various experiences, specific training and educational programs, special projects, and other learning activities planned for a predetermined time period. Ideally, these plans are developed with the help of the learning and development staff. These individual plans are most effective when:

- The employee has direct input into determining what the IDP should contain.
- The manager is directly involved in the assessment of the employee's developmental needs and in the preparation of the IDP.
- Employees have some responsibility for monitoring their own progress related to the IDP.
- Employees receive immediate, objective feedback on their progress.
- Learning and development staff support is provided to ensure that the IDPs are developed and reviewed on a timely basis and that the process is accomplished consistently.
- The IDP is modified as necessary after periodic progress reviews.
- The IDPs remain confidential and are available for review by managers and key shareholders.

Individual development plans come in a variety of formats. The plan usually have several target dates and are reviewed periodically—sometimes every six months. The specific actions on the plan are initiated and monitored by the individual, the manager, or the learning and development department.

The primary benefit of this approach is that it recognizes individual differences in the learning needs of employees, and it subsequently provides a tailored, efficient approach to meet those specific needs.

Mentor Relationships

Mentoring, an intriguing and increasingly common approach to development, exists informally in almost every organization. Some organizations capitalize on this principle, encourage the practice, and develop formal guidelines. A mentor is someone who helps other individuals with their career development. Specifically, mentors teach, guide, advise, counsel, and supervise, as well as serve as role models. The mentor may or may not be in the same department, division, plant, or location as the person being mentored. Recently, the concept of virtual mentoring began taking hold. E-mentoring is being used by many organizations where it is difficult for the mentor and mentee to meet (Hall, 2005).

Mentoring requires establishing a relationship with an experienced, influential professional, internal or external to the organization. For the relationship to be productive, there must be a good match between the mentor and the mentee. They must both be willing participants in the process. An awareness of what constitutes mentoring will allow many veteran managers to utilize their daily interactions to develop employees. The impact can be far greater than many expensive formal management or employee development efforts (Fourie, 2005).

A word of caution: Employees learn from poor role models as well as good ones. In practice, most successful managers have worked for several memorable bosses and have learned what not to do from role models almost as often as they have learned what to do. Therefore, an individual with several mentors holds an advantage over the individual with a single mentor, regardless of the competence of the mentor.

Coaching

Coaching provides a practical and sometimes informal approach to developing employees, particularly executives. Usually conducted by a specially trained internal coach or an external executive coach, this technique presupposes that the vast majority of learning will occur on the job as a result of guided experience under the direction of effective managers or coaches. Sometimes, managers provide coaching for their direct employees. Coaching is not a one-time effort but a continuous process that involves discussions between the coach and the individual being coached.

The coach observes the individual, provides feedback, and plans specific actions to correct deficiencies. Because the process is repeated regularly, individuals feel less anxiety toward coaching than toward typical manager-led performance reviews. While realistic performance feedback is vital, individuals sometimes confuse coaching with criticism and, consequently, avoid the process. Employees must thoroughly understand their duties and the standards by which they are evaluated. They must know and understand the goals, targets, and mission of their department, division, or organization.

Coaching is not a substitute for performance feedback from the immediate manager. Performance feedback must be specific, direct and non-emotional, and employees must know when their performance is acceptable and when it is unacceptable. Their managers are in the best position to provide this feedback.

Coaching should not be confused with cheerleading. Although a coach should consistently provide positive reinforcement and motivation, the coach attempts to raise morale only when it is an issue. Also, a mistaken belief exists that only high potential employees and marginal performers need coaching. In reality, all employees need some kind of coaching, including average performers. Coaching helps new employees become more productive in a shorter period of time. Coaching also helps marginal performers improve their performance to an acceptable standard. It helps average employees excel by identifying strengths and weaknesses and by helping them develop necessary skills. For the super-performers, coaching helps maintain their outstanding performance records, enabling them to advance to other jobs in the organization (Morgan, Harkins, and Goldsmith, 2005).

Although employees may come to view their coaches as role models, the coaching process is not intended to provide leadership. The coach is there to help the employee with a performance problem, not to solve the problem or perform the job. Effective coaching does not happen spontaneously; it must be planned, organized, and encouraged, and examples must be set throughout the organization.

Special Projects and Assignments

Using special projects and assignments to develop employees can be effective. This approach involves assigning special, nonroutine job duties to build skills needed in the current job, as well as to prepare for assignments in the future. Here are some typical projects:

- *Short-term projects.* Examples include participating in special investigations, solving a serious problem, exploring the feasibility of new technology, procedures, and products, or installing new equipment. These are sometimes sponsored by a CEO or another executive as part of an executive education program.
- *Task forces.* Examples include implementing enterprise software, implementing Six Sigma, or designing a new system.
- *On-loan assignments to other parts of the organization.* Examples include temporarily being assigned to research and development, briefly rotating to field sales, or managing a business unit.
- *Special assistance to schools and colleges.* Examples include helping a local vocational school develop a new curriculum, serving on an advisory committee for a community college, or teaching a business course at an evening college.
- *Special assignments to volunteer for nonprofit organizations.* Examples include fund-raising for the United Way, assisting the Red Cross in a disaster relief project, and implementing a human resources system in a child-care facility. The project should be selected on the basis of the development needs of the employee and the employee's willingness to participate in such activities.

Action Learning

Closely aligned to the project assignments discussed earlier is a process that varies considerably from traditional training—action learning. Typically, an action learning application involves three to four weeks of classroom learning consisting of interactive discussions and group participation. A project is assigned with individuals working as a team to achieve a specific goal, often with the support of colleagues. The projects are challenging and meaningful and represent problems or opportunities that need to be addressed. Participants are not only able to use what they learned in the classroom, but they have an opportunity to learn with and from each other by working on real problems and reflecting on their own experiences (Tunheim, Skoglund, and Cottrell, 1996).

Peer Teaching

A special type of on-the-job training involves the one-on-one learning opportunity often referred to as peer teaching, which is performed by a colleague or team member. Peer teaching is an organized and planned approach to develop other individuals using one-on-one instruction. The processes for developing peer or team member teaching are similar to the on-the-job training and the types of efforts and projects reflected in the job rotation method discussed earlier.

Just-in-Time Learning

Providing learning opportunities at the right time to the right employees and making sure they contain the right materials is not a new concept. It has been the desire of every CLO. However, because of the structure of traditional training, just-in-time learning has been difficult to achieve. With new delivery methods that move learning and development to the job site and use a variety of technology options, organizations are now able to provide just-in-time learning. Just-in-time learning requires a commitment to help employees, customers, distributors, and suppliers keep up with changes by providing them with timely information and instruction. Just-in-time learning is grounded in adult learning theory, which shows that adults are most keenly motivated to learn when they are grappling with immediate work problems. This process not only involves the method of delivery and the location of the learning program, it examines a process where needs are developed and met. It also involves examining communications and scheduling of learning opportunities, ensuring that no item is lost and that the learning is not provided too early or too late to be effective. This concept will continue to be a hot topic as time pressures become critical and the need for new skills becomes urgent.

As discussed earlier, the growing interest in alternative learning is based on the need to deliver information and facilitate workplace learning on a timely basis. Alternative delivery allows learning to be delivered virtually anywhere, particularly through multiple sites at the same time. Technology also allows for delivery on demand for the learner, compared with the set schedule of traditional training. Figure 6-3 illustrates this point. Traditional classroom learning is at point A in the figure, whereas alternative delivery methods, including technology, move up to points B and C.

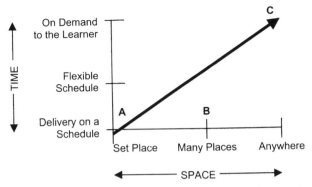

Figure 6-3. Classroom learning versus alternative delivery methods.

OUTLOOK

Technology

The positive impact of using technology for learning is substantial; for example:

- With the flexibility to add participants at no additional cost, more people can learn at a lower cost per participant.
- The quality of teaching increases due to utilization of expertise outside the learning facility during interaction between facilitators and participants.
- Participants learn at their own pace.
- Facility and resource costs drop because fewer classrooms, facilitators, and instructional supplies are required.
- Learning becomes decentralized, allowing it to occur at any place or time.
- Technology is always available to deliver learning and participants can count on consistent learning opportunities.

From all the evidence, it seems likely that technology applications will multiply dramatically and the development in software, hardware, and systems configurations will increase. Many issues involving technology will not only continue, but will intensify in the future. The CLO must deal with this issue reasonably.

A critical challenge is the overall approach to the use of technology. Almost every learning and development function has access to the technology described in this chapter. With the decreasing cost of software and hardware and the global availability of the Internet, the question is not *what* is available, but *how* the organization will take advantage of what is available. Table 6-3 illustrates two different approaches to the use of technology in learning and development: conservative versus innovative. As the table clearly illustrates, a conservative approach is a comfort zone that only uses completely obvious and proven technology, limiting applications only to those that have been tested by many others (Phillips, 1999).

A more innovative approach requires stretching and experimenting within each learning and development function. While technology has improved significantly, its application and use in learning and development has been limited and slow to develop. This would be a negative twist on an important development. Instead, we choose to examine the actual progress made by learning and development departments after they have significantly implemented technology. One point remains clear: the challenge is to use the technology that is available in the most appropriate and effective manner. Often, this means moving beyond the conservative approach and trying new innovative tools and techniques. Otherwise, the learning and development function will be pulled along in the technology revolution rather than being a driver to enhance performance. This is a great opportunity for the CLO.

Alternative Delivery

As with many of the other trends, this one has been developing for many years. However, in recent years it has mushroomed considerably with the development and availability of technology. Most CLOs welcome this transition and have explored different ways of making learning and development more efficient, responsive, and timely. However, some resistance may exist among individuals who prefer to be stand-up trainers. They may want to stay with the old ways because that is where they are most comfortable. Helping these people make the transition from traditional delivery will require education, coaching, and, ultimately, some goal setting.

Alternative delivery often requires additional time, particularly when using one-on-one delivery methods. Most organizations attempt this transition gradually, deliberately integrating alternative delivery and technology slowly so that it does not dramatically influence the budget at any one period.

Alternative delivery requires communication and training for the target audience and support group. The individual participants and

Table 6-3
Two Contrasting Approaches to Technology

Topic	Conservative Approach	Innovative Approach
Primary usage of computer capability	Imitate the old media, playing back electronic animated talking books.	Employ an enabling device used to experience an augmented reality with simulation, modeling, virtual reality, etc.
Views on Internet	Provide a super CD-ROM.	Provide the best colearning environment ever.
Implementation objective	Reduce training costs.	Improve performance by empowering learners.
Communication: dominant model	Establish one-to-one and one-to-many communication.	Establish many-to-many communication.
Main function	Exchange information.	Share experiences with VR, distributed simulations, and conferencing. Share information with workshop.
Main objective	Develop distance learning and flexible tutoring.	Facilitate access to multiple special interest groups, specialists, and resources.
Conferencing	Use teletutoring and distributed classrooms.	Encourage formal as well as informal communication.
Knowledge management	Drop in to collect information.	Share expertise, influence developments
Learning support produced	Produce electronic books and tools for trainers.	Produce experiential environments and tools for learners.
Favored authoring tool	Use multimedia and animation editors for electronic books.	Use the following authoring tools: simulation, distributed simulation, virtual reality and artificial intelligence.
Virtual reality	Re-create existing spaces like classrooms or labs.	Create new experiential and socialized spaces.

their immediate supervisors must understand how alternative delivery works and their roles in the process to make it successful. For most of them, selecting alternative delivery methods will be welcome news, as the process often provides them with more pleasing options, reduces their time commitment, and maximizes learning. However, participants may resist because they have become accustomed to traditional classroom training. This is particularly the case where organizations have been delivering learning programs at resort locations. A one-week-long program including social activities and recreational opportunities provides a relaxing opportunity for a break from the job routine. If individuals are attending programs for the wrong reasons, alternative delivery may not be attractive and may even be resisted.

Senior management usually welcomes this alternative delivery because it reduces the cost of facilities and the cost of delivering training, at least in most cases. Senior management usually supports the process and provides the necessary commitment to make it work.

FINAL THOUGHTS

This chapter has explored the topic of alternative delivery systems, including the use of technology. Facilitator-led classroom learning is routinely being replaced by a variety of learning and development methods that are delivered at or near the job, just in time of need, and often using technology. This shift represents a tremendous opportunity for the CLO to add value as learning is more efficient, more relevant, and is delivered just in time to the appropriate audience.

CLOs need to lead change within their own learning function. The pace of modern-day business is so rapid that the traditional models and approaches are not always viable. A wider variety of learning models are being utilized to keep up with the business needs—establishing peer-to-peer learning networks, taking the training closer to the workplace, and leveraging knowledge management systems, workplace coaching, and technology based solutions.

Bonnie Stoufer, Vice President for Learning, Training & Development, Boeing

REFERENCES

Allen, Michael. *Guide to E-Learning*. New York, NY: John Wiley, 2003.

Beck, Daryl. "Blended Learning: Getting the Right Mix," *CIPD Handbook*. London, England: Charted Institute for Professional Development, 2005.

Bell, Chip R. *Managers as Mentors*. San Francisco, CA: Berrett-Koehler Publishers, 1996.

Dolezalek, Holly. "Industry Report—2004," *Training*. October 2004.

Fourie, Leon. "Common Pitfalls and Lessons from Mentoring and Coaching Initiatives," *Skills Africa Summit IIR*, May 2005.

Hall, Liz. "E-Mentoring: Me and My Mentor," *People Management*. March 2005.

Levy, Jonathon. "The Future of Learning Technology," *Chief Learning Officer*. July 2004, 42–45.

Morgan, Howard, Phil Harkins, and Marshall Goldsmith. *The Art and Practice of Leadership Coaching: 50 Top Executive Coaches Reveal Their Secrets*. New York, NY: John Wiley, 2005.

Phillips, Jack J. *HRD Trends Worldwide*. Woburn, MA: Elsevier, 1999.

Snipes, Jeff. "Blended Learning: Reinforcing Results," *Chief Learning Officer*. September 2005, 56.

Tunheim, Katherine A., Judith Skoglund, and Dorothy Cottrell. "Action Learning." In *Action: Designing Training Programs*. Alexandria, VA: 1996, 271–287.

Van Dam, Nick. "Overcoming Challenges in Learning and Development," *Chief Learning Officer*. September 2005, 30.

CHAPTER 7

Managing for Value

> *A key difference between internal consultants, learning profes-*
> *sionals, and external consultants is that internal professionals*
> *are around for implementation, which enables them to have a*
> *broader perspective on all initiatives.*
> Allan Weisberg, Vice President of
> Organization Capability, Johnson & Johnson

Managing the learning and development function as a business is an
important part of the value-added equation. Within this context, the
CLO is constantly seeking ways to make the function more efficient,
resourceful, and effective in a variety of different areas. Four areas
comprise this chapter.

The first is the budgeting process, which is necessary to develop
the fiscal plans and learning implementation strategy for the next
year. The good news is that the budget is developed the same way
as in any other major function, thus underscoring the legitimacy of
learning and development as a business. The challenge is to select
the particular way in which the budget is developed and used in the
organization.

The second issue involves monitoring and controlling costs for
maximum effectiveness and efficiency. The rationale for monitoring
and controlling costs routinely is explored, as are ways to classify,
categorize, and report costs.

A third, more challenging issue for the learning and development
team represents utopia in terms of accountability—the development
of the profit center concept. This concept is explored, including its
benefits and challenges.

The fourth issue focuses on managing vendors and suppliers as
adjunct staff for the learning and development team. As learning
professionals become more strategic and more traditional learning

activities are outsourced, this topic becomes more challenging and necessary to ensure that the outsourcing is conducted efficiently and effectively and that it adds the appropriate value.

There are other issues involved in managing the learning and development function to add value. These include ensuring that the right staff members are selected and motivating and rewarding them to achieve exceptional performance. These issues are adequately addressed in many other books and are not explored in detail here.

THE BUDGETING PROCESS

As organizations recognize the importance and necessity for learning and development, annual budgets continue to increase by organization, industry, and country. Consequently, the process to develop a budget for a learning and development organization is becoming more structured.

A formal budgeting process, aligned with the business strategy, is considered one of the most important management tools for efficient and effective operation. Budgets are developed with other major functions and entities using the same budgeting guidelines and processes.

The budgeting process usually begins with delivery of a package containing specific guidelines, forms, procedures, and special instructions for developing the budget. It also contains the approval process, philosophy, concerns, and other issues often communicated along with budget packages. The good news is that the learning and development function is considered a mainstream activity in the organization—subject to the same control and budgeting requirements as other departments. For the CLO, the process has become more formal, organized, and accurate. The bad news is that the budget by itself can be constraining, take time, and may be inflexible in its administration.

The budget has become the most widely used tool of control for managers. Budgets enable the CLO to know where learning and development functions stand, to spot various trends, and to control resources during the fiscal year. When the budget is approved, it should communicate three things:

1. The learning and development plan for providing learning i
   tiatives and services must meet specific operational and
   gic business goals.

2. Each learning initiative should add value to the organization in some way, ultimately captured as increased performance revenue or a reduction of costs. In essence, almost all programs should increase productivity, improve quality, save time, reduce costs directly, or improve satisfaction for customers and employees.

3. Each learning initiative will have a specific unit cost associated with it. The total cost of all programs and services are included in the budget while the cost per program and per participant is included in the detail.

These three major statements characterize an ideal budget, a situation sought by many CLOs as the budget is developed each year. Unfortunately, some budgets fall short of providing the detail or connections of all three.

Collecting Information

In addition to information about specific program needs, several types of information should be collected when the budget is being developed. Table 7-1 provides a sampling of reports that might be

Table 7-1
Sampling of Documents Needed for Budget Development

- Operating plans of the organization
- Strategic plans or a multi-year operating plan
- Capital expenditure budget
- Operating performance of the organization
- Financial performance of the organization
- Major operating issues and concerns
- Special audit and investigative reports that address concerns or problem areas
- Customer satisfaction and commitment data
- Engagement and job satisfaction
- 360° feedback summaries
- Leadership inventories
- Succession planning documents
- Performance management process reports
- Talent management reports
- Specific projects in process

needed for budget preparation. These items can supply information that may help provide direction for budget implementation. New programs should be tied to specific business needs, which are addressed later. Several items in this table represent a wealth of opportunities to explore programs for the next year's budget.

A variety of business plans clearly indicate the direction of the organization, identifying some of the major issues and problems, which often translate directly into learning and development opportunities. This plan often alerts the CLO to strategic shifts that will occur in the business. Special audits and investigative reports uncover problems and issues, which represent a great source for program possibilities. Business issues, such as customer complaints, time to market, and delays of new products, are all business issues that can translate into learning opportunities for CLOs. Using these strategic business issues as a platform for developing curriculum and organizational solutions is the responsibility of an effective CLO.

Types of Budget

Although there can be many different types of budgets unique to an organization, three major categories often appear and each is briefly presented here. The specific application of these types can vary with the organization and culture.

Fixed and Variable Budgets. The fixed budget represents those costs that will not directly vary with the amount of work that is to be conducted. Facilities for learning and development, learning management systems, and overhead support staff fit into this category. The variable budget represents costs directly related to specific output, such as the number of programs or participants attending programs. Program materials, travel expenses, and facilitators are examples of variable costs. Some organizations use a charge-back model to manage learning budgets—users of learning in the business areas are charged a per-student fee to cover program costs. Other companies use an allocation model where budgets are "allocated" based on a flat fee per head count in a division or corporate area. Other organizations use a profit and loss model and are managed as business entities. All of these models have appropriate applications based on the business or organizational.

Planning, Programming, and Budgeting System. Initially launched by the federal government and now used by many organizations, this system is one where the budget is developed for specific programs. There are five basic steps to follow with this approach.

1. Specify and analyze basic objectives in each major area of activity.
2. Analyze the output of planned programs as defined by specific objectives.
3. Measure total cost of the programs for several years as a projection.
4. Analyze alternatives to the programs.
5. Make the approach an integral part of the budget.

Zero-Based Budgeting. Some organizations are using a system where the budget is developed from the ground up, with no holdover from the previous year. With this approach, every program or service is justified in the budgeting process. Zero-based budgets remove the temptation to add to the previous year's budget or to develop a budget based on what was accomplished in the previous year. When starting from zero, a careful analysis of the costs, as well as the value of various priorities, is required. With this approach, activities, programs, or services are developed into decision packages. Various services or programs are evaluated with resources allocated to those with the highest priority.

A realistic approach to budgeting could be a blend of all three of these types or a subset of just one.

Types of Programs

The process of identifying the specific types of programs is both necessary and challenging. The budget must be developed and plans must be established, along with a detailed summary of planned programs. It is challenging in that all the learning needs that will be generated during the year may be unknown. Also, the needs assessment and analysis process does not always coincide with the development of the budget. Basically, there are four types of programs and services.

- Ongoing programs that are repeated each year. For example, leadership development will be needed each year as new leaders are promoted or hired.
- New programs based on perceived needs or actual needs assessments. For example, customer service training for a particular job function based on predetermined needs assessment.
- Consulting services provided by the learning and development staff to help the organization improve performance. While some

projects can be predicted based on previous work, others would focus on perceived needs or actual needs as they are developed.

- Other services and support processes including administrative functions, such as tuition reimbursement. These services are often justified based on the level of activity or participation required.

Overall, determining specific types of programs may be the most difficult, but also crucial, part of the budgeting process. It must be completed with as much information as possible and be based on legitimate needs analysis. Many organizations create formal learning plans that are generated with input from business leaders. These plans provide a program, strategy, goal, and financial plan for all learning activities that are planned for the business. At QUAL-COMM, for example, an in-depth needs assessment process is conducted annually with 20 to 120 employees and managers in each business unit and functional area (See Figure 7-1). Needs are collected by the learning staff through an internal consulting process. These needs are put into a comprehensive strategic learning plan and are reviewed by the senior team and president of each division. This plan guides all learning initiatives for each business and is approved for accuracy, relevance, and budget. Plans are reviewed semiannually to provide updates to the executive team and progress is tracked. Processes and plans like this are not uncommon practices for CLOs who invest heavily in linking business and learning needs.

Using the Budget

Developing a learning and development budget is an essential part of managing any function, activity, or process in an organization. The trend toward more formal budgets is based, in part, on the legitimate role of learning. Budgets are a welcome tool for the learning and development staff because they make it possible to link learning to the business. Budgets can also act as a signaling device to take corrective action. When used properly, the budget can help the staff learn from past experiences. It also improves the allocation of resources within the department and helps communicate priorities. In some cases, budget performance can be an important element of the performance management process.

On the other side, budgets can become very complex, confusing, and time consuming. If the budget is not flexible, it may cause individuals to stick to the "numbers," regardless of the learning needs

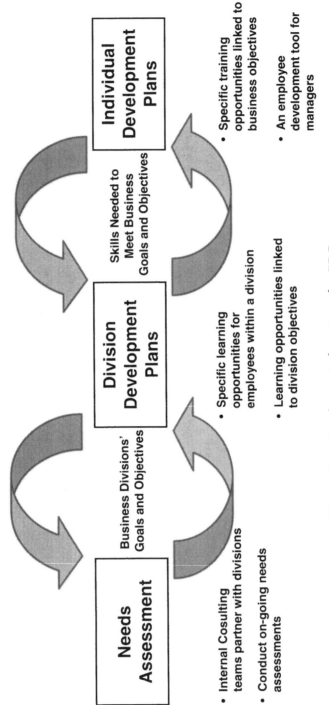

Figure 7-1. Qualcomm's learning plan/IDP process.

that may exist. Also, budgets can allow individuals to manipulate the funding, anticipating budget cuts and spending all of the money, whether it is needed or not.

MONITORING AND CONTROLLING COSTS

The cost of providing learning and development to employees is increasing. As CLOs scramble to fund their budgets, they must know how and why money is spent. Today there is more pressure than ever to report all costs of formal learning, referred to as a fully loaded cost profile. This goes beyond the direct cost of learning and includes the time that participants are involved in learning programs. Individual cost components are used to manage resources, develop standards, measure efficiencies, and examine alternative delivery processes. The total costs of a program can be used in an analysis to measure the actual return on investment (ROI) (Van Adelsberg and Trolley, 1999).

Why the Concern for Costs?

Many influences have caused the increased attention to monitoring and controlling learning costs accurately and thoroughly. Some of the more important ones are listed here.

Every CLO must know how much is invested in learning and development. Most CLOs calculate this expenditure and make comparisons with other organizations. The typical value is the cost of learning as a percentage of payroll. Others calculate learning and development costs as a percentage of revenue or develop learning and development costs on a per-employee basis. These categories were presented in Chapter 3. Total expenditures go beyond the overall budget for the learning and development department and include additional costs such as participants' salaries, travel expenses, replacement costs, facilities expenses, and general overhead. A few CLOs calculate and report this value.

Monitoring costs by program allows the learning and development staff to evaluate the relative contribution of a program and determine how these costs are changing. If a program's cost has risen, it might be time to reevaluate its impact and overall success. It may be useful to compare specific components of costs to other programs or organizations. For example, the cost per participant for one program could be compared to the cost per participant for a similar program. Significant differences may signal a problem. Also, costs associated with design, development, or delivery could be compared to other programs within the organization and used to develop cost standards. Competitive pressures are causing increased attention on efficiencies. Most learning and development departments have monthly budgets that project costs by various accounts and, in some cases, by initiative or program. Cost reports are excellent tools for spotting problem areas and taking corrective action. From a practical and classical management sense, the accumulation of cost data is a necessity.

Also, current costs are needed to predict future program costs, and historical costs provide the basis for predicting future costs. Sophisticated cost models provide the capability to estimate or predict costs with reasonable accuracy. Perhaps the most significant driver to collect costs is to prepare data for use in a benefits-versus-costs comparison. In this respect, cost data is as important as the program's economic benefits.

Cost data is needed for the human capital management system. A learning and development department must collect cost data so that these data can be integrated into existing databases for other human resource functions such as compensation, benefits, and recruiting. Including learning and development cost information in these databases provides information about the learning contribution to human resources costs. Some human capital systems monitor costs automatically.

Detailed costs are needed to plan and budget for future operations. The operating budget usually includes all of the expenditures within learning and development, and it may also include other costs such as participants' salaries and their associated travel expenses. In recent years, the budgeting process has come under closer scrutiny and a percentage increase to the previous year's budget is no longer acceptable for most organizations. More organizations have adopted zero-based budgets, in which each activity must be justified and no expenses are carried over from the previous year. An accurate accounting of expenditures enables the CLO to defend proposed ideas and programs in a line-item review with management.

Cost Classification Systems

Capturing costs is challenging because they must be accurate, reliable, and realistic. Costs can be classified in two basic ways. One is by a description of the expenditure such as labor, materials, supplies, travel, and so on. These are expense account classifications. The other is by placing them in categories in the learning process or function such as in analysis, program development, delivery, and evaluation. An effective system will monitor costs by account categories and include a method for accumulating costs by the process/functional category. While the first grouping is sufficient to present the total cost of the program, it does not allow for a useful comparison with other programs or indicate areas where costs might be excessive by relative comparisons. Therefore, two basic classifications are recommended to develop a complete costing system: process/functional classifications and expense account classifications (discussed next).

Process/Functional Classifications

Table 7-2 shows the process/functional categories for costs in four different ways. In Column A, there are only two categories: (1) support costs and (2) operating costs. Support costs include all administrative, overhead, development, and reassessment cost, or any other expenditure not directly related to conducting the program; operating costs include all expenses involved in conducting the program. While it is simple to separate the two, it does not provide enough detail to analyze costs on a functional basis. Column B adds a third category and provides a little more detail, but it does not provide information or program development costs—a useful item to have. Column C provides for development costs as a separate item, but it still falls short of an ideal situation. There is no way

Table 7-2
Process/Functional Categories for Cost

A	B
Support Costs	Classroom Costs
Operating Costs	Administrative Costs
	Participant Compensation and Facility Costs

C	D
Program Development Costs	Assessment Costs
Administrative Costs	Development Costs
Classroom Costs	Delivery Costs
Participant Costs	Evaluation Costs

to track evaluation costs, which are becoming a more significant part of the total process. Column D represents an appropriate cost breakdown: assessment, development, delivery, and evaluation. The administrative costs can be allocated to one of these areas or listed separately as a fifth category.

Needs assessment costs will usually be in the range of 10 to 15 percent of the learning and development budget. Development costs will run in the 15 to 25 percent range, while delivery is 55 to 75 percent of the budget. Evaluation is usually less than 5 percent. The actual breakdown will depend on how costs are accumulated in the organization and will vary considerably with each program, particularly in the development and delivery components. If a program is developed from one already in operation, development costs should be low. Similarly, in a lengthy program involving a large amount of participant time, the delivery costs may be much higher.

Expense Account Classifications

The most time-consuming step in developing a cost system is defining and classifying the various expenses. Many of the expense accounts, such as office supplies and travel expenses, are already a part of the existing accounting system. However, there may be expenses unique to the learning and development department that must be added to the system. The system design will depend on the organization, the type of programs developed and conducted, and the limits imposed on the current cost-accounting system. Also, to a certain extent, the expense account classifications will depend on how the process/functional categories have been developed, as discussed in the previous section.

Cost Monitoring and Reporting Issues

The most important part of cost monitoring is to define which specific costs are included in program costs. This involves decisions that will be made by the learning and development staff and are usually approved by management. If appropriate, the finance and accounting staff may need to approve the list. Table 7-3 shows the recommended cost categories to report for a fully loaded, conservative approach to estimating costs. These issues and categories go beyond the basic process/functional categories described earlier. Each category is described in the following pages.

Table 7-3
Learning Program Cost Categories

Cost Item	Prorated	Expensed
Needs Assessment	✓	
Design and Development	✓	
Acquisition	✓	
Delivery		✓
• Salaries/Benefits—Facilitators		✓
• Salaries/Benefits—Coordination		✓
• Program Materials and Fees		✓
• Travel/Lodging/Meals		✓
• Facilities		✓
Salaries/Benefits—Participants		
• Contact Time		✓
• Travel Time		✓
• Preparation Time		✓
Evaluation		✓
Overhead/Learning and Development	✓	

Prorated Versus Direct Costs. All costs related to a program are usually captured and expensed to that program. However, three categories are frequently prorated over several sessions of the same program: needs assessment, design and development, and acquisition. Some organizations will conservatively estimate one year of operation for the program; others may estimate two or three years. If there is some question about the time period, the finance and accounting staff should be consulted for the specific amount of time to use in the prorating formula. Learning and development overhead is usually allocated to each program as well.

Benefits Factor. When presenting the salaries of participants and staff associated with programs, the benefits factor should be included. This number is usually well known in the organization and used in other costing formulas. It represents the cost of all employee benefits expressed as a percentage of base salaries. In some organizations, this value is as high as 50 to 60 percent, while in others it may be as low as 25 to 30 percent; in the United States the average is 38 percent.

Needs Assessment. The cost of conducting a needs assessment is one item that is often overlooked. In some programs this cost is zero because no needs assessment is conducted. However, as more organizations increase their focus on needs assessment, this item will represent a more significant cost. All costs associated with needs assessment should be captured to the fullest extent possible, including the time of staff members conducting the assessment, direct fees and expenses for external consultants, and internal services and supplies used in the analysis. The total costs are usually prorated over the life of the program when the costs need to be allocated to a particular group, session, or individual. Depending on the type and nature of the program, the shelf life should be kept in the one- to two-year time frame. Of course, very expensive programs are an exception, where they are not expected to change significantly for several years.

Design and Development Costs. One of the more significant items is the cost of designing and developing the program. These costs include internal staff time in design and development, the use of consultants, and the purchase of supplies, videos, CD-ROMs, and other materials directly related to the program. Design and development costs are usually prorated, perhaps using the same time frame as the needs assessment—if there is a need to allocate to a session or individual. One to two years is recommended unless the program is not expected to change for many years.

Acquisition Costs. In lieu of development costs, many organizations purchase packaged programs to use directly or in a modified format. Acquisition costs include the purchase price for instructor materials, train-the-trainer sessions, licensing agreements, and other costs associated with the rights to deliver the program. These acquisition costs should be prorated using the same rationale as mentioned earlier. If the program requires modification or additional development, these costs should be included as development costs. In practice, many programs have both acquisition and development costs.

Delivery Costs. The largest segment of a learning program is usually comprised of the costs associated with delivery. The following five major categories are included:

Facilitators' and Coordinators' Salaries. The salaries of facilitators or program coordinators should be included. If a coordinator is involved in more than one program, the time should be allocated to the specific program. If external facilitators are used, all charges should be included for the session. It is important to capture all of the direct time of internal employees or external consultants working with the program. Benefits should also be included each time direct labor costs are involved.

Program Materials and Fees. Specific materials such as notebooks, textbooks, case studies, exercises, and participant workbooks should be included in the delivery costs, along with user fees and royalty payments. Pens, paper, certificates, and calculators are also included in this category.

Travel, Lodging, and Meals. Direct travel costs for participants, facilitators, or coordinators are included. Lodging, meals, and refreshments are included for participants during travel, as well as meals during the program.

Facilities. The direct cost of facilities for the training should be included. For external programs, this is the direct charge from the conference center, hotel, or training room. If the program is conducted in-house, the conference room should be estimated and included, even if it is not the practice to include facility cost in other reports.

Participants' Salaries and Benefits. Participants' salaries and employee benefits for the time involved in the program represent an expense that should be included. If the program has already been conducted, these costs can be estimated using average or midpoint values for salaries in typical job classifications. When a program is targeted for a comprehensive evaluation, participants can provide their salaries confidentially.

Evaluation. The total cost of the evaluation should be included to compute the fully loaded cost of a program. Evaluation costs include developing the evaluation strategy, designing instruments, collecting data, analyzing data, and preparing and distributing reports. Cost categories include time, materials, purchased instruments, or surveys.

Overhead. A final charge is overhead—additional costs in the learning function not directly related to a particular program. The overhead category represents any learning and development center cost not considered in the earlier calculations. Typical items include the cost of administrative support, office expenses, salaries of learning staff (including the CLO), and other fixed costs. In some organizations, the total is divided by the number of program participant days (or hours) for the year to obtain a per-day (or per-hour) estimate for allocation. This becomes a standard value to use in calculations.

Fully Loaded Costs

It is recommended that learning costs be fully loaded whenever possible. With this conservative approach, all costs that can be identified and linked to a particular program are included. The philosophy is simple: If it is questionable whether or not a cost should be included, it is recommended that it be included. Cost reporting should withstand even the closest scrutiny of its accuracy and credibility. The only way to meet this test is to ensure that all costs are included. Of course, from a realistic viewpoint, if the controller or CFO insists on not using certain costs, then it is best to leave them out.

From all indications, it appears that this trend will continue. Looking at fully loaded costs provides data that is essential for the management of the department, as well as other managers and executives who must make decisions about learning and development.

Recovering Training Costs

Another very important option for improving the efficiency and profitability of the learning enterprise is recovering the costs of training. In the United States, a variety of training grants, incentives, tax credits, and rebates are available to employers who provide needed training to employees. Employers can defray part of the cost of training by applying for reimbursements from local, state, or even federal agencies. In some states, this is provided in advance of the training, based on the types of programs eligible for these reimbursements. Others reimburse organizations for training that has already occurred—in some cases for years in the past. This arrangement takes place in other countries as well. A variety of governments in Europe, Africa, and Asia collect levies, taxes, and other fees directly from employers, then provide funds back to them as they invest in employee training. In almost every case, it is up to the employer to fully document the training and complete the application for the reimbursement. In some cases prior approval is required if reimbursement or refunds are planned.

The complexity of dealing with various government agencies and the difficulty of understanding how and when applications are made are leading many CLOs to turn to companies that help others navigate the reimbursement maze. For example, one organization, Wallace—The Training Cost Recovery Company (www. wraywallace.com), specializes in helping CLOs and their organizations recover training costs. Some learning and development centers with significant training expenses have been able to recover millions of dollars through this organization.

Exploring the Profit Center Concept

Some organizations have converted the operation of the learning and development department to a profit center rather than a cost center. Under the profit center arrangement, the department charges for products and services using a competitive fee schedule. Its clients, the managers in the organization, have the option of purchasing programs and services from the internal learning and development function or from external suppliers. Operating expenses are offset by revenues generated from program fees. Revenue exceeding operating cost generates a profit for the organization. While there has been a successful model for some organizations, many have opted for a more blended funding approach for learning. The profit center trend has been declining in recent years due to numerous challenges with this model, finding cuts being a major concern.

Why a Profit Center?

Several influences have driven the profit center concept over the years. It is perceived by some to be the ultimate level of accountability as far as evaluation is concerned, as shown in Figure 7-2. In a profit center model the learning and development department operates as if it were a business unit or a privately owned business with profits showing the true measure of economic success. Its customers

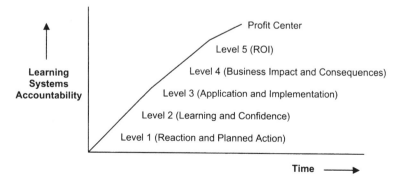

Figure 7-2. Levels of evaluation.

have complete autonomy to use the internal services or to shop externally. As Figure 7-2 implies, the other levels of evaluation must be firmly in place and thoroughly understood by clients before a profit center can be successful. In essence, managers need to understand that the learning programs and services are contributing to business unit performance and providing an excellent ROI before they will be willing to pay the prices demanded.

A key driver for shifting to the profit center concept is the challenge to provide products and services on a competitive basis. Most CLOs are convinced that they can offer superior programs for the same or lower price as external sources. They do not want to be perceived as an excess cost or financial burden to the organization and strive to demonstrate value through being a P&L center. However, many organizations that moved to a profit center model did not succeed and have changed their strategy, becoming corporate funded, a business unit charge-back, or fully allocated.

While there may be a need to evaluate the costs versus benefits of critical learning programs, the profit center concept lessens the need to calculate the ROI for most individual programs because the profit generated from revenues reflects the return on the total investment. Nonprofitable programs will either be subsidized by profitable programs or disappear.

Some professionals perceive the profit center as similar to an independent consulting firm. Hundreds of firms provide consulting services and learning and development programs as their sole source of revenue. They develop and customize in-house programs to meet their clients' needs with the goal of making a profit. The internal learning and development department should be able to provide the same programs or services, also at a profit.

In some cases, the management team demands this type of arrangement. Operating managers want the freedom to use any services they wish and not be required to always buy the services from the in-house training and education function. These client pressures force some organizations to gradually move to a profit center concept, giving managers more autonomy to buy services externally.

Successful cases have sparked enthusiasm among learning and development practitioners and senior executives. They perceive the profit center concept as a valuable way to address issues such as management support, increased funding, and concern over results. This model, however, does not fit every organization.

Sources of Revenue

If the profit center concept is effective, fees must be established for all products and services. A typical learning and development department has several sources of revenue, usually divided into the following categories:

> *Consulting and Professional Services.* User departments pay for services, including professional staff time devoted to conflict resolution, problem solving, needs analysis, organizational development, or other activities aimed at improving the organization. Service fees may also be collected for program development.
>
> *Program Fees.* Internal clients pay fees for seminars, workshops, or other learning programs. Fees cover the costs of delivering the program as well as overhead, analysis, development, and evaluation.
>
> *Products.* Product sales include self-contained packaged programs and materials for departments or divisions within the organization. For example, a self-sufficient learning module with all the materials and a facilitator's guide that does not necessarily require support from the staff are sold at a fixed price.
>
> *Administrative Services.* User departments are charged fees for routine services provided by the learning staff. Examples include processing tuition refund requests, coordinating external seminar participation, or processing 360-degree feedback instruments.

A few organizations also receive income from external sales of services and programs. DuPont, Disney, General Motors, Ford, Microsoft, Cisco Systems, and Xerox are only a few of the many organizations that sell their programs to the public (Gordon, 2005).

Fee/Price Determination

The determination of fees or prices for revenue items is critical to the success of a profit center model. Prices must be high enough to generate the desired profit, yet low enough to be competitive. Three basic approaches are available for setting fees:

> *Fee Negotiation.* The learning and development staff and the client can negotiate a fair and equitable fee for the services offered.

This approach is particularly useful when determining the fee to charge for professional assistance and support. Some consideration must be given to using a rate similar to those set by external consulting firms providing the same or similar services.

Competitive Pricing. Another possibility is to price the program or service equal to or less than the market price for the same or similar items. This is probably the best approach with commonly available programs. The prices must compete with those that are commercially available and, ideally, they should be lower. Of course, the enhanced quality and custom tailoring should be a definite plus. This approach is difficult when a program is needed and no comparable programs are commercially available. In this situation, programs similar in terms of length, content, and difficulty may be used for comparison purposes.

Administrative Service Charges. A third approach is to establish a charge for providing administrative services to the organization. This charge, determined internally with input from finance and accounting personnel, should be fair and equitable. An example is a 10 percent service charge (of tuition paid) for processing all tuition refund applications. Thus, the user department is charged the amount of the refund plus 10 percent.

Variations of the Profit Center Concept

The concept just described represents a typical profit center. With fixed or negotiated fees and prices, the revenue offsets the expenses, and the extra amount is considered profit generated by the department. The ROI is the department earnings divided by the total investment in resources to deliver the products and services. Other variations discussed here, which are short of the typical profit center, may be appropriate for some organizations.

Protected Profit Center. When a profit center is subsidized to ensure the availability of resources, it is called a protected profit center. This approach involves pricing some services and products and subsidizing other programs and essential services. This approach assumes that it is difficult to establish prices for some necessary services. Departments may not use the learning staff to supply those services, and the result may cause inefficiencies. For example, if a client department is unwilling to pay the 10 percent administrative service charge for the tuition refund program and insists on processing its own tuition refunds, it could jeopardize the program's standards. An easy way to avoid this problem is to subsidize the department to provide funds necessary to administer those programs.

Cost Center. Another approach involves estimating the cost of various services and products delivered and charging the client for those costs. All department costs are allocated in some way to user departments. This approach requires detailed and accurate cost forecasts and cost accumulation. Also, when parts of the organization refuse to use programs or services, the cost for providing those products and services to other parts of the organization may increase. Suppose ten departments share the cost of a program and two departments decide not to participate. All costs, including prorated development costs, must be spread over eight departments instead of ten, raising the overall cost for those departments. This approach provides little incentive for the learning staff to minimize costs, eliminating the opportunity for a profit.

Break-Even Center. This variation is similar to the cost center concept, except that fees and prices are established to enable the department to reach a break-even point at the year's end. Higher prices are established for popular or frequently offered programs to offset losses on programs or services that are difficult to price or represent a loss. With this approach, users may pay more for some programs and less for others when they should cost approximately the same. A disadvantage is the lack of opportunity for the learning and development center to make a profit.

Considerations for Moving to the Profit Center Model

Several critical factors, discussed here, should be considered when converting to the profit center concept. The strength or weakness of these factors may determine if such a move is feasible.

Gradual Change. A conversion from an expense-based department to a profit center requires gradual change. Management may have concerns about the concept of paying for these services. One organization approached the conversion with the 10 sequential steps shown in Table 7-4. It took this organization approximately 5 years to move from a centralized, budget-based department to a self-sufficient profit center.

Table 7-4
Gradual Steps in One Profit Center Conversion

1. Establish learning accounts in each department.
2. Allocate all costs of outside programs/seminars to user departments.
3. Allocate the costs of special, nonroutine programs.
4. Charge each user department for tuition refunds of their employees.
5. Charge a fee for participation in major programs.
6. Set prices for all formal programs.
7. Charge all management trainee salaries to the sponsoring department.
8. Negotiate fees for new program development.
9. Negotiate fees for consulting work.
10. Charge an administration fee for all regular support services.

Effective Products. Products and services provided by the organization must be effective and viewed as worthwhile investments. The CLO and staff must have an excellent reputation for success with previous programs; otherwise, such a conversion could be disastrous.

Management Support. A successful conversion requires good management support and commitment at all levels. Management must see the need for effective learning programs and be willing to pay for it—investing today for a return tomorrow. Also, managers must be willing to encourage employees to participate in programs and become more involved in the development and implementation of new programs.

Committed Staff. Commitment to the conversion to a profit center must include the entire learning and development staff. Too often, major programs are implemented at the initiation of one key individual in the learning and development organization.

Competitive Prices. Revenue items must be competitively priced. Charging more than the competition on the premise of providing a better product may not influence profit-minded executives. Operating department managers are seeking results, and they must be convinced that they will receive a superior product at a fair price.

Simplicity Is Key. Simple and equitable methods for charging departments must be devised. One problem that may surface is duplicate charging. In some organizations, the learning and development department is funded through direct charges or allocations to all operating departments, regardless of their participation in programs. If a department is charged an additional fee for employee participation in a program, there is a double charge. This perception has caused some conversion efforts to fail. A more realistic approach is to credit a predetermined amount to those departments and charge only if the fees or prices of the products and services used become greater than the allocated amount.

Impact. The impact of the profit center concept across the organization must be considered. This analysis includes the types of courses delivered, services provided, reaction of the management group, and reaction of the learning staff. Some courses, particularly those perceived as unnecessary, will be eliminated because no one will be willing to pay for them. This may be cause for concern; for instance, suppose all team leaders, supervisors, and managers were required to participate in a valuing diversity workshop. The company feels that all leaders need to understand the applicable laws and the company's commitment to diversity. If some managers do not perceive the program as essential and worthwhile, they may be reluctant to send participants. These issues must be addressed before conversion is initiated.

Some insight into impact may be gained by surveying management to determine their willingness to use the learning center's services if managers must pay directly for them. Negative attitudes might signal problems ahead or pinpoint areas where attention is needed before implementing a conversion plan.

It is important to examine the philosophy and structure of the organization before implementing the profit center concept. This concept is not as effective if training is decentralized to the lowest level in the organization because it is difficult to pinpoint precise costs to be charged to the user organization. In essence, a highly centralized approach moves the cost of training to the user organization, which makes this action a step toward the concept of paying for services provided.

Staff Resistance. The most significant obstacle for implementation will be the resistance from the learning and development staff. Staff members may not see the need for the process and will fear that the programs in which they are involved will not be purchased and, thus, eventually disappear. Also, they may fear what will happen to the function if the management team does not buy their services. These fears can turn into realities if the programs are not delivering results.

Current Success. To ensure that current programs produce results, most organizations implement the profit center after level four and five evaluations have been applied in a comprehensive and effective way. When the management team sees the value of the programs—in terms of business impact and ROI—they will purchase internal programs. Managers support proven results. Thus, level four and five evaluations are considered a prerequisite for the implementation of the profit center concept.

As with any significant change, the profit center will be accepted if the model fits the organization, is aligned with the business direction and ensures employees are informed and prepared for the change.

Outlook

Overall, the profit center approach is a legitimate, viable alternative for some organizations. In the past few years it has declined in popularity. Many organizations with this model have decided to move to an allocation model or a blended approach for finding learning and development investments. It should be pursued only if it fits the business model of the organization. A conversion that succeeds can be very rewarding to the learning team; a failure can be disastrous to all (Zeinstra, 2004).

MANAGING SUPPLIERS FOR VALUE

Because of the increased use of outsourcing, managing suppliers or vendors becomes a critical issue. When outsourcing a part of the function such as the use of specialized facilitators and SMEs, the issue is not as serious. When outsourcing reaches the point where almost all of the function is outsourced to a variety of suppliers (or even one major partner), the accountability of the supplier relationship is critical and the opportunity to add value by managing this relationship properly is vast (Foreman, 2004). Using outsourcing as a way to augment staff and capabilities is an excellent way to leverage the learning function. It is best to determine the business's case for outsourcing. For example, at QUALCOMM, the role for the staff in the learning center is to be experts in QUALCOMM business and understand QUALCOMM's technology, employees, and culture. The role does not involve being content experts or trainers. Therefore, outsourcing development and delivery of programs is an effective model. All needs assessment, evaluation, customization, and reporting is done by internal staff.

Outsourcing Strategy

The extent of outsourcing is usually decided when the strategy of the learning and development department is defined. Chapter 2 focuses on this issue and shows the possibilities for outsourcing. Outsourcing is definitely a trend because of the great benefits that can be derived from the process. Outsourcing allows a more flexible and responsive learning team; in some cases, outsourcing can bring capabilities not readily available, thus improving the variety of services and products offered. By outsourcing tasks, key learning staff focus their efforts on other value-added possibilities.

Recently, outsourcing has been explored because of financial considerations—that is, it provides services and additional products at a lower cost than can be obtained internally. Cost reduction can be an important benefit, but only if the process is managed appropriately and outsourcing partners are selected carefully.

Outsourcing Decision

The decision to outsource parts—either minor or major—of the learning and development function must be approached carefully and managed properly. It is essential to treat outsourced vendors as adjunct staff and provide them with knowledge and guidance about the organization. They are dependent on the learning staff to help them be successful, and if they are successful, the learning function will be as well. The important element in this process is to ensure that the correct decision is made for the different outsource partners, whether the partner is a facilitator, a firm that provides the up-front analysis, or a vendor for a learning management system. The selection will rest on several key issues. Table 7-5 shows a checklist of the issues that must be considered in making this selection (Hale, 2006).

Most of these issues are self-explanatory, but a few deserve some attention. The left column of the table is fairly standard in the supply partner selection. The right side contains issues that may not be defined clearly. The most important one is the measurement of

Table 7-5
Checklist for Selecting Supplier Partner

• Experience	• Measurement of success
• Credentials	• Reporting and monitoring
• Quality of team	• Deliverables
• Technology capabilities	• Implementation issues
• References	• Schedule
• Work samples	• Fees and expenses
• Demos	• Reviews
	• Termination provisions

success. The supplier should specify what the proposed measure of success will be in the project, in concert with defined requirements. Also, reporting and monitoring will be critical from the supplier's perspective, detailing the specific reports provided and the data monitored to provide a summary of progress made and the success of the project. It is important to define the deliverables. With some suppliers this is easy. For others it may be more difficult (e.g., major consulting projects). In terms of implementation issues, the supplier is indicating what must take place to make the process operate smoothly and efficiently, defining particular problems that may cause a disturbance in the relationship. Schedule, fees, and expenses are necessary. Private reviews are often inserted to explain the progress and review the relationship. Provisions for termination are necessary in today's legal environment. These issues should not be taken lightly, even when one individual is being compared with another to provide consulting or facilitation services.

Managing the Partnership

Managing the ongoing relationship is critical. Suppliers are extremely valuable to the CLO, and they must be managed to obtain maximum value. Table 7-6 shows a checklist for routinely managing these partnerships. A few of these issues should be underscored. Appropriate communication channels must be established up front so that the supplier always has access to the proper individuals in the learning and development function. Expectations for success should be defined up front and on an ongoing basis so that both parties have a clear understanding of the issues.

Table 7-6
Managing the Partnership

• Establishing contacts/ communications	• Resolving issues
• Defining expectations/success	• Monitoring progress
• Clarifying roles and responsibilities	• Keeping communication open
• Minimizing resistance	• Providing care to maintain a productive relationship
• Delivering the service	• Taking action for improvement

Clarifying roles and responsibilities is standard and leads to an important issue: minimizing resistance from the staff. When functions are outsourced, the current staff may be concerned about losing their jobs. In some arrangements, the current staff joins the outsource provider. This approach to outsourcing is a major change effort and specific plans and actions should be implemented to ensure that resistance is minimized or removed. Staff members accept outsourcing more readily when they understand the need and advantages and are involved in some of the issues. Issues must be resolved, progress consistently monitored, and communication open. Both sides must take care to maintain a productive relationship and be willing to take action when improvements are needed. These partnerships are critical and without the appropriate attention, the value of outsourcing could be missed. In extreme cases, results could be disastrous.

Monitoring Performance

Absent from the previous list is the topic of monitoring performance. Since this is where the value is added, it deserves additional attention. Deliverables are the first to consider. Delivery must be on time and include quality commitments. Beyond those items are the routine data that could be captured; these types of data discussed in the next chapter.

Guaranteeing Results

In the last few years, vendors and suppliers have been a part of fees and expenses, but not all are guaranteeing results. Under this arrangement, results must be clearly defined, in some cases, using the actual ROI. The product or service delivered to the supplier must be recommended properly and supported adequately, and all stakeholders must understand and respect these roles for success. When applied appropriately, this approach is a tremendous win-win for all parties (Phillips, 2006). It represents the way to achieve maximum value from the supplier. It also keeps the learning team and other stakeholders on the same page, clearly showing what must be done to support the supplier; otherwise, the guarantee is null and void.

FINAL THOUGHTS

This chapter explored four major areas where the CLO can add value through effectively managing the learning and development function. Setting the budgets is the first step to add value. Controlling costs is critical to managing processes efficiently. Exploring the possibility of a profit center, or implementing at least parts of the process, may be a very important step for the CLO. Finally, outsourcing small parts or much of this function may be another important way to deliver value.

CLOs should provide external development to suppliers and customers. These people are part of the supply chain, and their knowledge is important to the success of the business. Providing development to them can assist in building greater alignment for the company.

Bill Wiggenhorn, Former President, Motorola University and Vice Chairman of Global Ed-Tech Management Group

---

REFERENCES

Foreman, Katherine O., Ph.D. "Working with Vendors," *Chief Learning Officer.* April 2004, 28.

Gordon, Jack. "Selling on the Side," *Training.* December 2005, 35.

Hale, Judith. *Outsourcing Training and Development: Factors for Success.* San Francisco, CA: Pfeiffer, 2006.

Phillips, Jack J. *The Consultant's Companion.* New York, NY: McGraw-Hill, 2006.

Van Adelsberg, David, and Edward A. Trolley. *Running Training Like a Business.* San Francisco, CA: Berrett-Koehler Publishers, 1999.

Zeinstra, Bob. "Converting from a Training Department to a Profit Center," *Chief Learning Officer.* December 2004, 32–37.

CHAPTER 8

Demonstrating Value from the Learning Enterprise, Including ROI

> *Level 3, 4, and 5 evaluations are done on 2 to 3 courses corporate-wide every year using an ROI process model. Results are shared. We use these results to ensure value delivery and to improve our efficiency and effectiveness as well as demonstrate results.*
>
> David Vance, President, Caterpillar University

One of the most important challenges facing the CLO is to demonstrate the success of the learning investment. For almost a decade, measurement and evaluation have dominated conference agendas and professional meetings. Journals and newsletters regularly embrace this concept with increasing print space. More than 25 books provide significant coverage of the topic. Special conferences have been devoted to it. Even top executives have stepped up their appetite for impact and return on investment (ROI) data.

Although interest in measurement and evaluation has heightened and much progress has been made, they are still issues that challenge even the most sophisticated and progressive learning and development professionals. While some CLOs argue that it is difficult to have a successful evaluation process, others quietly and deliberately implement effective evaluation systems. The latter group is gaining tremendous support from the senior management team and is making much

187

progress. Regardless of the position one takes on the issue, the reasons for demonstrating the value of learning and evaluation are intensifying. Almost all CLOs share the concern that they need to link learning to the business and must eventually show results on their learning investment. Otherwise, funds may be reduced or the CLO may not be able to maintain or enhance his or her present status and influence in the organization. In the CLO futures survey of almost 500 CLOs, measuring impact was listed as one of the critical challenges they face (L'Allier, 2005).

The dilemma surrounding the value of learning is a source of frustration for many senior executives—even the CLO. Most executives realize that learning is a basic necessity when organizations are experiencing significant growth or increased competition. They intuitively feel that there is value in providing learning opportunities, logically anticipating a payoff in important bottom-line measures such as productivity improvements, quality enhancements, cost reductions, time savings, and customer service. Yet the frustration comes from lack of evidence to show that the process is really working. While results are assumed and learning programs appear to be necessary, more evidence is needed; otherwise, funding may be adjusted in the future. A comprehensive measurement and evaluation process represents the most promising way to show this level of accountability (Long, 2004).

TRENDS AND ISSUES

Global Evaluation Trends

Measurement and evaluation have been changing and evolving, in both private and public sector organizations, across organizations and cultures not only in the United States, but throughout all the developed countries. The following trends have been identified in the ROI Institutes' benchmarking studies of over 200 organizations using a comprehensive measurement evaluation process over 5 years:

- Organizations are increasing their investment in measurement and evaluation with best practice groups spending 3 to 5 percent of the learning and development budget on measurement and evaluation.
- Learning staffs are spending more time learning about effective measurement of learning.
- Organizations are moving up the value chain away from measuring reaction and learning to measure application, impact, and occasionally, ROI.

- The increased focus on measurement and evaluation is largely driven by the needs of the clients and sponsors of learning projects, programs, initiatives, and solutions.
- A shift from a reactive approach to a more proactive approach is developing, with evaluation addressed early in the cycle, even to the point of forecasting ROI prior to program launch.
- Measurement and evaluation processes are systematic and methodical, often designed into the delivery process.
- Technology is enhancing the measurement and evaluation process, enabling large amounts of data to be collected, processed, analyzed, and integrated across programs.
- The use of ROI is emerging as an essential part of the measurement and evaluation mix. Benchmarking studies show it is a fast growing metric—70 to 80 percent of companies have it on their wish list.
- Many CLOs have created internally accepted practices for demonstrating the value of learning that focuses on the value of the investment—not necessarily the financial ROI.

These trends are creating demand for more information, resources, knowledge, and skills in the measurement and evaluation process.

Evaluation Challenges

While evaluation seems to be a popular topic, why aren't all organizations doing it, and what keeps the evaluation process from being effective? The barriers to conducting meaningful evaluation can be summarized with these basic challenges:

Too many theories and models. Dozens of evaluation books have been written just for the learning and development community. Add to this the dozens of evaluation books written primarily for the social sciences, education, and government organizations. Then add the 25-plus models and theories for evaluation offered to practitioners to help them measure the contribution of learning and development, each claiming a unique approach and a promise of calming evaluation woes along with bringing world peace.

Lack of understanding of evaluation. It hasn't always been easy for practitioners to learn this process. Some books on evaluation have over 600 pages, making it impossible for a practitioner to absorb the process just through reading. Not only is it essential to understand evaluation processes, but also the entire learning and development staff must learn parts of the process and understand how it fits into their role. To remedy this situation, it is essential for the organization to focus on developing and disseminating expertise within the organization. Add to this the search for statistical precision. The use of complicated statistical models is confusing and difficult to absorb for many practitioners. Statistical precision is needed when a high-stakes decision is being made and when plenty of time and resources are available. Otherwise, very simple statistics are appropriate.

Evaluation is considered a postprogram activity. When evaluation is considered an add-on activity, it loses the power to deliver the needed results. The most appropriate way to use evaluation is to consider it early—prior to program development—at the time of program conception. When this happens, an evaluation is conducted efficiently and the quality and quantity of data is enhanced.

Lack of support from key stakeholders. Important customers, who need and use evaluation data, sometimes do not provide the support needed to make the process successful. Specific steps must be taken to win support and secure buy-in from key groups including senior executives and the management team. Executives must see that evaluation produces valuable data to improve programs and validate results. When stakeholders understand what is involved, they may offer more support.

Evaluation hasn't delivered the data senior managers need. Today, clients and sponsors are asking for data beyond reaction and learning. They need data on the application of new skills on the job and the corresponding impact in the business units. Sometimes they want ROI data for major programs. They are requesting data about the business impact of learning—both from short-term and long-term perspectives. Ultimately, these executives are the ones who must continue funding for learning and development. If the desired data are not available, future funding could be in jeopardy.

Improper use of evaluation data. Improper use of evaluation data can lead to four major problems:

- *Too many organizations do not use evaluation data at all.* Data are collected, tabulated, catalogued and filed, and are never used by any particular group other than the individuals who initially collected the data. This results in wasted resources and missed opportunities to communicate success and improve the program.

- *Data are not provided to the appropriate audiences.* Analyzing the target audiences and determining the specific data needed for each group are important steps when results are being communicated.

- *Data are not used to drive improvement.* If it is not part of the feedback cycle, evaluation falls short of what it is intended to accomplish.

- *Data are used for the wrong reasons—to take action against an individual or group or to withhold funds rather than improving processes.* Sometimes the data is used in political ways to gain power or advantage over another person.

Inconsistency and lack of standards. For evaluation to add value and be accepted by different stakeholders, it must be consistent in its approach and methodology. Tools and templates need to be developed to support the method of choice to prevent perpetual reinvention of the wheel. Without this consistency, evaluation consumes too many resources and raises too many concerns about the quality and credibility of the process. Closely paralleled with consistency is the use of standards. Evaluation standards are rules for making evaluation consistent, stable, and equitable. Without standards there is little credibility in processes and stability of outcomes.

Sustainability. A new evaluation model or approach often has a short life. It is not sustained. Evaluation must be integrated into the organization so that it becomes routine and lasting. To accomplish this, the evaluation process must gain the respect of key stakeholders at the outset. The evaluation process must be well documented, and stakeholders must accept their responsibilities to make it work. Without sustainability, evaluation will be on a roller-coaster ride, where data are collected only when programs are in trouble and less attention is provided when they are not.

Necessity. Many corporate executives understand the value of learning. They hired CLOs, grew learning functions, and have been intimately involved in creating learning strategies for their companies (Jack Welch at GE, for example). CLOs in companies with this learning commitment are not too concerned about evaluation systems; they already have support for learning initiatives and continue to demonstrate the value of their work through extensive linkage with the business.

Benefits of Measurement and Evaluation

Although the benefits of measurement and evaluation may appear obvious, several distinct and important payoffs can be realized.

Satisfy client needs. Today's executives and key clients need information about application and implementation in the workplace and the corresponding impact on key business metrics. In some cases, they are asking for ROI data. Developing a comprehensive measurement and evaluation system can be an effective strategy to meet client requests and requirements.

Justify budgets. Some CLOs use evaluation data to support a requested budget while others use evaluation data to prevent the budget from being slashed, or—in drastic cases—eliminated entirely. Additional evaluation data can show where programs add value and where they fall short of the mark. This approach can lead to protecting successful programs as well as pursuing new programs.

Improve program designs and processes. A comprehensive evaluation system should provide information to improve the overall design of a program, including the critical areas of learning design, content, delivery method, duration, timing, focus, and expectations. These processes may need to be adjusted to improve learning, especially during implementation of a new program. Evaluation data can determine whether the upfront analysis was conducted properly, thereby aligning the program with the organizational needs. Additional evaluation data can indicate whether nonlearning and development interventions are needed. Finally, evaluation data can help pinpoint inadequacies in implementation systems and identify ways to improve them.

Enhance the transfer of learning. Learning transfer is perhaps one of the biggest challenges facing the learning and development field. Research still shows that 60 to 90 percent of job-related skills and knowledge acquired in a program are still not being implemented on the job. A comprehensive evaluation system can identify specific barriers using learning. Evaluation data can also highlight supportive work environments that enable learning transfer.

Eliminate or expand. Evaluation processes can provide rational, credible data to help support the decision to implement a program or discontinue it. In reality, if the program cannot add value, it should be discontinued. One caveat: Eliminating programs should not be a principal motive or rationale for increasing evaluation efforts. Although it is a valid use of evaluation data, program elimination is often viewed more negatively than positively. The flipside of eliminating programs is expanding their presence or application. Positive results may signal the possibility that a program's success in one division or region can be replicated in another division if a similar need exists.

Enhance the respect and credibility of the learning and development staff. Collecting and using evaluation data—including application, impact, and ROI—builds respect for learning and respect for the staff. Appropriate evaluation data can enhance the credibility of the CLO when the data reveal the value added to the organization. It can also help shift the perception of learning from a dispensable activity to an indispensable value-adding process.

Increase support from managers. Immediate managers of participants need convincing data about the success of learning. They often fail to support these processes because they cannot see the value in taking employees away from the job to be involved in a program with little connection to their business unit. Data showing how learning helps these managers achieve their objectives will influence their support.

Strengthen relationships with key executives and administrators. Senior executives must perceive the CLO as a business partner who can be invited to the table for important decisions and meetings. A comprehensive measurement and evaluation process, showing the contribution of the learning function, can help strengthen this relationship. A comprehensive evaluation process may influence these managers to view learning as a contributing process and an excellent investment.

Set priorities for learning and development. A comprehensive measurement system can help determine which programs and projects represent the highest priority. Evaluation data can show the payoff or potential payoff of important and expensive programs, or those supporting strategic objectives.

These key benefits, inherent with almost any type of impact evaluation process, make additional measurement and evaluation an attractive challenge for the learning function. Some organizations develop an annual review of activity and progress under the label of Value of Investment (VOI) Table 8-1 shows an example of this type of data from QUALCOMM.

THE LEARNING VALUE CHAIN

It may be helpful to examine measurement and evaluation of learning as a value chain where various types of data (levels) are collected at different times (sometimes from different sources) to generate a balanced profile of success, providing the value desired by the various stakeholders of the process. Figure 8-1 shows this value chain, which is fundamental to much of the current work in evalu-

Table 8-1
Reporting VOI

Contents of QUALCOMM's Annual Learning and Development Executive Report

- Total Training Expenditures as a Percent of Payroll
- Total Training Expenditures per Employee
- Outside Payments as a Percent of Total Training Expenditures
- Ratio of Training Staff to Employees
- Percentage of Employees Trained
- Employee Participation in Learning and Development
- Top Program Enrollments
- Customized Programs
- Total Enrollments in Programs by Division as Compared to Total Headcount
- Percentage of All Programs Completed in Each Content Area
- Courses Completed by Job Function as Compared to Total Headcount
- Enrollments by Manager and Above Employees as Compared to Total Headcount
- Executive participation (by hours) in learning and development
- Percentage of participants who believe that the program related directly to a business objective
- Percentage of participants who believe that they are prepared to apply what they've learned in the program to their job
- Outcomes/business results linked to programs/initiatives

Level	Measurement Focus	Key Questions
0 Input and Indicators	Measures input such as volume and efficiencies	What is the number of participants, hours, and programs and what are the costs?
1 Reaction and Planned Action	Measures participant satisfaction with the project and captures planned actions	Was the learning relevant, important, useful, and helpful to participants in the job environment? Did the participants plan to use the content in the program?
2 Learning and Confidence	Measures changes in knowledge, skills, and attitudes	Did participants increase or enhance knowledge, skills, or perceptions and have confidence to use them?
3 Application and Implementation	Measures changes in on-the-job behavior or action	What did the participants do differently in the job context? Was the program implemented effectively? What changes were made on the job?
4 Impact and Consequences	Measures changes in business impact variables	What are the consequences of the application in terms of output, quality, cost, time, and satisfaction?
5 ROI	Compares project benefits to the costs	Did the monetary benefits of the learning program exceed the investment in the program?

Figure 8-1. The learning value chain.

ation and provides the framework for CLOs to measure the success of learning.

This concept shows how value is developed from different perspectives. Some stakeholders are interested in knowing about the inputs so that they can be managed and made more efficient. Others are interested in reaction measures so that adjustments can be made to obtain more positive reactions. Still others are interested in learning to identify weaknesses in the learning design. More recently, clients and sponsors are more interested in actual behavior change (application) and the corresponding impact in the work units. Finally, a few stakeholders are concerned about the actual ROI.

It is helpful to view the learning value chain as a chain of impact that is necessary for learning to create value from a business perspective. The chain can be broken at any point. For example, if participants have an adverse reaction to a learning program, all is lost at that point because there will be little, if any, learning. Even if there is a positive reaction, participants may not be learning new skills, gaining new knowledge, or changing their perceptions, consequently, there would be no value from the program. Also, if there is no application of skills and knowledge, there is no corresponding business impact. Without business impact, the ROI is very negative—as much as 100 percent negative. It is helpful to remind all the stakeholders that these important data sets represent a chain of impact that must exist for learning to add business value. Collecting data along the value chain provides evidence that learning is making a difference. The additional step of isolating the effects of learning provides the proof that a learning program is adding value. This issue will be discussed later in this chapter.

Setting Goals

Because more organizations are moving up the value chain, it may be helpful to assess the current status at these different levels and set specific goals over a defined period to achieve desired targets. Figure 8-2 lists the levels and provides space for targets. Also included are

| | Percent of Programs Evaluated at This Level | | |
Value Level	Current	Target	Best Practices
Inputs and Indicators	100%	100%	100%
Reaction and Planned Action			100%
Learning and Confidence			60-80%
Application and Implementation			25-30%
Impact and Consequences			10-25%
ROI			6-10%

Figure 8-2. Evaluation targets.

the percentages from best practice organizations—those organizations that have developed a comprehensive measurement and evaluation process. This target is sometimes established as part of a transition plan to move from the current state to a desired future state. Current assessments can be estimated from the learning and development staff, or they may come from the learning management system. Either way, it is important to take stock of the current status and set goals for improvement.

The concept of micro-level and macro-level scorecards should be underscored at this point. When a project or program is evaluated with all types of data, including ROI, a micro-level scorecard is developed. The six types of data represent data collected at different times from different sources, reflecting both quantitative and qualitative data. This equates to a balanced scorecard for that specific program. However, when there are dozens—if not hundreds—of programs, the challenge is to collect data across programs so that there is a meaningful scorecard for the overall learning contribution. This is a macro-level scorecard, and the concept is fairly simple. Whenever a program is evaluated at Level 1 (reaction), for example, a few of the measures are collected for integration into the macro-level scorecard. In each of the succeeding levels, a few measures are taken to insert into the overall macro-level scorecard. The concept is illustrated in Figure 8-3. As this figure shows, the key is to identify the measures at each level that are important to consider in the macro-level scorecard and integrate the data for meaningful reports either monthly, quarterly, or

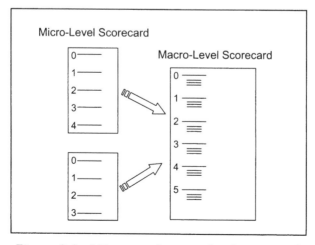

Figure 8-3. Micro- and macro-level scorecard.

annually—in some cases, instantaneously for a fully automated system.

Input and Indicators

The most fundamental level of measurement is the capture of inputs into the system. This represents a variety of measures showing the scope, volume, and efficiencies as well as costs. The typical benchmarking measures are included in Table 8-2.

Participant count is a common measure. This measure could represent participants in various job groups and various status, and it could be presented in categories such as employees, suppliers, customers, and the general public. Counting *hours* is another issue, particularly when CLOs have a target for a certain number of learning hours per person. This accounting becomes more meaningful with extensive use of e-learning, but it also has drawbacks since hours of training are not an effective measure of what was learned. *Cost profiles* are typical, reflecting costs per participant in job groups, and could include all the direct costs associated with providing learning. Some CLOs are reporting indirect costs, such as those associated with taking participants off the job, using average salaries for the time participants are away from normal job duties. The problem with this metric is that it assumes learning is separate from the job

Table 8-2
Typical Inputs and Indicators

Participants	Efficiencies
Total	Show-up rate
By job group	Completion rate
Hours	**Delivery Profile**
Total	Percent instructor-led
By employee	Percent e-learning
By job group	Percent blended
Costs	Percent on-the-job
Total	
Per participant	
Per employee	
Per hour instructor-led	
Per hour e-learning	

and is treated as an extracurricular activity instead of a job necessity. *Delivery mechanisms* are often presented in this level and they show how the delivery processes are changing. Categories include conventional facilitator-led learning, e-learning, and blended learning; a balanced mix of these is often a goal of the organization. Job rotations, on-the-job learning, coaching, and mentoring are sometimes reported. When delivery methods are reported, it is important to set goals, accept changes, and track shifts. *Efficiencies* reflect a variety of measures such as the time it takes individuals to complete programs, the percentage of learners completing programs, and the percentage of individuals who attend follow-up sessions. These measures are important because they show how well the system is functioning and how data flows throughout the learning and development function.

Reaction and Planned Action

All programs are usually evaluated at this level. Direct feedback is needed from participants to capture the planned actions from the learning process. Failure to secure a reaction about a program sends a message to participants that their feedback is not important and does not enable learning professionals to improve programs based on feedback. Consequently, 100 percent coverage is recommended. Typical topics covered are listed in Table 8-3.

The measures at this level can vary significantly in the organization depending on the needs for data and methods used to collect it. At times, different types of methods may be used. The method is not

Table 8-3
Typical Learning and Confidence

Typical Reaction Measures

Program Design	Potential Use
• Program objectives	• Planned improvements
• Program content	• Intent to use
• Instructional materials	• Relevance to job
• Assignments	• Importance to job
Program Delivery	• Amount of new information
• Method of delivery	• Recommend to others
• Facilitator/instructor delivery	**Overall Satisfaction with Program**
• Facilities/learning environment	

as important as having standard approaches. Some are standardized along the intensity level. Low intensity is a quick reaction questionnaire appropriate for e-learning or a program of short duration. Moderate intensity gets deeper into the topics listed in Table 8-3 and represents most of the programs. High intensity gets into much more detail, perhaps detailing the planned action more significantly. High intensity feedback is needed to evaluate programs where detailed feedback is required. Regardless of the set of data, it is important to be consistent, standardized, and allow for integration of data across programs.

Some reaction measures tend to have more value than others. For example, some are predictive in their ability to forecast or correlate with actual use of the skills on the job. The five measures listed in Table 8-4 have the strongest correlation to actual use based on a variety of studies in and across organizations. Although planned actions cannot be summarized in a meaningful way across programs, the percent of participants providing planned actions may be a useful measure at this level. Still, this is only reaction data, and the learning and development staff must move beyond this type of data to demonstrate other values in the value chain.

Learning and Confidence

The first measure at the learning level is the percent of programs evaluated at this level. This measure not only varies with the needs of the organization, but with the definition of a learning measure. Some CLOs do not count a learning measure unless it is objective and formally structured, such as a test, demonstration, or simulation. Other CLOs consider self assessment and facilitator assessment to be learning measures, and thus the percentage should be quite high. If the latter approach is taken, a target of 80 to 90 percent or,

Table 8-4
High Levels of Correlation

Reaction Items with Predictive Capability

- This program is relevant to my current work.
- This program is important to my job success.
- I intend to use this material on the job.
- This program contains new information.
- I would recommend this program to others in my job category.

in some cases, 100 percent coverage is possible. Because of this, it is helpful to integrate learning measures with the reaction questionnaire at the end of the program. The measures shown in Table 8-5 are examples of the types of learning measures that can be integrated into the reaction instrument. The advantage of these measures is that they can easily be integrated across programs that ultimately appear in the overall learning and development scorecard. The disadvantage is that this does not represent enough detail to address issues that may surface if there are problems with a particular program's content, delivery, learning design, or the readiness of participants.

Thus, these measures must be implemented in conjunction with other learning measures that are more detailed about the program. For example, it may be common to include a role play demonstration to measure the confidence in using a particular skill. The success of the demonstration is measured to provide feedback for the learner, program facilitators, and designers. Multiple choice tests, problems, and simulations are very useful for gauging skills and knowledge increases. Learning measures are meaningful at the program level only and cannot be easily included in the macro-level scorecard.

Some organizations detail the types of learning measures in a profile on the macro-level scorecard. Here, the CLO's interest in learning measures may be detailed and divided into formal and informal learning methods. The trend here is two-fold: first, self assessment measures are obtained and should be taken at high percentages across programs; second, there is a move to more objective methods that can be defended when the testing is challenged.

Application and Implementation

This level becomes more important as CLOs are concerned about how behavior changes, on-the-job application, guidelines, and the

Table 8-5
Typical Learning and Confidence Measures

- Skill acquisition
- Knowledge acquisition
- Perception changes
- Objectives met
- Capability
- New networking contacts
- Confidence to use skills

actions being taken by learners are connected to learning programs. The first measure at this level is the percent of programs evaluated. Typically, a best practice target is approximately 30 percent. This number involves sampling from two perspectives: 30 percent of the programs are evaluated, and only a sample of the participants in a particular program are usually included in the evaluation. At this level of measurement, there is both a micro and macro view. The micro view involves measures that provide enough detail to understand how the program is driving change and how it is implemented. Specific questions, tailored to the type of program, may be relevant here. The macro view is needed to compare one program follow-up with another and to be consistent with the types of issues. Table 8-6 shows typical application questions that would be appropriate for any type of learning and development program. These measures can then be compared across programs in the macro-level scorecard.

The barriers to the transfer of learning in the workplace are significant and must be measured. Whether labeled inhibitors, obstacles, or impediments, these measures represent serious roadblocks to application. Table 8-7 shows the barriers often collected across all programs. These barriers can be very powerful for understanding what the impediments are to the transfer of learning in an organization.

To complement the barriers, the enablers are often captured. Whether labeled enhancers, supporters, or enablers, these measures represent the processes that support the use of learning on the job. The combination of barriers and enablers can be very powerful to ensure that there is an adequate level of application and implementation. Without them, the programs may not add significant value to the organization. When forced choice options are used, there is a

Table 8-6
Typical Application and Implementation
Measures

- Use of skills
- Use of knowledge
- Frequency of use
- Success of use
- Progress with implementation
- Barriers
- Enablers

Table 8-7
Barriers to Transfer of Learning

- Immediate manager does not support the learning.
- The culture in the work group does not support the learning.
- No opportunity to use the skills.
- No time to use the skills.
- Didn't learn anything that could be applied to the job.
- The systems and processes did not support the use of the skills.
- Didn't have the resources available to use the skills.
- Changed job and the skills no longer apply.
- Skills taught are not appropriate in our work unit.
- Didn't see a need to apply what was learned.
- Could not change old behaviors.

possibility for reporting data from across the programs, thus enabling the CLO and executives to understand these issues on a macro-level.

Impact and Consequences

Some CLOs and sponsors believe the impact and consequences level should contain the most important data. The first measure at this level is the percentage of programs evaluated. Best practice organizations typically measure 10 to 20 percent of their programs at this level. Sampling is used in two ways: to determine the number of programs and the number of participants in the programs. The types of data driven or influenced by a learning and development program can vary significantly and can include both hard and soft data, as shown in Tables 8-8 and 8-9.

Data at this category are more meaningful at the micro-level where the learning program is linked to specific impact measures. This provides valuable data to make adjustments or to show the contribution in a credible way. This is covered in more detail later.

Rolling up the data across programs becomes a little more difficult, but possible. One potential rollup to the macro-level scorecard is a standard question that would appear on all follow-up questionnaires (whether at Level 3 or 4). This question, shown in Table 8-10 as an example, lists the most important measures in the organization. Ideally, senior executives should identify their most

Table 8-8
Types of Hard Data

Output	Time
Units produced	Equipment downtime
Items assembled	Overtime
Items sold	On time shipments
Forms processed	Time to project completion
Loans approved	Processing time
Inventory turnover	Cycle time
Patients visited	Meeting schedules
Applications processed	Repair time
Productivity	Efficiency
Work backlog	Work stoppages
Shipments	Order response time
New accounts opened	Late reporting
	Lost time days

Costs	Quality
Budget variances	Scrap
Unit costs	Rejects
Cost by account	Error rates
Variable costs	Rework
Fixed costs	Shortages
Overhead costs	Deviation from standard
Operating costs	Product failures
Number of cost reductions	Inventory adjustments
Accident costs	Percent of tasks completed
Sales expense	properly
	Number of accidents

critical 10 or 12 measures, in order of importance, and include the list in the questionnaire. Participants indicate the extent to which this program has influenced each measure, using a 5-point scale. Alignment is achieved when the priorities listed by senior executives mirror the participant response. For example, if customer satisfaction is the number one measure with executives, it would be ideal if that measure was the one most influenced by learning and development programs. Guidelines are needed to decide the depth of influ-

Table 8-9
Types of Soft Data

Work Habits	Customer Satisfaction
Absenteeism	Churn rate
Tardiness	Number of satisfied customers
Visits to the dispensary	Customer satisfaction index
First aid treatments	Customer loyalty
Violations of safety rules	Customer complaints
Excessive breaks	

Work Climate	Development/Advancement
Number of grievances	Number of promotions
Number of discrimination claims or charges	Number of pay increases
Employee complaints	Number of training programs attended
Job satisfaction	Requests for transfer
Employee turnover	Performance appraisal ratings
Litigation	Increases in job effectiveness

Job Attitudes	Initiative
Job satisfaction	Implementation of new ideas
Organizational commitment	Successful completion of projects
Perceptions of job responsibilities	Number of suggestions implemented
Employee loyalty	Number of goals
Increased confidence	

ence—such as obtaining a rating of 4 or 5 on a scale of 1 to 5—and to decide how to integrate the data. Ultimately, this can reveal the top 10 measures influenced by the organization.

Another measure sometimes captured at this level is the method used to isolate the effects of learning on those measures. For a credible impact study, it is important to isolate the effects of learning on the impact data. When this is accomplished, it is helpful to understand which methods are being used, as some methods are more credible than others. Although this information is not as easy to accumulate and compare, it is some of the most powerful data captured and communicated by the CLO.

Table 8-10
Linking with Impact Measures

Business Measure	Not Applicable	Applies but No Influence	Some Influence	Moderate Influence	Significant Influence	Very Significant Influence
A. Work output	☐	☐	☐	☐	☐	☐
B. Quality	☐	☐	☐	☐	☐	☐
C. Cost control	☐	☐	☐	☐	☐	☐
D. Efficiency	☐	☐	☐	☐	☐	☐
E. Response time to customers	☐	☐	☐	☐	☐	☐
F. Cycle time of products	☐	☐	☐	☐	☐	☐
G. Sales	☐	☐	☐	☐	☐	☐
H. Employee turnover	☐	☐	☐	☐	☐	☐
I. Employee absenteeism	☐	☐	☐	☐	☐	☐
J. Employee satisfaction	☐	☐	☐	☐	☐	☐
K. Employee complaints	☐	☐	☐	☐	☐	☐
L. Customer satisfaction	☐	☐	☐	☐	☐	☐
M. Customer complaints	☐	☐	☐	☐	☐	☐
N. Other (please specify)	☐	☐	☐	☐	☐	☐

ROI

ROI is calculated on a selected number of programs and the percent evaluated at this level is reported. Best practice companies target 5 to 10 percent of the programs, using specific criteria detailed throughout this chapter. Most of the data at this level are in the micro-analysis category. The data are only meaningful relative to the individual study and must be communicated to interested stakeholders.

When the ROI is captured, all the other data types exist as well, and they provide some of the most valuable data for senior executives. In a macro-level scorecard, it may be helpful to include a summary of the studies presented in the timeframe the scorecard is developed (annual, monthly, etc.).

The issue of converting data to money is included in ROI analysis because a monetary value is required to compare the costs to develop the ROI. This enables executives to see the financial contribution compared to the costs of the learning program. Because there are a variety of methods used to convert data, it is important for executives to understand how a particular method was used to make that conversion. Consequently, the method used to convert data to monetary value is captured. For most situations, standard values will be used, but other methods are available. This issue is covered later in this chapter. A word of caution: It is dangerous to show an average ROI percent because sample size is small at this level and the numbers can vary significantly. It can be very misleading.

A COMPREHENSIVE EVALUATION PROCESS

Evaluation Planning

Figure 8-4 shows a comprehensive evaluation process labeled the ROI Process (Phillips, 2003). The process begins with planning, overall and individually, for each program. When evaluation is conducted only at reaction levels, not much planning is involved, but as evaluation moves up the value chain, increased attention and efforts need to be placed on planning. During the typical planning cycle, it is helpful to review the purpose of evaluation for the specific learning solutions and to determine where the evaluation will stop on the value chain. The feasibility of evaluating at different levels is explored, and two planning documents—the data collection plan and the analysis plan—are developed when the evaluation migrates to

The ROI Process

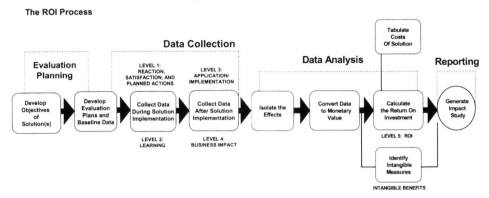

Figure 8-4. ROI methodology. (Source: Phillips, 2003. Used with permission.)

application, impact, and ROI. These documents are sometimes used in combination but are often developed separately.

Objectives

One of the most important developments in measurement and evaluation is the creation of higher levels of objectives. Program objectives correspond to the different levels on the value chain. Ideally, the levels of objectives should be in place at the highest level desired for evaluation. Essentially, the levels of objectives are as follows:

- Input objectives (number of programs, participants, hours, etc.) (Level 0)
- Reaction objectives (Level 1)
- Learning objectives (Level 2)
- Application objectives (Level 3)
- Impact objectives (Level 4)
- ROI objectives (Level 5)

Before an evaluation is conducted, these objectives must be identified and developed. Ideally, they should be developed early as the program is designed. If they are not readily available, they will have to be included to take the evaluation to the desired level.

Collecting Data

Three issues are addressed with data collection. First, the timing of collection must be established. In some cases, preprogram measurements are taken to compare with postprogram measures and, in a few cases, multiple measures are taken. In other situations, preprogram measurements are not available and specific follow-ups are still taken after the program. The key issue is to determine the timing for the follow-up evaluation, which can vary from three weeks to six months.

Second, the source of data must be considered. For much of the data, the learner is the source. Other common sources include managers, direct reports, team members, external experts, and internal records and databases.

Third, the most important issue is the method used. Data are collected using the following methods:

- *Surveys* are taken to determine the extent to which participants are satisfied with the program, have learned skills and knowledge, and have utilized various aspects of the program.
- *Questionnaires* are usually more detailed than surveys and can be used to uncover a wide variety of data. Participants provide responses to several types of open-ended and forced-response questions.
- *Tests* are conducted to measure changes in knowledge and skills. Tests come in a wide variety of formal (criterion-referenced tests, performance tests and simulations, and skill practices) and informal (facilitator assessment, self assessment, and team assessment) methods.
- On-the-job *observation* captures actual skill application and use. Observations are particularly useful in customer service training and are more effective when the observer is either invisible or transparent.
- *Interviews* are conducted with participants to determine the extent to which learning has been utilized on the job.
- *Focus groups* are conducted to determine the degree to which a group of participants has applied the training to job situations.
- *Action plans and program assignments* are developed by participants during the program and are implemented on the job after the program is completed. Follow-ups provide evidence of program success.
- *Performance contracts* are developed by the participant, the participant's supervisor, and the facilitator, who all agree on job performance outcomes.
- *Business performance monitoring* is useful where various performance records and operational data are examined for improvement.

The challenge is to select the method or methods appropriate for the setting and the specific program, within the constraints of the organization. There is no one way to collect the data; CLOs need to tailor the measurement for their organizations based on the needs of the executives and employees.

Analysis

Evaluation requires analysis. Even if the evaluation stops at reaction, analysis is required, usually involving simple averages and standard deviations. As organizations progress up the value chain, additional analyses are required. In some cases, not only are the averages and standard deviations used, but simple hypotheses testing and correlations may be required; however, these are very unusual situations. For the most part, analysis is simply tabulating, organizing, and integrating data and then presenting results in meaningful ways for the audience to understand and appreciate.

Isolating the Effects of Learning

An often-overlooked issue in some evaluations is the process of isolating the effects of learning on output data. This step is important because there are many factors that will usually influence performance data after a learning program is conducted. Several techniques are available to determine the amount of output performance directly related to the program. These techniques will pinpoint the amount of improvement directly linked to the program, resulting in increased accuracy and credibility of the evaluation data. The following techniques have been used by organizations to tackle this important issue:

- A *control group* arrangement is used to isolate the program's impact. With this strategy, one group participates in a program, while another similar group does not. The difference in the performance of the two groups is attributed to the program. When properly set up and implemented, the control group arrangement is the most effective way to isolate the effects of learning and development.
- *Trend lines and forecasting* are used to project the values of specific output variables as if the learning program had not been undertaken. The projection is compared to the actual data after

the program is conducted, and the difference represents the estimate of the impact of learning. Under certain conditions, this strategy can accurately isolate the impact of learning.

- *Participants or managers* estimate the amount of improvement related to the learning and development program. With this approach, participants or managers are provided with the total amount of improvement, on a pre- and post-program basis and are asked to indicate the percentage of the improvement that is actually related to the program.

- *Other experts*, such as customers, provide estimates of the impact of learning on the performance variable. Because the estimates are based on previous experience, the experts must be familiar with the type of program and the specific situation.

Converting Data to Monetary Values

To calculate the ROI, business impact data collected in the evaluation are converted to monetary values and compared to program costs. This requires a value to be placed on each unit of data connected with the program. In many cases, standard values are available as organizations have attempted to place value on measures they want to increase and develop costs for measures they want to avoid. When such values are not available, internal experts can estimate the value of the measure. Several techniques are available to convert data to monetary values:

- *Output data is converted to profit contribution or cost savings.* With this strategy, output increases are converted to monetary value based on their unit contribution to profit or the unit of cost reduction. These values are readily available in most organizations.

- The *cost of quality is calculated* and quality improvements are directly converted to cost savings. These values are available in many organizations.

- For programs where employee time is saved, the participants' *wages and benefits are used for the value of time.* Because a variety of programs focus on improving the time required to complete projects, processes, or daily activities, the value of time becomes an important and necessary issue.

- *Historical costs and current records are used* when they are available for a specific variable. In this case, organizational cost data are used to establish the specific value of an improvement.

- When available, *internal and external experts may be used* to estimate a value for an improvement. In this situation, the credibility of the estimate hinges on the expertise and reputation of the individual.
- *External databases are sometimes available* to estimate the value or cost of data items. Research, government, and industry databases can provide important information for these values. The difficulty lies in finding a specific database related to the situation.
- *Participants estimate the value of the data item.* For this approach to be effective, participants must be capable of providing a value for the improvement.
- *Supervisors of participants provide estimates* when they are both willing and capable of assigning values to the improvement. This approach is especially useful when participants are not fully capable of providing this input or in situations where supervisors need to confirm or adjust the participant's estimate.
- *Senior management provides estimates* on the value of an improvement when they are willing to offer estimates. This approach is particularly helpful to establish values for performance measures that are very important to senior management.
- *Education and training staff estimates may be used* to determine a value of an output data item. In these cases, it is essential for the estimates to be provided on an unbiased basis.

This step is necessary for determining the monetary benefits from a learning program. The process is challenging, particularly with soft data, but it can be methodically accomplished using one or more techniques.

Tabulating the Cost of Learning

The cost of learning is usually developed from two perspectives. For budgets, program approvals, and general information requests, the costs are often reported systematically in the organization, and usually include only the direct costs. Executives and administrators are interested in the direct costs. In some cases, these reports are changing to include other indirect costs. When the actual ROI is calculated, the costs must be fully loaded to include both the direct and indirect costs. In these situations, the cost components should include the following:

- *Needs assessment, design, and development*, possibly prorated over the expected life of the program;

- All program *materials* provided to each participant;
- *An instructor/facilitator,* including preparation time as well as delivery time;
- *Facilities* for the learning program;
- *Travel, lodging, and meal* costs for the participants, if applicable;
- *Salaries,* plus employee *benefits* of the participants who participated in the learning program;
- *Administrative and overhead* costs of the learning and development function, allocated in some convenient way; and
- *Evaluation,* including planning, data collection, analysis, and reporting.

The conservative approach is to include all of these costs so that the total is fully loaded.

Calculating the ROI

The complete ROI process model for ROI development and analysis is shown in Figure 8-4. This reinforces the processes described in this chapter. When the ROI is developed, it should be calculated systematically, using standard formulas. Two formulas are available. The benefits/cost ratio (BCR) is the program benefits divided by cost:

$$BCR = \frac{\text{Program Benefits}}{\text{Program Costs}}$$

The ROI uses the net benefits divided by program costs. The net benefits are the program benefits minus the costs. In formula form, the ROI becomes:

$$ROI\,(\%) = \frac{\text{Net Program Benefits}}{\text{Program Costs}} \times 100$$

This is the same basic formula used in evaluating other investments where the ROI is traditionally reported as earnings divided by investment.

Identifying Intangible Benefits

In addition to tangible benefits, most learning programs will influence intangible, nonmonetary benefits. Intangible benefits may include items such as:

- Branding of the learning organization
- Increased job satisfaction
- Increased organizational commitment
- Improved teamwork
- Improved customer service
- Reduced complaints
- Reduced conflicts

During analysis, hard data such as output, quality, and time are usually converted to monetary values. The conversion of soft data is attempted. However, if the process used for conversion is too subjective or inaccurate, and the resulting values lose credibility in the process, then the data are listed as an intangible benefit with the appropriate explanation. For some programs, intangible, nonmonetary benefits are extremely valuable, often carrying as much influence as the hard data items.

Reporting Data

This critical step often lacks the proper attention and planning to ensure that it is successful. This step involves developing appropriate information—such as impact studies, executive summaries, one-page summaries, and other brief reports. The heart of this step includes the different techniques used to communicate to a wide variety of target audiences. In most situations, several audiences are interested in and need the information. Careful planning to match the communication method with the audience is essential to ensure that the message is understood and appropriate actions follow.

Operating Standards

To ensure consistency and replication of evaluation studies, operating standards should be developed and applied in the measurement and evaluation process. It is extremely important for the results of an evaluation to stand alone and not vary depending on the individual conducting the study. The operating standards detail how each step and issue of the process will be addressed. Here are examples of general standards:

- When a higher level evaluation is conducted, data must be collected at lower levels.
- When an evaluation is planned for a higher level, the previous level of evaluation does not have to be comprehensive.

- When collecting and analyzing data, use only the most credible source.
- When analyzing data, choose the most conservative among the alternatives.
- If no improvement data are available for a population or from a specific source, it is assumed that little or no improvement has occurred.
- Estimates of improvements should be adjusted (discounted) for the potential error of the estimate.
- Extreme data items and unsupported claims should not be used in the analysis.
- Intangible measures are defined as measures that are purposely not converted to monetary values.
- Evaluation data must be communicated to all key stakeholders.

These specific standards not only serve as a way to consistently address each step, but they also provide a much needed conservative approach to the analysis. A conservative approach will build credibility with the target audience.

Implementation Issues

A variety of organizational issues and events will influence the successful implementation of measurement and evaluation. These issues must be addressed early to ensure that evaluation is successful. Specific topics or actions may include these:

- A policy statement concerning results-based learning and development;
- Procedures and guidelines for different elements and techniques of the evaluation process;
- Meetings and formal sessions to develop staff skills with measurement and evaluation;
- Strategies to improve management commitment and support for measurement and evaluation;
- Mechanisms to provide technical support for questionnaire design, data analysis, and evaluation strategy; and
- Specific techniques to place more attention on results.

Measurement and evaluation can fail or succeed based on these implementation issues.

BRANDING THE LEARNING AND DEVELOPMENT ENTERPRISE

A very important intangible measure has been evolving in the learning and development community: developing a brand for the learning organization. Branding has been a critical issue in the marketing area for many organizations. Successful companies and organizations often develop a strong, identifiable, and compelling brand and stick with it. The same case can be made for the learning and development function, requiring attention to the elements described in this section. In essence, the brand reflects all of the measures and measurement processes described in this chapter. Collectively, the data provides evidence of the role, importance, success, and value from the learning and development processes. Capturing the brand, and developing and presenting it effectively, enables the stakeholders to clearly understand what can be expected from the learning and development enterprise whatever their position: participant, supporter, or sponsor.

Brand Discovery

The American Marketing Association (AMA) defines a brand as a "name, term, sign, symbol or design, or a combination of them, intended to identify the goods and services of one seller or group of sellers to differentiate them from those of the competition" (www.marketingpower.com).

The first step in developing a brand for the learning and development organization is to explore the issues covered in Chapter 2. It is from this development that the role, function, process, capabilities, and outcomes are defined. Discovering the brand includes developing brand elements that identify the different parts of a brand and analyzing what attracts individuals to learning and development center and the results that are expected. The brand is then developed to reflect all of the issues in Chapter 2.

Brand Essence

Brand essence is the fundamental issue around the brand, reflecting the values, beliefs, attitudes, and opinions of those involved. It is the heart and soul of the brand. It identifies what the learning stands for, what value can be expected, what makes the learning center successful, and what can make the experience compelling. According to Brad VanAuken, author of *Brand Aid*, the exercise of developing a brand will "make you think through what value you add, identifying the proof points—anecdotes, case studies, testimonials, statistics, third-party reports validating learning's importance and benchmarking from other organizations, etc.—brand essence brings out these proof points" (VanAuken, 2003).

Successful brands offer more than a product and provide more than a service; they offer an experience. For example, Disney is not just in the business of running theme parks, but providing family fun. Starbucks sells time to relax, not just coffee. Nike sells athletic performance, not just shoes. Therefore, a critical component of a successful brand is understanding the value and experience your customers are seeking, and being able to communicate and deliver that experience (Travis, 2004).

Brand Identity

The actual identity of the brand is usually the tagline or logo of value statements that reflect what the brand intends to offer. Unfortunately, while attempting to brand, many learning organizations move directly to this step without thinking through previous steps. With a clear focus, the brand discovery, in essence, must be developed first.

The identity can reflect the essence of the brand. The brand identity should include logos, web sites, key presentations, marketing material, and handouts. Consistency, clarity, and instant recognition are very important. The focus on creating value for the corporate university—the brand and its identity—should reflect key words such as performance, results, improvement, value, success, accomplishment, growth, and achievement. These are deliverables that individuals, particularly executives, are seeking in the learning and development enterprise.

Brand Building

After deciding on the brand, the next challenge is to build the brand. This requires promoting the brand, and what it stands for, in newsletters, articles, brochures, and e-mails. Wherever programs and processes are communicated, they should relate directly to the brand and its identity, always ensuring that the customer and key stakeholder identify with what the brand stands for.

Living the Brand

The next step is living up to the brand. The old adage, "Actions speak louder than words," is very true in brand development and use. Reactions of the learning and development staff members, the success of the programs, the quality of the materials, the value of the experience, and the results are all connected to the brand in some way. If there is a breakdown in delivering the value perceived in the brand, the brand is destroyed. If the service, offerings, experience, and success do not align with the brand, the value of the brand will disappear, opening up opportunities for ridicule. If the brand is to deliver unmistaken value, the value must exist; if the brand is creating results through learning, the results must be evident. This will require constant focus on branding, on ensuring that the brand becomes an important consideration in the development of new programs, on the design and delivery of the programs, and on the data that are constantly developed to provide the proof points. A successful learning brand will drive ancillary benefits for an organization. External press about a company with a successful learning organization will be attractive to potential candidates and potential learning partners (vendors, trainers, etc.). Internal press about a successful learning function will be important for retention of employees and can influence learning participation and executive involvement.

Brand Discipline

The final step is the discipline to maintain the brand. Branding is not a one-time event; it is a continuous and consistent process to ensure that stakeholders are engaged in the brand, identify with the brand, and are constantly reminded of the brand. Year-to-year marketing should reflect the brand, and the proof points should be a constant string of data to convince all stakeholders that the value of the brand exists.

Call to Action

To consider focusing more on branding requires immediate and productive steps. Table 8-11 provides a checklist of what the CLO can and should do to ensure that a brand is developed and is providing the payoff. The CLO is the catalyst for developing the brand and, to the extent possible, represents the heart and soul of the learn-

Table 8-11
Branding Checklist

	Yes	No
1. Does your brand support the organization's strategic objectives?	❏	❏
2. Does your brand promise and deliver value as defined through the eyes of your customer?	❏	❏
3. Do you adequately understand the competition?	❏	❏
4. Have you defined what you do and what you don't do?	❏	❏
5. Does your brand name communicate your organization's value, identity, and promise?	❏	❏
6. Do your learning offerings reflect your brand vision and convey your value?	❏	❏
7. Do you have a marketing plan in place to build brand awareness?	❏	❏
8. Is there a direct link between your learning brand and your customer's experience?	❏	❏
9. Do you have systems and standards to ensure brand discipline and consistency?	❏	❏
10. Does your brand have an emotional connection with your customers?	❏	❏

Source: *Chief Learning Officer*, 2004. Used with permission.

ing organization. The brand provides a way of demonstrating that the learning organization stands for something and creates a unique value from learning experiences. The brand also provides an opportunity for emotional connection with the participants, suppliers, leaders, and a variety of stakeholders involved in the learning process.

FINAL THOUGHTS

There is almost universal agreement that more attention is needed for measurement and evaluation. Its use is expanding; the payoff is huge; the process is not very difficult or impossible; and the approaches, strategies, and techniques are not overly complex and can be useful in a variety of settings. The combined and persistent efforts of CLOs will continue to refine the techniques and create successful applications. Ultimately, this will show the business value and contribution of a learning and development organization.

> *IBM executives still look at participant feedback and the five levels of evaluation based upon knowledge gain, reported behavior change, or business improvement. Sharing metrics is valuable for executives but will not change the mind of those executives that don't believe in training.*
>
> Ted Hoff, Vice President of Learning, IBM

REFERENCES

L'Allier, James J. "The CLO's Role: Preparing for Future Challenges," *Chief Learning Officer.* March 2005, 26–28.

Long, Larry N. "Analytics: The CLO's Case in the CEO's Language," *Chief Learning Officer.* September 2004, 22–28.

www.marketingpower.com

Phillips, Jack J. *Return on Investment in Training and Performance Improvement Programs*, Second ed. Woburn, MA: Butterworth-Heinemann, 2003.

Phillips, Patricia P., and Jack J. Phillips. *ROI Basics*. Alexandria, VA: ASTD, 2005.

Travis, Lisa. "Branding Enterprise Learning," *Chief Learning Officer.* October 2004, 28–32.

VanAuken, Brad. *Brand Aid: An Easy Reference Guide to Solving Your Toughest Branding Problems and Strengthening Your Market Position*. New York, NY: Amacom, 2003.

CHAPTER 9

Managing Talent for Value

> No *amount of training and development will make up for a fundamental error in placing people in the wrong jobs. The CLO has a significant opportunity to help individuals learn about themselves and the kinds of jobs in which they will flourish and how to navigate around the tempting traps that can seriously damage career choices.*
> Fred Harburg, Managing Partner, Third Rivers Partners LLC

> *A learning strategy should provide strategic value and ensure that it addresses developing an optimal workforce—the right people with the right skills assigned to the right jobs that are aligned with business requirements.*
> Ted Hoff, Vice President of Learning, IBM

Talent management is one of the most important strategic objectives for many of companies today; many CLOs have the primary responsibility for the talent management system. The CLO's role represents a great opportunity to add value to the organization by acquiring, developing, and retaining critical talent. This chapter explores the importance of talent in the organization. From every viewpoint, talent is essential and is often regarded as a key strategy in maintaining a competitive advantage. A systems approach to talent management is needed for success, efficiency, and consistency. The systems approach follows a step-by-step process, beginning with attracting talent and ending with retaining talent.

221

TALENT MANAGEMENT ISSUES

Critical Jobs

The CLO should create a process for evaluating critical roles within the organization. Sometimes, people who are in critical jobs are not the best performers and the best performers are not in critical jobs. A successful talent management system identifies critical jobs in the organization and finds ways to ensure current and backup incumbents are top performers. Figure 9-1 provides an example of the type of data collected for talent management.

High Potentials

Another key element of a successful talent management system is a clear process for identifying and developing high potentials, people in the organization who are identified as the next leaders in the company. Many organizations carefully review and manage a small segment of their talent as high potentials. Other companies do not clearly segment out this group or provide preferential development or treatment. Either way, understanding who the top performers are in the company and fostering their development provides higher chances for business and leadership success.

First Name	Current Title	Dept Head	Capability Rating	Contribution Rating	Retention Rating	Top Leader?	Critical Role	Short-Term Successor
John	VP Engineering	Jan Smith	5	4	5	Yes	Yes	Mary White
Jane	Director of Learning	Billy Jones	3	3	6	No	No	Betty Boop
Kathy	VP Manufacturing	Joe Johnson	5	5	5	Yes	Yes	SpongeBob

Figure 9-1. QUALCOMM critical jobs chart.

Succession Planning

A good talent management system also plans for organizational transitions. Some companies have extensive succession plans for several layers of management; others only create plans for the top leaders in the company. To avoid disruption in business performance, the CLO must plan for departures of talent or, in the words of McDonald's Corporation, backups in case someone "gets hit by the bun truck." Evaluating ready-now talent, growing internal leaders, and sourcing external talent are all responsibilities of CLOs who manage talent in their companies.

Talent Movement

Companies inherently struggle with movement of talent because of the gaps this can leave in the organization. Talent mobility occurs when movement of talent happens regularly and has minimal impact on the business. If an employee's skills can be better used in another function, the business leaders should support moving that individual. Unfortunately, managers become territorial and fear gaps in their departments. Planning for these gaps and creating a culture that believes talent belongs to the company—not a specific department—takes time and effort. When managed appropriately, there should be no talent gaps because the talent management system is so robust that it can fill the openings quite quickly.

Centralized Talent Pools

Before the Securities and Exchange Commission's (SEC's) rules on segment reporting, many companies had centralized talent pools that could be used across the company transparently. For example, a centralized engineering function would enable engineering leads in the businesses to pull on resources with specific skill sets. Today, companies have typically aligned functional employees in a business, which limits movement or rotations. Formal rotation programs have flourished to simulate the concept of a centralized pool of talent. These programs enable a person, a new graduate, or existing employees to work for different managers in different functions during their rotational assignment. Finance departments, for example, use this model quite frequently with new MBA graduates. A rotation program that exposes the new grad to financial accounting, financing strategy, financial analysis, and, sometimes, tax/treasury provides robust experiences and develops talent effectively for future career mobility. At the end of the formal program, the employee can select a function, manager, or group for his or her work assignment. This provides the employee with exposure to different functions and develops his or her skills, which enables more growth and talent readiness as needs arise.

Talent Management Outcomes

Many CLOs share information about company-wide organizational talent with the executive team and sometimes communicate about talent to the board of directors. Giving exposure to management about the number of employees with international experience, the number of leaders with marketing education, or the percentage of employees with advanced degrees can provide critical information for business planning. Boards have an increasing interest in understanding the talent within a company as well as their strategies for employee acquisition, development, and retention. CLOs are in a critical position as keepers of the talent profile of a company.

The Conference Board has identified eight elements of talent management that, when truly integrated, create a holistic talent management system in an organization (Morton, 2005). These elements are critical for CLOs to consider as they create comprehensive strategies for talent management in their companies.

- *Recruitment.* College recruitment, experienced hires, recruitment programs, and onboarding processes.
- *Retention.* Retention and total rewards programs.
- *Professional Development.* Professional development systems, assessment centers, learning and training programs, and mentoring programs.
- *Leadership/High Potential.* Stretch assignments, high-potential development programs, executive coaching, cross-functional and international opportunities, short-term special assignments, succession planning, and talent reviews.
- *Performance Management.* Competency profiles, performance management systems, reward/recognition programs, and flexible compensation.
- *Feedback/Measurement.* Exit interviews, regular employee surveys, and Balanced Scoreboard.
- *Workforce Planning.* Forecasting talent needs and demands and talent skills development.

Table 9-1
Measuring Success of Talent Management

Traditional

- 3 job groups defined as critical talent.
- 6 recruiting channels utilized.
- 2,439 new employees recruited.
- Cost per hire reduced by 10% over the last year.
- Time to fill jobs reduced by 30% in two years.
- IDPs developed for 95% of high potentials.
- 92% of managers and executives involved in 360° process.
- 7 formal talent development programs in place.
- 5 informal talent development programs in place.
- 1,479 individuals involved in the talent development programs.
- Turnover rate below industry average.

Emerging

- Recruiting effectiveness increased by 30%.
- 85% of IDPs completed within one year.
- Promotion readiness rating increased by 42%.
- External hire ratio reduced by 35%.
- Performance ratings of newly promoted managers increased 36%.
- Manager/executive failure rate sliced in half.
- Avoidable turnover for three critical talent groups 30% below industry average.
- In sales and marketing, talent management system adds $15 million in sales.
- In IT, talent management systems saved $2.3 million in costs.
- 3 ROI studies in talent management completed with an average of 139%.

- *Culture.* Corporate values, internal communication, diversity, flexible workplace, and brand value proposition.

Table 9-1 shows how the talent management measurement systems are changing. The traditional group of measures of talent management focused on activity; the emerging group is focused on results, using the methods described in Chapter 8.

WHY TALENT IS CRITICAL TO SUCCESS

Talent is considered the most critical source of success in an organization, and no executive will argue this point. How did it get this way? How critical is it now? How critical will it be in the future? There are several major reasons why talent is so important and will be even more critical in the future. Some of them are briefly described in the following pages.

Stock Market Mystery

When considering the value and importance of talent, executives need look no further than the stock market. Investors place a tremendous value on human capital in organizations. For example, consider QUALCOMM, a leader in developing and delivering innovative digital wireless communication products and services. Based in San Diego, QUALCOMM is included in the S&P 500 Index and is a Fortune 500 company traded on the NASDAQ stock market. QUALCOMM is a very profitable company with revenues of $5.7 billion in fiscal 2005, a gross margin of 7 percent proforma, and a net income of $1.7 billion (QUALCOMM Annual Report, 2005).

QUALCOMM reported total assets on its balance sheet of $12.5 billion at the end of fiscal 2005; however, the market value was much higher. The stock price in late-2005 was approximately $45 per share, and the company had a market value of approximately $74 billion. In essence, total assets represented only 17 percent of the market value and included not only the current cash assets of cash, marketable securities, accounts receivable and inventories, but property, plants, equipment, and even goodwill.

Thus, investors see something in QUALCOMM that has a value much greater than the assets listed on the balance sheet. This "hidden value," as it is sometimes called, is the intangible assets, which now represent major portions of the value of organizations, particularly those in knowledge industries, such as QUALCOMM. It is helpful to understand what comprises the intangible assets; human capital is certainly a big part.

The Best Idea Will Fail Without Proper Talent and Execution

Talent management is fundamentally about ensuring that the right people are positioned in the right places and utilized to the fullest potential for the optimal success of the organization. Business leaders clearly understand their talent pool. They work hard to identify the key players who have critical relationships with customers and suppliers, and then they work even harder to nurture and keep those key resources.

A number of business leaders have asserted that coming up with the best talent for their companies is the most important task they have to perform. Some, such as former GE chairman Jack Welch and Honeywell International's Larry Bossidy, spent an inordinate amount of time searching for the best talent within their own employee pools, hoping to build leadership that way. Both Welch and Bossidy have frequently said that all the great strategies in the world will have little effect on a company unless the right people are chosen to execute those strategies (Hartman, 2004).

Leaders understand this and put a premium on keeping the talent they need for growth. They do what is necessary to ensure that key people are secure and do not leave because of low morale, thus preventing a defection domino effect.

Human Capital as the Last Major Source of Competitive Advantage

Today's organizations have access to the key success factors. Financial resources are available to almost any organization with a viable business model. One company no longer has an advantage over another to access the financial capital needed to run a business. Access to technology is equal; a company can readily adapt technology to a given situation or business model. It is difficult to have a technology advantage in an information technology society.

Businesses also have access to customers, even if there is a dominant player in the market. Newspapers are laced with stories of small organizations taking on larger ones and succeeding. Having entry and access to a customer database is not necessarily a competitive advantage. What makes the difference, clearly, is the human capital—the talent—of the organization. With relatively equal access to all the other resources, it is logical to conclude that the human resources are where a strategic advantage can be developed (Fitz-enz, 2001).

The Great Places to Work

Probably no activity about the importance of talent is more visible than the list of organizations selected as the 100 Best Companies to

Work For in America. This list is published each year in *Fortune* magazine and has become the bellwether for focusing on the importance of talent. Although other publications have spin-offs, this is the premier list that organizations strive to make. The most important factor in selecting companies for this list is what the employees themselves have to say about their workplace. For a typical list, at least 350 randomly selected employees from each candidate company fill out an employee-produced survey created by The Great Place to Work Institute, San Francisco (Levering and Moskowitz, 2005). The annual list presents each company in rank, along with the following statistics:

- Total employment, detailed by the percent of minorities and women
- Annual job growth (percent)
- Number of jobs created in the past year
- Number of applicants
- Voluntary turnover rate
- Number of hours of training per year
- Average annual pay, detailed by professional and hourly
- Revenues

These lists are alive with tales of how the employers focus on building a great place to work and building employee respect, dignity, and capability. These firms are successful in the market. A typical list includes well-known and successful companies such as American Express, Cisco Systems, FedEx, Genentech, Eli Lilly and Company, Marriott International, General Mills, Merck, Microsoft, Procter & Gamble, QUALCOMM, and others. Inclusion in the list has become so sought after by organizations that they change many of their practices and philosophies in an attempt to make this list. Table 9-2 shows the 22 companies that have made the list every year since its inception in 1998 (Harrington, 2005).

This list underscores the importance of talent and how much emphasis companies place on it. It shows how diversity, job growth, turnover, and learning make a significant difference in the organization. For the most part, these organizations are investing heavily—far exceeding those on any other list. Investment, in their minds, translates into payoff.

Most Admired and Successful Companies

Two other important lists are *Fortune*'s America's Most Admired Companies and The World's Most Admired Companies. These lists

Table 9-2
Hall of Fame of Great Places to Work

The Consistent Best Places to Work

These 22 companies have appeared on our list every year since its 1998 inception.

A.G. Edwards	Nordstrom
Cisco Systems	Publix Super Markets
FedEx	REI
First Horizon National	SAS Institute
Four Seasons Hotels and Resorts	Synovus
Goldman Sachs	TDIndustries
JM Smucker	Timberland
Marriott International	Valassis
MBNA	W.L. Gore & Associates
Microsoft	Wegmans Food Markets
	Whole Foods Market

are unique because the ranking is determined by peer groups. To develop the list, the Hay Group starts with the 10 largest companies (by revenue) in 64 industries, including foreign firms with US operations. Then, they ask 15,000 executives, directors, and security analysts to rate the companies in their own industries with 8 criteria, using a scale of 1 to 10. The respondents selected the 10 companies they admired most in any industry. From a talent perspective, it is interesting that 3 of the 8 key attributes focused directly on talent: employee talent, quality of management, and innovation. The other 5 are indirectly related. The key point is that investors and business people admire companies that are placing important emphasis on the human capital aspects of their business (Useem, 2005).

Perhaps the most publicized list is the grouping of superstars. As there are superstars in almost every area in life, so are there superstar organizations—those perceived as being extraordinarily successful, based on major accomplishments. We all know them by reputation, success, and contribution. The literature is laced with showplace examples of these extraordinary companies-including SAS, QUALCOMM, SAP, GE, Southwest Airlines, Honda, and USAA, to name a few. One common denominator for the superstar organizations is that each recognizes the people factor—the talent.

Executives at superstar organizations always give recognition to the people who have created the outstanding performance.

Most executives not only declare that their people are their most important asset, but they make statements such as, "We could not have done it without the people." Some will argue that the success of an organization can only be defined in terms of employees. Success cannot be generated in any way without successful people, not only at the top, but at all levels. People *are* the most important asset and no organization has been successful without them.

The Cost of Competent Talent

Successful talent acquisition and management is expensive. The total investment in competent talent is the total HR department expenses plus the salaries and benefits of all other employees. In essence, this includes every function that exists in the chain of talent acquisition and management. Attracting, selecting, developing, motivating, compensating, and managing talent are all accounted for in this total cost. Because the traditional HR department expenses do not include salaries of other functions, this measure has the effect of showing the total cost. It should be reported as a percent of operating costs or revenue, or on a per-employee basis to show realistic comparisons with other organizations. All of the direct employee-related costs are included in the human capital measure (Phillips, 2005).

Executives in some organizations realize the magnitude of these expenses and have a desire to manage them efficiently. Although the costs do not include the costs for office spaces and support expenses, they are still very significant, often two to three times the annual pay. In many—if not most—industries, the cost of talent is the largest operating expense category. Recruiting fully competent employees avoids some of the cost of initial training, development, and on-the-job learning, although the salary and benefits may be higher than those of less skilled employees. Because talent is so expensive, it must be managed carefully and systematically.

The Cost of Talent Departures

When talent leaves, the costs are high. Executives see the direct cost of recruiting, selection, and initial training, but may not understand other impacts. The total cost of turnover is not calculated routinely in organizations. When the cost is estimated, it is often

Figure 9-2. The turnover cost categories.

underestimated. Also, estimations of the total cost are not communicated throughout the organization, leaving the management team unaware of the potential costs. If turnover is a problem, the costs are always significant. In some cases, the actual impact can be devastating and can result in the organization's demise.

The total cost of turnover involves both the direct and indirect costs. Figure 9-2 lists the costs in the sequence in which they occur. This figure suggests that there are many different costs, some of which are never known with certainty but can be estimated if enough attention is directed to the issue.

When the total costs are calculated, it is often expressed as a percent of annual pay for a particular job group, as shown in Table 9-3. As this table shows, these costs, arranged in a hierarchy of jobs, are significant. The data for this table were obtained from a variety of research studies, journals, and academic publications as well as from publications for industries where turnover has become an issue, such as those for nurses, truck drivers, bank tellers, or software designers. Collectively, these external studies provide a basis for understanding the total cost of this issue; understanding the impact of turnover is the first step toward tackling it. There is healthy turnover in any organization—people who retire, leave to work in nonprofit organizations, or go back to school.

The area of most concern in managing talent is when top performers or critical employees depart their jobs unexpectedly. The

Table 9-3
Turnover Costs for Selected Job Groups

Job Type/Category	Turnover Cost Ranges (Percentage of Annual Wage/Salary)*
Entry level—hourly, unskilled (e.g., fast food worker)	30–50
Service/production workers—hourly (e.g., courier)	40–70
Skilled hourly—(e.g., machinist)	75–100
Clerical/administrative (e.g., scheduler)	50–80
Professional (e.g., sales representative, nurse, accountant)	75–125
Technical (e.g., computer technician)	100–150
Engineers (e.g., chemical engineer)	200–300
Specialists (e.g., computer software designer)	200–400
Supervisors/team leaders (e.g., section supervisor)	100–150
Middle managers (e.g., department manager)	125–200

*Percentages are rounded to reflect the general range of costs from studies. Costs are fully loaded to include all of the costs of replacing an employee and bringing him/her to the level of productivity and efficiency of the former employee.

CLO's role is emerging to manage this turnover successfully and onboard new employees quickly. In an ideal scenario, the CLO is prepared with talent sources, so there are no gaps in organizational performance or product road maps. Managing talent in an organization is a critical responsibility. Hence, many CLOs are integrating the staffing or recruitment function into their scope of responsibility. They are aware of talent needs, know the sourcing strategies for aligning great talent, are prepared with learning to build capable talent internally, and manage the employment brand.

Summary: Why Talent Is Critical

It may be helpful to summarize this information, which clearly details the critical role of talent in the organization. Table 9-4 provides a quick summary, showing many of the reasons why talent is critical to success. The remainder of this chapter describes a system to provide the focus, attention, and care needed for this strategic issue.

Table 9-4
Why Talent Is Critical

Why Talent Is Critical to Success
1. We cannot be successful without talent.
2. Talent adds to the market value.
3. Talent executes the ideas.
4. Talent is the last source of competitive advantage.
5. Great workplaces attract and retain talent.
6. The most successful and admired companies have great talent.
7. The cost of competent talent is high.
8. The cost of turnover of talent is high.
9. The competitive environment has created a retention crisis.
10. Retention can be managed.

NEEDED: A SYSTEM FOR TALENT MANAGEMENT

The most effective way to tackle talent management is to use a systems approach, ensuring that the different elements and pieces of the process are working in concert to acquire and integrate talent into the system. Several issues support the need for this system.

Disconnected Efforts

The traditional way to deal with this issue is to have the responsibility assigned to various groups that traditionally cut across functional HR lines. Recruiting, learning and development, reward systems, and employee relations are traditional functional groups. Several problems may surface with this approach. First, in this traditional HR model style, talent management is in a reactive mode, reacting to critical issues, problems, and talent shortages. There are few early signs—other than the lack of communication between groups—to signal an impending problem. Also, because individuals involved are not tightly integrated with open communication, inefficiencies abound in the processes, often creating duplications and delays throughout the system. Consequently, this is a very expensive approach to the problem—one that fails to generate the success needed and leaves voids, omissions, and delays. The results can be disastrous for an organization in need of talent and attempting to

Figure 9-3. The traditional talent management process.
(Source: Deloitte, 2004.)

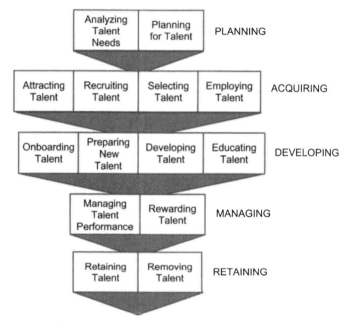

Figure 9-4. Talent management system.

grow. Most of all, the traditional approach creates confusion—not only in the roles and responsibilities but in the process of designating who is in charge. This confusion has been minimized by a systems approach.

A Systems Approach

Figure 9-3 shows the traditional model for a talent management process where the focus is on acquiring and retaining talent (Deloitte, 2004). Today, more issues must be addressed and integrated.

A systems approach to talent management is presented in Figure 9-4. It includes the major issues of planning, acquiring, developing, managing, and retaining employees. These are often subdivided into responsibility areas, as outlined in the figure. Traditionally, many of these have been under different sections, apart from the typical learning and development area of responsibility. This is a system that must work together in close coordination and integration, ideally under the direction of a central person whose key responsibility is talent management—namely, the CLO. When in place, the benefits are tremendous from the client's perspective. First, this approach presents consistent attention throughout the process. Problems can be spotted quickly and adjustments can be made. Second, talent acquisition can be more effective, ensuring that adequate talent is recruited and integrated into the system and the appropriate quality and quantities are secured. Finally, there is value added as costs are reduced when the process is more efficient and duplications are avoided. The systems approach is not only rational and logical, but it is an economic way to address talent management.

A Scenario

In the traditional model, Company X needs to quickly hire 30 multimedia engineers for a new technology deployment. The staffing lead receives notification, opens 30 position requisitions, creates an advertisement, posts the job on a web site, and begins the candidate screening process. In an ideal model, the CLO would be working closely with the executive team and know that the business strategy is moving toward multimedia. The CLO could scan a database of talent profiles that would identify 20 internal candidates that either have multimedia skills or need a few courses/development opportunities to acquire the skills. In this case, the request for external talent drops to 10 and the ramp-up time for these internal employees in these new roles is much shorter. Time to full productivity is cut in half. The CLO then works to backfill the jobs that were filled by employees who are now in the multimedia jobs. This is a true talent management model—the CLO deploys resources where they are needed most and develops internal talent for optimum performance and long-term value to the company.

Defining the Critical Talent

Before describing the mechanics of talent management, it is helpful to define the critical talent in the organization. The critical talent is made up of the employees who drive a major part of the company's business performance and who generate above average value for customers and shareholders. Typically, the critical talent possess highly developed skills and deep knowledge. They don't just "do their job," but they go above and beyond to contribute to the organization's success. Surprisingly, these are not always the high-tech or highest paid employees; often they are the valuable employees that are seldom mentioned in the annual report. Take FedEx, for example—the world's largest overnight package delivery firm. One report suggested that the couriers might be more critical to the operation than the pilots who fly the packages through the night. The couriers have direct contact with the customers and must make continual decisions that impact efficiency and the effectiveness of the supply chain, such as how to reconfigure a route and how long to wait for a customer's packages (Deloitte, 2004).

Critical talent can vary considerably by industry and organization. At Bristol-Myers Squibb, critical talent may include the scientists and clinicians who discover and develop pharmaceuticals that fuel the company's growth. At BP Global, it may include the geologists and petroleum engineers who find and extract oil. At DaimlerChrysler, it may be the machinists who perform precision operations to develop parts for automobiles using Six Sigma standards. At Wal-Mart it may be the inventory managers who ensure that the right goods are in the right store at the right time. Recruiting wars often erupt when there's a shortage of critical talent, leading to much inefficiency and cost and many disruptions in the talent management system.

A Starting Point

Over the past several years, there has been a tremendous focus on the use of competencies characteristics and traits of individuals. Some experts indicate that attracting talent can only be achieved if there is a focus on identifying competencies and using them throughout the talent system. Competency models are fundamental to human capital systems. Many organizations use a unique language when describing recruiting standards, training requirements, and promotional criterion. The problem is exacerbated when the organizations span cultures and countries. By using an agreed-upon competency model, the organization can communicate via a common language that describes performance from one unit to the next (Berger and Berger, 2004).

As shown in Figure 9-5, competencies may drive the entire talent management system. A competency is a reliably measurable, relatively enduring characteristic (or combination thereof) of a person, community, or organization that causes or statistically predicts a

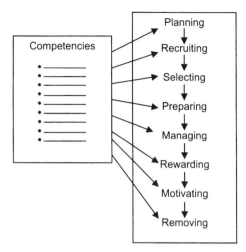

Figure 9-5. Competencies may drive the talent management system.

criterion or level of performance. Competency characteristics are knowledge, behavioral skills, competency processing (IQ), personality traits, values, motives, and occasionally other perceptional capabilities (Spencer, 2004). Competencies are a critical part of planning, recruiting, and selecting talent at the beginning of the process. Preparing and developing talent focuses on the same competencies, as does managing, rewarding, and motivating employees. The competencies for a particular job—even similar jobs—can vary.

An example of competencies is shown in Table 9-5. While these can be typical competencies for organizations, they are not necessarily for *every* organization. They have to be specific in terms of what is important to an organization and the skills, knowledge, and value systems needed. Competencies can be evaluated through interviews and previous work experiences. Once on the job, competencies are often observable and translate directly into success or lack thereof. The steps needed to develop competencies are beyond the scope of this book, and are contained in other works (Lucia and Lepsinger, 1999).

The key challenge is to determine, to the extent possible, the competencies needed for talent in specific divisions, groups, functions, or even job categories and to use them to drive the talent management system. Some companies use behavioral dimensions, leadership characteristics, or behavioral quotients instead of competencies. Whatever the language, it is important that the basis for the talent management system fit the organization.

Table 9-5
Sample Competencies

Competency	Competency Definition
Action Orientation	Targets and achieves results, overcomes obstacles, accepts responsibility, establishes standards and responsibilities, creates a results-oriented environment, and follows through on actions.
Communication	Communicates well both verbally and in writing. Effectively conveys and shares information and ideas with others. Listens carefully and understands various viewpoints. Presents ideas clearly and concisely and understands relevant detail in presented information.
Creativity/Innovation	Generates novel ideas and develops or improves existing and new systems that challenge the status quo, takes risks, and encourages innovation.
Critical Judgment	Possesses the ability to define issues and focus on achieving workable solutions. Consistently does the right thing by performing with reliability.
Customer Orientation	Listens to customers, builds customer confidence, increases customer satisfaction, ensures commitments are met, sets appropriate customer expectations, and responds to customer needs.
Interpersonal Skill	Effectively and productively engages with others and establishes trust, credibility, and confidence with others.
Leadership	Motivates, empowers, inspires, collaborates with, and encourages others. Develops a culture where employees feel ownership in what they do and continually improve the business. Builds consensus when appropriate. Focuses team members on common goals.
Teamwork	Knows when and how to attract, develop, reward, and utilize teams to optimize results. Acts to build trust, inspire enthusiasm, encourage others, and help resolve conflicts and develop consensus in creating high-performance teams.
Technical/Functional Expertise	Demonstrates strong technical/functional proficiencies and knowledge in areas of expertise. Shows knowledge of company business and proficiency in the strategic and financial processes, including P&L planning processes and their implications for the company.

Source: Berger and Berger, 2004. Used with permission.

Table 9-6
The Changing Role of the CLO in Talent Management

The CLO's Role in Talent Management

System Component	Traditional	New
• Talent planning and analysis		✓
• Attraction and recruiting		✓
• Selection and employment		✓
• Orientation and onboarding	✓	
• Learning and development	✓	
• Performance management		✓
• Rewards and recognition		✓
• Retention management		✓
• Layoff management		✓

The CLO's Role

In the past, the responsibility for talent management has not been assigned to the executive responsible for learning and development. This has changed in many organizations. As shown in Table 9-6, the roles are changing, and in many organizations, the CLO is now responsible for the entire system, including recruiting and managing performance and retention. In this sense, the chief learning officer becomes the chief talent officer, ensuring that the proper talent is selected, properly developed, and managed. The CLO has the opportunity to change the mindset of the organization and can have a key impact on lowering recruiting and turnover costs and offering employees new growth and opportunities that may not have been visible before. While recruiting organizations have been pointed outward in the past, learning organizations are pointed inward, toward the organization's most valuable asset—its people (Averbook, 2005).

PLANNING FOR TALENT

Planning is perhaps the area that has been most neglected in many talent management systems. The objective of planning is to have a forecast for acquiring the appropriate types of employees to meet the needs of the organization, given the constraints of market forces and the available labor supply. The three areas that are often addressed, sometimes by separate individuals or units within the talent management system, are discussed in the following pages.

Analyzing Talent Needs

Several factors will determine the need for talent, as defined earlier. First, the growth of the organization often translates into the largest component of talent requirements. The CLO must be aware of the organization's strategy, both short- and long-term. Needs are sometimes driven by shifts in products and services, acquisitions, mergers, and routine growth through expansion. Whatever the reasons, this action translates into a specific number of individuals in different job categories.

Second, replacement needs create openings as employees leave the organization. If the turnover is excessive, replacement needs become significant. If there is low turnover, replacement needs are minimal. In the context of managing retention, only the avoidable turnover is considered. However, when replacements are needed, all types of turnover must be considered-including those individuals who retire, leave due to disability, or transfer to other regional areas. Just the retirement issue is a critical problem for many organizations. NASA, for example, faces a tremendous loss of talent as much of the science and engineering capability will be retiring in the next few years. This situation will have a tremendous impact on their talent management system; they need to ensure that the proper talent is recruited and prepared for their assignments.

A third area that translates directly into needs is the changes in skills and competencies. As technology advances, markets change, and products shift, a different set of skills and competencies is sometimes needed, either in addition to or beyond those currently in the organization. These three areas generate needs that must be translated into specific numbers and forecasted, in both short- and long-term scenarios.

Market Analysis

Since the majority of needs must be filled from the available labor market, a market analysis is critical. When examining the labor market, one must take several issues into consideration. First, the supply of labor in the recruiting area—this is a critical issue for some organizations because of labor shortages. This may require the relocation of facilities to ensure a better source of labor. For example, many automobile companies that are based outside the United States are developing plants in record numbers in the southern part of the United States. For example, Toyota, Honda, Mercedes Benz, and Hyundai have all developed major plants in Alabama, making this state the automobile capital of the south. A major part of the attraction is the available labor supply—in both quality and quantity—as well as a strong work ethic.

Planning for Talent

After the labor needs have been developed and the market is analyzed, the plans are developed, generating a schedule of the number of employees that will be acquired at what times, from what sources, and, sometimes, by job group. If it becomes apparent that the market will not be able to supply the required resources, the shortages must be addressed and alternatives must be developed. For example, due to the difficulty of recruiting fully trained nurses, hospitals have created their own nursing schools, sometimes in conjunction with a university, at other times on their own. This is a classic case of attempting to regulate supply versus demand—taking control of the situation and creating the supply. This situation creates an important issue that must be part of the talent planning—scenario planning. Because all forecasts contain errors and there are many events that can have a significant effect on the sources, different scenarios should be developed, including worst-case conditions. This process provides insight into what can, should, and perhaps must be done to ensure that available talent is onboard when needed.

ACQUIRING TALENT

Acquiring talent has four key components: attracting—in essence, creating a talent magnet; recruiting—getting them into the organization; selecting—making the selection decision; and employing— getting them on the payroll. Each of these is an important step, often performed by different individuals.

Attracting Talent

Attracting talent is a long-term issue. The attraction of a place to work covers several issues, but two very important ones relate to the issue of developing a talent magnet. One issue is being an employer of choice, representing a great place to work. The second is the overall reputation, or employment brand, of the organization. Employers of choice have several things in common. They recognize and organize a work/life balanced program that meets needs across the business; they have professional and personal development opportunities for all; they possess the ability to make a contribution to the firm tied to personal responsibility; they enjoy a friendly and culturally rich environment ("being with others I can relate to"); and they operate a business that is responsible to the community as a whole (Johnson, 2002). In the United States, employer-of-choice issues are developed by a variety of organizations and publications. The most common is the one developed by *Fortune* magazine—The 100 Best Companies to Work For in America, described earlier in the chapter.

Organizations are working harder to polish their image in the eyes of prospective talent. Some have staff who do little other than keep the firm's name in front of both faculty and students and promote their "employer brand." GE focuses on 38 universities where it actively promotes itself as an employer. PricewaterhouseCoopers (PWC) targets 200 universities and gives a partner responsibility for each. PWC says that each of these partners spends up to 200 hours per year building relationships on campus. That particular investment seems to have paid off. Each year, Universum, an employer-branding consultant, asks some 30,000 American students to name their ideal employer. As shown in Table 9-7, PWC was ranked second (up from fourth in 2004) in a 2005 survey, topped only by BMW. Yet the German carmaker, which knocked Microsoft off the top spot, steers clear of campuses, relying, says Universum Communications, on the "coolness" of its products for its popularity (Economist, 2005).

The reputation is based on several factors. Harris Interactive and the Reputation Institute published a corporate reputation poll based on the views of almost 30,000 respondents. They developed six categories to rank reputation:

- Emotional appeal
- Products and services
- Workplace environment
- Social responsibility
- Vision and leadership
- Financial performance

The reputations, particularly for those issues about a place to work, are often evolved and developed over time and have to be driven by

Table 9-7
The Good Workplace Guide

American Undergraduates' Ideal Employers

Company	2005	2004
BMW	1	2
PricewaterhouseCoopers	2	4
Ernst & Young	3	6
Boeing	4	7
Johnson & Johnson	5	17
Deloitte	6	8
Coca-Cola	7	5
Microsoft	8	1
CIA	9	14
FBI	10	138
Merrill Lynch	11	12
IBM	12	11
Apple Computer	13	41
KPMG International	14	16
JPMorgan Chase & Co.	15	18

Source: Universum Communications, 2005. Used with permission.

senior leadership. A few scandals, ethical concerns, or ineffective leadership can spoil an otherwise superb reputation. Many companies work very hard to ensure that their image, from a talent attraction perspective, is superb. In essence, they are attempting to brand their organization as a great place to work as well as a great place to invest. Sears perfected this sentiment in their overall strategy to create a compelling place to shop, a compelling place to invest, and a compelling place to work, putting the customers, shareholders, and employees on equal footing.

Recruiting Talent

Recruiting has changed significantly in the last decade; not only the methods, but the overall approach. Table 9-8 shows how the recruiting strategies have shifted. The newer approaches involve constant recruiting, using many sources, branding, and involving many individuals.

Table 9-8
The Shifting Strategies of Recruiting

Old Recruiting Strategies	New Recruiting Strategies
Grow all your own talent.	Recruit talent at all levels.
Recruit only for vacant positions.	Search for talent all the time.
Go to a few traditional sources.	Tap many diverse sources of talent.
Recruiting is limited to a few individuals.	Every employee is a recruiter.
Advertise to job hunters.	Find ways to reach passive candidates.
Specify a compensation range and stay within it.	Break the compensation rules to get the candidates you want.
Recruiting is about screening.	Recruiting is about selling as well as screening.
Hire as needed with no overall plan.	Develop a recruiting strategy for each type of talent.
Keep a low profile except during employment growth.	Create and brand an employer of choice.

Adapted and updated from Michaels, 2001.

Table 9-9
Shift in Recruiting Methods

Traditional Recruiting Methods	Nontraditional Recruiting Methods
Job service agencies	Web resources
Recruiting ads	Open houses
Professional recruiters	Receptions at conferences
Campus recruiting	Information seminars
Employment support groups	Military recruiting
Community recruiting	Employee talent scouts
Job fairs	Networking
Online applicants	Employee referrals
Trade and professional associations	Current events monitoring
Employment hotline	Preemployment programs

Table 9-9 shows the shift in the actual methods of recruiting. Although the traditional methods are still being used, newer methods are being adopted, particularly those involving web resources and networking. Monitoring current events in specific areas to understand where the talent may be located or what may be driving available talent is an effective tactic. Using employees as talent scouts is another useful approach. Because of the scarcity and competition for quality talent, a talent war is being waged in certain industries. Nontraditional recruiting methods are often needed to capture the interest of the passive prospect. Recruiting has become so subtle that some organizations—such as Cisco Systems—have a philosophy of not hiring candidates who are actually looking for a job.

Selecting Talent

Recruiting brings the prospects for consideration. Next comes one of the most critical talent decisions—the employment decision. How it is made, who makes it, when it is made, or whether it is accepted are important issues. Although the selection is only one component in the talent management system, it must be consistent. It is at this stage that the most scrutiny comes in terms of being fair and equitable. An inconsistent selection process is doomed to be challenged and may be difficult to defend. A systematic process is followed for each selection so that no candidate is subject to disparate treatment and the selection does not represent an adverse impact. Figure 9-6 shows the selection system for a commercial banking officer for a large banking firm in the United States. The figure shows steps in the process and where the applicant can be rejected. Because there are so many components in a typical selection process, it has to be organized very carefully so that the selection time is minimized.

Just as the recruiting methods have changed, so have the selection methods. Table 9-10 shows the nontraditional selection methods now being used to make a better employment decision. Executives are anxious to ensure a good fit for the employee before the ultimate selection is made. After it is made, it becomes expensive, time consuming, and disruptive to make adjustments or changes.

Employing Talent

Employing talent comprises the processing and administrative steps. Timing and convenience are the concerns as new talent joins the organization. All payroll tax forms and employee benefits forms are completed. An organized system is the key to handling these steps efficiently, effectively, and with as little frustration as possible. Two important problem areas must be avoided: administrative delays in the processing and unpleasant surprises, particularly those that can create a negative impression.

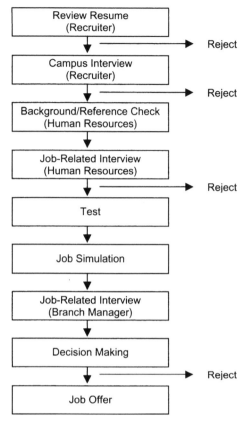

Figure 9-6. Selection system for commercial banking officer.

Table 9-10
Shifts in Selection Methods

Traditional Selection Methods	Nontraditional Selection Methods
Resumes	Behavioral interviews
Background checks	Job simulation
Reference checks	Preemployment training
Testing	Assessment center
Physical exams	Work samples
Drug testing	Referral profile
Interviews	

DEVELOPING TALENT

After the talent is on board, the learning and development process begins with onboarding, initial training and learning for the job, and development to refine processes and improve capability as well as prepare individuals for other job positions.

Onboarding New Talent

Initial orientation or onboarding, as it is sometimes called, creates early impressions that are lasting. It is important for new talent to have a positive first day on the job and an outstanding first week. In some job situations where employees have an opportunity to move quickly to another job with little investment, an unpleasant experience in the first week of work may result in an early turnover. The early turnover measure is the number of departures in the first month of employment. When this number is excessive, 10 percent for example, this is an indication that either the selection was improper or that something happened in the early days of employment to change the employee's opinion.

Onboarding helps the individual align with the organization, its values, mission, philosophy, policies, practices, and people. Employees must understand the guidelines, practices, and policies—even the unwritten ones—so that initial success can be ensured. It is important to avoid frustrating experiences, missteps, miscues, and unpleasant surprises. At the same time, this is the best opportunity to secure the employee's commitment to the organization. Both the motivation and the potential for engagement is extremely high. Both the efficiency and effectiveness of handling the orientation are important.

Preparing New Talent

Regardless of the level of talent, a certain amount of preparing for the job is necessary. For some, it may be significant, as in preparing for skills or applications unique to the job. For most, it will be a matter of adjusting to the situation and learning specific practices, technology, and procedures. If the competencies are already in place, significant skillbuilding will not be needed. If these competencies do not exist, significant training may be required.

Developing New Talent

A variety of learning and development programs must be available to continue to improve performance, refine skills, learn new techniques, and adjust to changing technology. A variety of development methods used by the CLO were covered in Chapter 6, with specific emphasis on the nontraditional ones.

Educating New Talent

Education is defined as preparation for the current and next job. Because today's employees are interested in all types of career movement and development opportunities, several approaches are utilized and explored. Succession planning is part of this as well as other types of replacement planning. The methods discussed in Chapter 6 are used to develop employees for new jobs as well.

Managing Talent

With talent in place and performing, the next challenge is to ensure that performance improves as employees are highly motivated and thoroughly utilized. Managing talent involves two new responsibilities for the CLO: managing the performance and rewarding talent appropriately. In most cases, these functions have previously been performed by the compensation function, but now many CLOs also have this responsibility.

Managing Talent Performance

To ensure that performance is discussed, recognized, rewarded, and understood appropriately, many organizations are focusing renewed efforts on performance management systems. The old approach was through the traditional performance review conducted quarterly, semiannually, or annually, which was usually a one-way conversation from a manager to an employee. All parties typically disliked the process. Managers didn't like to do it because there was the potential for conflict and they did not have the skills or the confidence to do it properly; employees didn't like it because it did not meet their needs and often left them confused, frustrated, and sometimes angry. The human resources staff didn't like it because it wasn't conducted properly, effectively, or consistently.

Figure 9-7. Performance management system example.

CLOs are attempting to make this process less painful by automating the system. For example, a typical approach to performance management is to develop briefing sessions and maybe even e-learning modules that show how the process should work and the benefits of conducting these types of discussions. Discussions are often more frequent, and there is a meeting between the employee and the manager to discuss performance improvement and to set individual goals that align with organizational goals. These goals are entered into an online system, and are posted for constant review, follow-up, and adjustment. As progress is made, the status is updated. Performance data are available to others who need to keep track of key issues and see how well the system is working overall. Progress is monitored and the feedback is obtained in a variety of follow-up discussions. This approach brings constant overview, feasible goals, challenging assignments, and alternative delivery, and it saves time and provides excellent documentation. Figure 9-7 shows the performance management system at a credit card division of a financial services firm. An important challenge for the CLO is to track and manage this type of process so that it becomes a motivational tool to drive performance instead of a headache that creates confusion.

Rewarding Talent

Rewarding performance, accomplishments, and milestones is very important. If used appropriately, recognition is one of the most effective motivators; and one of the best ways to motivate is to tie bonuses and incentives directly to performance. Nonmonetary rewards can often be just as motivational. The development of these programs is beyond the scope of this book and can be found in many other references.

When providing recognition, both the substance and the style must be considered. Substance is the value of the reward or recognition from the perspective of the person receiving it. If that person places no value on the reward, it will have very little motivational effect. The style is the manner in which the recognition is provided, including how, when, and where. The style relates to the sincerity of the communication and is just as important as the substance.

RETAINING TALENT

Keeping talent is perhaps one of the most critical challenges for the CLO, representing one of the newest responsibilities. This principle involves managing the retention process, which is now a CLO responsibility in some organizations. A strategic accountability approach, outlined in Figure 9-8, is needed to tackle the retention issue (Phillips, 2003). This approach has five important advantages.

1. *It considers the retention issue to be an important part of strategy.* The executive team is very involved in the retention issue.
2. *The retention issues are measured with bottom-line results.* Accountability is built in throughout the process so that those involved can fully understand the cost of the problem, the cost of the solutions, the potential impact of the solutions, and the actual impact of the solutions—all in monetary terms.
3. *The approach moves logically from one issue to another.* A series of steps, not necessary to manage the process, are followed with this approach.
4. *The approach is a discipline and a methodology.* With this approach, it's easy to stay on track because each of the different issues has to be addressed before moving on to another issue.
5. *It is a continuous cycle of improvement.* Starting with a problem ultimately leads to a reduction in turnover. The process continues until turnover is at the desired level.

Ultimately, the approach positions the organization in a preventative stance working to maintain the appropriate level of staffing and reducing the risk of turnover. Each segment of the strategic

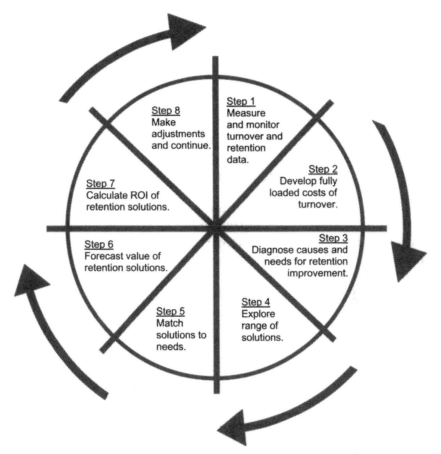

Figure 9-8. Strategic accountability approach.

accountability approach is briefly discussed in the remainder of the chapter.

Measure and Monitor Turnover

For many organizations, turnover is defined as voluntary. For others, resignations and terminations based on unsatisfactory performance are included in the definition. The cleanest definition to use is avoidable turnover—employees leaving (voluntarily) or being forced to leave (involuntarily) when such departures could have been prevented. It is important for the classification to match the definition in benchmarking studies, industry reports, or trade publications. Turnover by demographics should be reported, showing the regions, divisions, branches, plants, and departments as well as the sex, age, and personal characteristics of the individual employees. Job groups are also important.

When using benchmark data and other comparisons, trigger points for action must be developed. When should an alarm sound? Is the turnover a rising trend or a sudden spurt? Is the measure going up when it should go down? Each of these could signal that action is necessary to begin exploring causes and creating solutions.

Develop the Fully Loaded Cost of Turnover

The impact cost of turnover is one of the most underestimated and undervalued costs in the organization. It is often misunderstood because it does not reflect the actual costs of a turnover statistic, and it is not regularly reported to the management team who are left unaware of the actual cost. Although turnover rates and percentages are reported routinely, additional reporting of actual costs can be more effective. The fully loaded cost of turnover, see Figure 9-2, should be reported, even if it is only an estimate. The total cost will attract the attention of the senior management team, revealing the true impact that turnover is having in the organization.

Diagnose Causes and Needs for Retention Improvement

The cause of turnover must be determined. Some causes appear obvious, where others can be deceptive. Collecting appropriate data is often a challenge because of the potential for bias and inaccuracies that surface during the data collection process. Several diagnostic processes are available. A variety of tools are available for use with turnover analysis, beginning with analyzing trends and patterns in particular groups and demographic categories to pinpoint the problem area. As Table 9-11 lists, the tools range from conducting a survey to coordinating a focus group to uncover the causes of turnover.

Explore a Range of Solutions and Match Solutions to Needs

Creative approaches to the turnover problem have resulted in hundreds of excellent solutions. In fact, because there are so many potential solutions to the problem, confusion often results. The solution must be appropriate and feasible for the organization. When matching solutions to needs, five key issues are considered:

Table 9-11
Tools to Diagnose Turnover Problems

- Diagnostic tools
- Demographic analysis
- Diagnostic instruments
- Focus groups
- Probing interviews
- Job satisfaction surveys
- Organizational commitment surveys
- Exit interviews
- Exit surveys
- Nominal group technique
- Brainstorming
- Cause and effect diagrams
- Force field analysis
- Mind mapping
- Affinity diagrams
- . . . and the list continues

1. Avoid mismatches.
2. Discourage multiple solutions.
3. Select a solution for maximum return.
4. Verify the match early.
5. Check the progress of each solution.

Forecast the Value of Solutions

Forecasting is an expert estimation of what a solution should contribute; the process can be difficult, challenging, and risky. When a forecast for the value of a solution is developed, this allows the team to establish priorities, work with a minimum number of solutions, and focus on solutions with the greatest ROI. When as much data as possible is accumulated, the estimate is supported and credibility is built around the process. The payoff value can be developed if the percentage of expected turnover reduction can be related to it.

Ideally, the forecast should contain an expected ROI value, particularly if the solution is expensive. However, a more realistic approach is to offer a range of possible ROI values, given certain assumptions, thus removing some of the risk of making a precise estimation. This step is perhaps one of the most difficult parts of the process.

Calculate ROI for Turnover Reduction Solutions

Another commonly neglected step is the calculation of the impact of a turnover reduction strategy. This step is often omitted because it appears to be an unnecessary add-on process. If accumulating solutions is the measure of success of turnover reduction or prevention, the impact to those solutions may appear to have no value. From a senior executive's point of view, accountability is not complete until impact and ROI data have been collected, at least for major solutions.

Make Adjustments and Continue

The extensive set of data collected from the ROI process will provide information that can be used to make adjustments in turnover reduction strategies. The information reveals success of the turnover reduction solution at all levels from reaction to ROI. It also examines barriers to success, identifying specifically what kept the solution from being effective or prevented it from becoming more effective. This information also identifies the processes in place that enable or support a turnover reduction solution. All of the information provides a framework for adjusting the solution so that it can be revised, discontinued, or amplified. The next step in the process goes back to the beginning—monitoring the data to ensure that turnover continues to meet expectations—and then the cycle continues.

FINAL THOUGHTS

Talent management is fast becoming a critical strategic objective for growing organizations. This responsibility represents an excellent opportunity to create value. The importance of hiring competent talent is evident in any direction. Talent is a key focus—now and in the future. It is the last source of competitive advantage.

Although CLOs have always had the responsibility for the employee development portion of talent management, only recently have CLOs been involved in some of the other issues such as acquiring, managing, and retaining employees. These are key responsibilities that can make an enormous difference and add significant value. A complete talent management system with a single individual in charge—the CLO—is needed. In some organizations, the CLO has become the chief talent officer.

> *The job of a CLO is really two roles in one: the CLO role and the leadership development role. The CLO is responsible for the total package of talent management, development, retention programs, consistency of the internal message, competencies, and alignment with the business. They must understand change management, organization design, and business and educational technology. This is a large role that is continuously growing.*
>
> Bill Wiggenhorn, Former President, Motorola University and Vice Chairman of Global Ed-Tech Management Group

REFERENCES

"In Search of the Ideal Employer," *The Economist.* August 20, 2005, 49.

Averbook, Jason. "Connecting CLOs with the Recruiting Process," *Chief Learning Officer.* June 2005, 24.

Berger, Lance, and Dorothy R. Berger. *The Talent Management Handbook: Creating Organizational Excellence by Identifying, Developing, and Promoting Your Best People.* New York, NY: McGraw-Hill, 2004.

Deloitte Research. *It's 2008: Do You Know Where Your Talent Is? Why Acquisition and Retention Strategies Don't Work.* Deloitte Development LLC, 2004.

Fitz-enz, Jac. *ROI of Human Capital.* New York, NY: Amacom, 2001.

Harrington, Ann. "Hall of Fame," *Fortune.* January 24, 2005, 94.

Hartman, Amir. *Ruthless Execution: What Business Leaders Do When Their Companies Hit the Wall.* Upper Saddle River, NJ: Prentice Hall, 2004.

Johnson, Mike. *Talent Management: Getting Talented People to Work for You.* London, England: Prentice Hall, 2002.

Levering, Robert, and Milton Moskowitz. "2005 Special Report: The 100 Best Companies to Work For." *Fortune.* January 24, 2005, 61.

Lucia, Anntoinette D., and Richard Lepsinger. *The Art and Science of Competency Models: Pinpointing Critical Success Factors in Organizations.* San Francisco, CA: Jossey-Bass/Pfeiffer, 1999.

Michaels, Ed, Helen Handfield-Jones, and Beth Axelrod. *The War of Talent.* Boston, MA: Harvard Business School Press, 2001.

Morton, Lynne. *Talent Management Value Imperatives.* New York, NY: The Conference Board, 2005.

Phillips, Jack J. *Investing in Your Company's Human Capital: Strategies to Avoid Spending Too Much or Too Little*. New York, NY: Amacom, 2005.

Phillips, Jack J. *Managing Employee Retention: A Strategic Accountability Approach*. Woburn, MA: Butterworth-Heinemann, 2003.

QUALCOMM Annual Report. Available from http://www.qualcomm.com. Accessed September 2, 2004.

Spencer, Lyle M., Jr. "How Competencies Create Economic Value," *The Talent Management Handbook: Creating Organizational Excellence by Identifying, Developing, and Promoting Your Best People*. New York, NY: McGraw-Hill, 2004, 64.

Useem, Jerry. "America's Most Admired Companies," *Fortune*. Universum Communications, March 7, 2005, 67.

CHAPTER 10

Developing Productive Management Relationships

> *The CLO's role is to ensure that the culture supports, drives, and thrives on learning. They must be aware of the inhibitors of learning and ensure systems are in place to transfer and pull knowledge across the organization.*
>
> Bob Corcoran, Vice President of Corporate Citizenship and Chief Learning Officer and President of GE Foundation

The CLO and other leaders on the learning and development team must develop productive relationships with executive teams and key managers in their organizations. With emphasis on working with business leaders, these relationships are developed to reach common goals and improve performance as employees participate in learning programs and use resources from the learning and development function. Building this relationship involves direct actions to improve management commitment and support, enhance reinforcement to learners, secure active involvement in the process, and maintain productive partnerships. As a prerequisite, CLOs must understand the business, the business drivers and challenges, and the leadership focus areas. Building executive relationships is essential for CLOs to be successful and align with the company.

KEY CONCEPTS

Major Influences

Some consider partnering to be a logical, rational approach, which is long overdue. Partnering and collaborating has been an ongoing practice in many Asian countries. Only recently has it spread significantly to other countries. As information about management practices continue to proliferate, and the successes of effective techniques are publicized, effective management practices are being adopted by a wide variety of cultures. Partnerships represent an important tool for the CLO.

Developing a productive relationship with business leaders is a win-win relationship. It creates value by helping the business achieve goals while providing direction and guidance for the learning and development staff. When operating effectively, business impact can be significant and enables CLOs to have a "seat at the table."

Establishing effective collaborative relationships with management is the best route to success with learning and development programs. Input from the management team is an integral part of the process. Management involvement is sometimes critical to successful implementation of a program. An effective relationship can help guarantee success with quality input and cooperation.

The partnership relationship is an outgrowth of the learning organization movement. Most major organizations have been transformed (or are in the process of being transformed) into a learning organization. In the classic definition of the learning organization, the management team takes a more active role in the learning process and partners with learning providers to ensure that employees acquire the skills and knowledge necessary for success. In essence, management becomes a willing partner in the process.

Finally, many success stories about partnering relationships have been publicized, causing others to pay more attention to this process. Many CLOs have deliberately planned and organized attempts to build the relationship to a productive level. These success stories have created additional interest for others to pursue the process.

Why Managers Don't Always Support Learning

It is helpful to understand why managers don't support learning. Their reluctance can be linked to a variety of reasons. Some are valid, while others are based on misunderstandings about the learning and development function and its impact in the organization. An analysis of the current level of support usually reveals the most common problems, outlined in the following pages.

No Results. Management is not convinced that job-related learning adds value. They do not see programs producing results in ways to help them reach their objectives. Managers are rarely asked, "Is this learning program working for you?" or "Is it adding value to your department?" Learning and development professionals deserve much of the blame for this situation. The effectiveness of learning all too often is determined by the reactions of participants and measures of learning during the program. Managers need more application and impact data in terms they understand and appreciate.

Too Costly. Management has the mistaken perception that formal learning is a double or triple the actual cost. The direct cost for learning and development is ultimately taken from the operating profits and sometimes charged to their departments. They also see formal learning programs as taking employees away from their jobs, which results in a loss of productivity. They experience the cost it takes them to find ways to get the job done while an employee is involved in a program. They must rearrange work schedules to meet deadlines, find new ways to meet service requirements, redistribute the workload, or secure staff replacement.

No Input. Management does not support learning because their input is not part of the process. They are not asked for their views about the content or focus of a program during needs assessment or program formulation process. They are rarely provided with objectives that link learning to job performance improvements or business results. Without input, managers do not develop a sense of ownership for learning and development.

No Relevance. Management has little reason to believe that learning programs have job relevance or will help their departments or work units. They see content descriptions that bear little resemblance to work-related issues, and they hear comments about learning activities that are unrelated to current challenges faced by the team. Managers have many requests and demands for resources. They quickly eliminate the unnecessary tasks and what they perceive to be busy work. No relevance equals no need, which equals no priority and eventually leads to no support.

No Involvement. Management does not support learning because they are not actively involved in the process in a meaningful way. Even in some of the best organizations, the manager's role is severely limited; sometimes by design and other times by default. To build respect for the learning and development function, managers should have some type of active involvement in the process.

No Time. Management does not have the time to support formal learning and development. They are busy with ever-increasing demands on their time. When establishing daily priorities, the specific actions necessary to show support for learning just do not make it to the top of the list. Consequently, nothing happens. Managers often perceive that requests for increased support always require additional time. In reality, many supportive actions *do not* require much time; it is often a matter of perception.

No Preparation. Sometimes, management lacks the skills necessary to provide reinforcement to participants after they attend programs. Although they may be willing to offer support, managers may not know how to provide feedback, respond to questions, guide participants through specific issues, or help achieve results with programs. Specific skills are needed to provide effective reinforcement, just as specific skills are required for planning, budgeting, delegating, and negotiating.

Lack of Knowledge. Management is not always aware of the nature and scope of learning and development. They do not fully understand the different steps involved, ranging from needs assessment to development, delivery, and evaluation. They see bits and pieces of the process, but may not know how they are integrated to create an effective process. Perhaps they know that it is a legitimate function necessary to equip new employees with specific skills and knowledge required for the job, but beyond that, they are not fully aware of what learning and development can provide for the organization. It is difficult for managers to support a process they do not completely understand.

Collectively, these reasons for not supporting learning and development equate to challenges for the CLO and represent opportunities for managers. If the issues are not addressed in an effective way, management support will not exist, transfer of learning will be diminished, and, consequently, results will be severely limited or nonexistent.

Definitions

Management's actions and attitudes have a significant influence on the impact and success of learning and development programs. This influence, and the environment external to program development and delivery, is the focus of this chapter. Although the learning and development staff may have no direct control over some of these factors, they can exert a tremendous amount of influence on them.

Several terms need additional explanation. Management commitment, management support, management involvement, reinforcement, maintenance of behavior, and transfer of learning are overlapping terms and are sometimes confusing. *Management commitment* usually refers to the top management group and includes their pledge or promise to allocate resources and support to the learning and development effort. *Management support* refers to the actions of the entire management team, which reflects their attitude toward the learning and development process and staff. The major emphasis is on middle and first-line management. Their supportive actions can have a tremendous impact on the success of learning programs. *Management involvement* refers to the extent to which managers and other professionals outside the learning and development department are actively engaged in the learning process in addition to just participating in—sponsoring—programs. Since management commitment, support, and involvement have similar meanings, they are used interchangeably in current literature.

Reinforcement, maintenance of behavior, and transfer of learning also have similar meanings. *Reinforcement* refers to actions designed to reward or encourage a desired behavior. The goal is to increase the probability of the behavior occurring after a participant attends a learning program. *Maintenance of behavior* refers to the organization's actions to maintain a change in behavior on the job after the program is completed. *Transfer of learning* refers to the extent to which the learned behavior from the program is used on the job. The term *operating manager* is used to represent key managers involved in producing, selling, or delivering the products and services. Table 10-1 summarizes the key management actions needed, defining the target group, scope, and payoff.

IMPROVING COMMITMENT FOR LEARNING

Commitment is necessary to secure the resources for a viable learning and development effort. The 10 general areas of emphasis for strong top management commitment are shown in Table 10-2. These 10 areas need little additional explanation and are necessary for a successful learning effort.

Table 10-1
Comparison of Key Management Actions

Management Action	Target Group	Scope	Payoff
Management commitment	Top executives	All programs	Very high
Management support	Middle managers, first-level supervisors	Usually several programs	High
Management reinforcement	First-level managers	Specific programs	Moderate
Management involvement	All levels of managers	Specific programs	Moderate

Table 10-2
Top Management Commitments to Learning

Top 10 Commitments

For strong top management commitment to learning and development, the CEO should:

1. Develop or approve a mission for the learning and development function. Provide input and perspective.
2. Allocate the necessary funds for successful learning and development programs. Initial funding may be based on benchmarking. Later, it is based on value added.
3. Allow employees time to participate in learning and development programs. Encourage, but don't require, a minimum level of participation.
4. Get actively involved in learning and development programs and require others to do the same. This involves conducting parts of formal programs and getting involved in coaching or mentoring.
5. Support the learning and development effort and ask other managers to do the same. Define and communicate ideal support.
6. Position the CLO in a visible and high-level place on the organization chart, ideally reporting directly to the CEO or other chief executive.
7. Require that each learning and development program be evaluated in some way, recognizing that most evaluations should include reaction and learning data only.
8. Insist that learning and development programs be cost effective and require supporting data, including a few ROI studies each year.
9. Set an example for self-development. Show that continuous improvement is necessary in a learning organization.
10. Create an atmosphere of open communication with the CLO. Schedule quarterly reviews with the CLO to discuss progress, opportunities, and issues.

Now for the big question. How can top management commitment be improved? Quite often the extent of commitment is fixed in the organization before the CLO becomes involved with the function. The amount of commitment varies with the size, nature, and scope of the organization. It usually depends on how the function evolved, the top management group's attitude and philosophy toward learning, and how the function is administered. The key to the question of increasing commitment lies in how the effort is managed. The staff can have a significant effect on future top management commitment by focusing on the following six important areas: getting results, encouraging management involvement, exhibiting professionalism, communicating needs, showing resourcefulness, and taking a practical approach.

Results

Top management commitment will usually increase when programs or initiatives obtain desired results. As illustrated in Figure 10-1, this is a virtuous cycle because commitment is necessary to create effective programs and to obtain desired results. When results are obtained, commitment is increased. Nothing is more convincing to a group of top executives than programs with measurable results in terms they can understand. When a program is proposed, additional funding is usually based solely on the results the program is expected to produce.

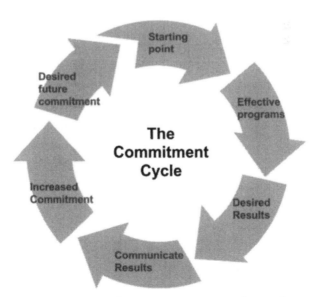

Figure 10-1. The commitment-results cycle.

Management Involvement

Commitment is increased when there is extensive involvement at all levels of management. This involvement, which can occur in almost every phase of the learning process, shows a strong cooperative effort toward developing employee potential within the organization. Chief executives want their managers to make a concerted effort to increase their staffs' and departments' skills and knowledge. Specific techniques for increasing involvement are covered later in the chapter.

Figure 10-2 shows an example of ownership at different levels at the British Airports Authority (BAA). This large organization manages the airports in Great Britain and has made significant efforts in building relationships with the management team, getting them more involved, and increasing commitment from different levels of managers and executives. As this figure shows, the ownership and involvement is at different levels of the organization. The learning boards are perhaps the most important part. Each board is chaired by a single director; other members come from senior specialists in the area covered by the zone. For example, one zone is airport operations. The learning and development representative supports the group by advising on best practice approaches to learning. The boards—not the learning and development function—make the decisions about what to make available, what resources to allocate, and what requests of learning cannot be processed (Thomas, 2005).

BAA University

University Council

> Senior managers and specialists within the business ensure our learning is adding
>
> value, monitor funding, and convert business priorities into learning priorities.

Learning Zone Boards

> Chaired by "deans" with boards of subject specialists, the B Learning Zones
>
> develop the university curriculum and learning offers.

Local Learning Forums

> Local learning forums with union involvement will support local learning
>
> initiatives (e.g., key skills).

Figure 10-2. Involvement at different levels at BAA.

Many companies have learning advisory boards made up of leaders from across the company. These boards serve many CLOs well, as they engage support and sponsorship for the learning function and secure management support.

Professionalism

A highly professional learning and development group can help influence the commitment from the management. Achieving excellence is the goal of many professionals and should be the mandate of the CLO. The learning and development staff must be perceived as professional in all actions-including being open to feedback and criticism, adjusting to the changing needs of the organization, maintaining productive relationships with other staff, setting examples throughout the company, and practicing what is taught in programs. Professionalism will show up in attention to detail in every program and every initiative—detail that is often overlooked by nonprofessionals.

Communicating Needs

The CLO must be able to communicate development needs to top management and make them realize that learning is an integral part of the organization. This communication may be in the form of proposals or review sessions with the top management team. When chief executives understand the need, they will respond through additional commitment. CLOs must be advocates for learners from across the organization. The CLO's role is to translate learning needs and objectives into actions for the company. Management relies on CLOs to identify needs and create solutions for improving individual and organizational performance.

Resourcefulness

The learning and development function should not be a narrowly focused group. Too often, learning and development staff are regarded as experts in technical training, team development, or sales training, but not problem solving or consulting. When the learning and development team is viewed as versatile, flexible, and resourceful, they can be used to help solve organizational performance problems and not be confined to formal development activities. The result: additional commitment on the part of management. Learning and development staff define the function. Their willingness to develop their capabilities and those of individuals across the organization is critical for business success.

Practical Approach

The CLO must take a practical approach. A learning and development staff that focuses too much on theories and philosophical efforts may be regarded as noncontributors in the organization. While there is a place for theoretical processes, learning solutions should be followed by practical application. Programs should be relevant and taught by experienced people who understand the content as well as the business. This practical approach will help ensure additional commitment.

BUILDING MANAGEMENT SUPPORT

Ideal Support

Middle- and first-level managers are also important for success. Before discussing the techniques involved in improving the support for programs, it is appropriate to present the concept of ideal management support. Ideal support occurs when a manager reacts in the following ways to a participant's involvement in a learning and development program:

- Encourages participants to be involved in programs.
- Volunteers personal services or resources to assist with learning and development.
- Makes an agreement with the participant prior to attending the program that outlines what changes should take place or what tasks should be accomplished after the program is completed.
- Reinforces the behavior change taught in the program; this reinforcement may be demonstrated in a variety of ways.
- Conducts a follow-up of the results achieved from the program.
- Rewards participants who have achieved outstanding accomplishments linked to the program.

This type of support represents utopia for the CLO. Support is necessary before and after the program is conducted. Actions prior to a program can have a significant impact on learning in the program and application on the job. Follow-up actions are also very important to drive results. Often, management actions do not follow this path. It is imperative that individuals in organizations take responsibility for their own development and make changes in their performance independent of management. People tend to manage as they were managed, unless they learn different skills.

Degrees of Support

A key area of support involves postprogram activities. In this context, the terms "support" and "reinforcement" are almost synonymous because when support is exhibited, it helps reinforce what the participants have learned. Before pursuing specific techniques for improving postprogram support and reinforcement, it is useful to classify managers into four different types according to their degree of support. Here, the term *manager* is primarily used to represent the supervisor of a participant in a program. The same analysis can apply to other managers above that level. A label has been attached to each type of manager that best describes his or her attitude and actions toward learning and development.

A *supportive* manager is a strong, active supporter of all learning efforts and is involved in programs and anxious to have his or her employees take advantage of every appropriate opportunity. This manager vigorously reinforces the material presented in programs and requires participants to apply it. He or she publicly voices approval for learning and development, provides positive feedback to the CLO and other staff members, and frequently calls on the staff for assistance, advice, and counsel. This manager is an ally and a valuable asset.

A *responsive* manager supports learning and development but not as strongly as the supportive manager. He or she allows employees to participate in learning and development programs and encourages them to get the most out of the activities. This manager usually voices support for programs, realizing that it is part of his or her responsibility, but usually does not go out of his or her way to aggressively promote learning programs or activities. This manager reinforces the material presented in the program, probably at the prodding of the learning and development staff. This manager views the support for formal learning programs no differently than the support for budgeting—it is something that must be done, but he or she is not excited about it.

A *nonsupportive* manager privately voices displeasure with formal learning programs. He or she reluctantly sends participants to programs, doing so only because everyone else does or because it is required. This manager thinks the organization spends too much time with learning and development and does not hesitate to explain how he or she achieved success without any formal learning programs. When participants return from a program, there is very little, if any, reinforcement from this manager. This manager's actions may destroy the value of the program. A typical comment after a program will be, "Now that the program is completed, let's get back to work."

A *destructive* manager works actively to keep participants from being involved in learning and development programs. This manager openly criticizes the CLO and the learning and development programs, believing that all learning and development should be accomplished on the job in the "real world," not in a formal classroom setting. He or she requires that all e-learning programs be taken at night or on the weekends. When participants return from a program, there is usually negative reinforcement, with typical comments such as, "Forget what was discussed in that program and get back to work." Fortunately, this type of manager is rare in today's organizations; however, there may be enough of these individuals to cause some concern.

When development is a key area of accountability for managers or executives of a company, management support is much easier to obtain. Businesses today realize that learning is a competitive advantage and the cost of not learning is too great for an organization. Management has begun to take the impact of learning seriously and, in many cases, managers who refuse to support learning are not going to be successful and neither will their businesses.

Improving Support

The degree of management support is based on the value management places on learning, the function and role of learning, and, in some cases, the actions of staff members. To improve management support, the CLO and the learning and development staff should carefully analyze each situation and work to improve relationships with individual managers or the management group. This requires a series of critical steps.

First, key managers, whose support is necessary, are identified. The target group may be the decision makers, the entire middle management group, or all of senior management.

Managers are then analyzed and classified, based on their degree of support, following the descriptions in the previous section. Input

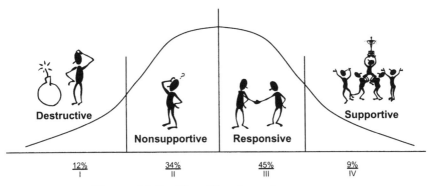

Figure 10-3. Classification of managers.

from the entire staff may be helpful to classify all key managers. As shown in Figure 10-3, manager support follows a normal distribution curve. The percentages represent the allocation in one organization—a construction materials firm—not known for having strong supporters of learning. The goal is to shift the curve to the right; the responsive to the supportive and nonsupportive to the responsive. In addition, the destructive need to be shifted to nonsupportive, if possible (or neutralized).

Next, the reasons for support or nonsupport are analyzed. Managers will usually show support (or nonsupport) for learning and development based on a series of facts, beliefs, and values related to learning and development.

Then, the best approach for each manager is selected. The strategy for improving a relationship with a particular manager depends on his or her degree of support. A later section in this chapter on building partnerships explores specific strategies to improve relationships.

Finally, the approach is adjusted, if necessary. Managers are individuals and what works for one may not work for another. If an attempt to change a manager's behavior does not work, perhaps another approach will succeed.

Here are typical actions to enhance support:

- Utilize preprogram agreements and commitments to determine specific goals and objectives for participants in the program.
- Clearly define responsibilities of managers in the learning and development process.
- Provide clear instructions and expectations to managers.

- Encourage managers to attend programs designed for their direct reports.
- Conduct follow-up discussions with managers to review success of programs using application and impact data.
- Encourage managers to provide advice and counsel to the learning and development staff on key issues, concerns, and business challenges.

INCREASING REINFORCEMENT OF LEARNING

With results-based learning, there must be an effective relationship between the facilitator, the participant, and the participant's immediate manager. This relationship can be viewed as part of a three-legged stool representing the major stakeholders. One leg of the stool is the discussion leader, who conducts the program. The next leg is the participant, who experiences the program. The third leg is the participant's manager, who reinforces what is being taught. If any leg is missing, the application of learning collapses.

The importance of involving the participant's manager as an integral part of the process cannot be understated. Too often, participants return from a program to find roadblocks to successfully applying what they have learned. Faced with these obstacles, even some of the best participants revert to old habits and forget most of what was learned in the program. Regardless of how well the program is conducted in the classroom, unless it is reinforced on the job, most of the effectiveness is lost.

The reason for this lies in the nature of learning. In learning a skill, participants go through a frustrating period when using the new skill feels uncomfortable and the desired results are not being produced. This period represents a results decline and is difficult for most participants. However, those who persist gain the expected reward that is obtained from the new behavior. If the participant continues to exercise the new behavior or skill, it eventually feels more natural and performance improves. However, without proper reinforcement, particularly during the time when results decline, participants may abandon the acquired skills. They may revert to the old, familiar way of behavior with no change.

Although self-reinforcement and peer-reinforcement are helpful, the learner's immediate manager is the primary focus for reinforcement efforts. These managers exert significant influence on the participant's postprogram behavior by providing reinforcement in the following ways:

- Help participants diagnose problems to determine if new skills are needed.
- Discuss possible alternatives for handling specific situations and act as a coach to help the participants apply the skills.
- Encourage participants to use the skills frequently.
- Serve as a role model for the proper use of the skills.
- Give positive rewards to participants when the skills are successfully used.

Each of these activities will reinforce what has been taught and can have a tremendous impact on participants' use of skills and knowledge.

IMPROVING MANAGEMENT INVOLVEMENT

Management involvement in learning and development is not a new process; organizations have been practicing it successfully for many years. Although there are almost as many opportunities for management's involvement in the learning and development process as there are steps in a learning design model, management input and active participation will generally occur only in the most significant ones. Line management should be involved in most of the key decisions of the learning and development department. The primary vehicles for obtaining or soliciting management involvement are presented here.

Program Leaders

The key to involving management and professional personnel is to use them as leaders or facilitators. The concept of leaders teaching leaders has become a very effective way to deliver customized leadership development. Jack Welch, former chairman of GE, was involved in management development programs regularly at GE's Management Development Center. Welch would allocate several days per month to teaching in certain programs. This approach presents some unique challenges for the learning and development department. Not everyone has the flair for leading discussions in a development program. The extent to which managers are involved in programs can vary considerably. In some efforts, the learning and development staff conducts the entire program. At the other extreme, some programs are conducted entirely by operating management. The right combination depends on these factors:

- The capability of the learning and development staff.
- The capability of operating management and other professional staff.
- The value placed on having operating management and other professional staff identified with the program.
- The size and budget of the learning and development staff.
- The physical location of the program as compared to the location of operating managers.

There may be other factors specific to the organization. The use of leaders to teach programs creates a strong atmosphere of commitment and support and can provide critical knowledge and information that cannot be achieved with external facilitators.

Advisory Committees

As mentioned in Chapter 9, some organizations have developed committees to enhance management involvement in the learning and development process. These committees, which act in an advisory capacity to the CLO, may have other names such as councils or people development boards. As shown in Table10-3, committees can

Table 10-3
Types of Committees

Responsible For	Examples
Individual Program	New Team Leader Development Committee
	Account Executives' Learning Committee
	Product Knowledge Course Committee
	Apprenticeship Training Committee
Specific Function	Sales Training Committee
	Nurse Professional Development Committee
	IT Training Committee
	Underwriting Training Committee
Multifunctions	Management Development Committee
	Faculty Development Committee
	Skills Training Committee
	Government Compliance Training Committee

be developed for individual programs, specific functions, or for multiple functions. They can be one-time committees or standing committees, depending on the duration of the initiative. Committees can be used in many stages of the process, from needs analysis to communicating program results. The learning and development staff benefits from management input, and from its commitment as well, when the committee buys into a specific program. It is difficult for managers to criticize something when they are a part of it.

Task Forces

Another potential area for management involvement is through the use of a task force. The task force consists of a group of employees—usually management—who are charged with the responsibility for developing a learning and development program. Task forces are particularly useful for programs beyond the scope of learning and development staff capability. Also, a task force can help reduce the time required to develop a program.

A major difference between the function of a task force and that of a committee is that the task force is required to produce a deliverable. They must devote a considerable amount of time on a project or program. The time required may vary from a two-week assignment to a six-month, full-time project. This time span, of course, depends on the nature of the program being developed and the availability of assistance for the task force.

The task force approach is very economical. It relieves the learning and development staff of time-consuming program development that may be an impossibility in a subject unfamiliar to the staff. Additional involvement on the part of management and professional staff can help improve the program's credibility and enhance the results.

Managers as Experts

Managers may provide expertise for program design, development, or implementation. Subject matter experts (SMEs) provide a valuable and necessary service while developing attachment to the program. For example, at one of Whirlpool's refrigerator manufacturing plants, managers served as experts in a major job redesign project. The traditional assembly line was replaced with a work cell arrangement. The expertise of the managers was critical to program success.

Managers as Participants

Managerial participation can range from attending all of a program to auditing a portion to examining its content. However, participation may not be feasible for all types of programs, such as specialized courses designed for only a few individuals. This approach is best when one or more of these conditions exist:

- A high percentage of the manager's subordinates will attend the program.
- Support and reinforcement from the manager are essential to the program's success.
- It is essential for the manager to have the same knowledge or skills that the subordinates will learn from program attendance.

Involving Managers in Analysis and Evaluation

Another area where managers can be involved is in analysis and evaluation. In analysis, managers review the needs assessment data and confirm the training needs to approve a solution. Sometimes, managers are directly involved in assessment and analysis. Manager involvement in evaluation is usually through a team or committee arrangement. One approach requires managers to examine collectively the application and business impact of learning. Here are some possibilities:

- Invite managers to participate in focus groups about program success.
- Ask managers to collect application and impact data.
- Ask managers to review success data.
- Ask participants to interpret results.
- Convene managers to share overall results.
- Ask managers to communicate data to their teams.

Involving managers and showing them how evaluation can work increases commitment and support.

Sometimes executives are involved in planning annual learning initiatives. At QUALCOMM, the learning and development staff conduct annual needs assessments with division executive teams and their staff. The annual learning needs are compiled into a learning plan, which is reviewed and approved by the Division President and their senior team. This has proved to be an excellent way of obtaining management support across the organization.

New Roles for Managers

The approaches just described are traditional ways to involve managers in the learning and development process when the focus is on achieving results. Many other ways are available for involvement. Management involvement may define new training roles for managers in an organization, such as these:

- Coordinate/organize learning programs.
- Participate in needs assessments.
- Provide expertise in program design.
- Facilitate learning programs.
- Reinforce learning.
- Evaluate learning, application, and impact.
- Drive actions for improvement based on evaluation data.

Table 10-4 summarizes the opportunities for manager involvement along the traditional steps in the learning and development cycle. The potential strategy for involvement is identified.

Table 10-4
Manager Involvement Opportunities

Step in the Results-Based Process	Opportunity for Manager Involvement	Most Appropriate Technique
Conduct analysis.	High	Taskforce
Develop measurement and evaluation system.	Moderate	Advisory committee
Establish program objectives.	High	Advisory committee
Develop program.	Moderate	Taskforce
Implement program.	High	Program leader
Monitor costs.	Low	Expert input
Collect and analyze data.	Moderate	Expert input
Interpret data and draw conclusions.	High	Expert input
Communicate results.	Moderate	Manager as participant

Link Pay to Involvement

A great way to get a manager's attention on an issue is to link compensation to it. Therefore, an effective strategy for some companies is to link manager bonuses to involvement in learning and development. A difficulty of this approach is selecting the proper measures. While managers might not agree with the construction of the metrics or the measures as targets, managers will become more aware of the organization's people development goals. Survey data from the Conference Board suggest that putting employee development measures in bonus plans correlates with successful links between business strategies and certain people measures. However, this is still a minority practice, with only 39 percent of firms rewarding managers systematically based on the measures (Bates, 2004).

Benefits of Management Involvement

In summary, there are six major benefits from involving management and professionals in the learning and development process.

1. Credibility of the programs is enhanced.
2. Management ownership of programs and projects increases since they have been involved in the process of developing, conducting, or evaluating them.
3. Participants and the learning and development staff have more interaction with management, which enhances relationships and improves needs assessments.
4. The skills of managers involved are enhanced.
5. Internal leaders teaching classes can lower the cost of external facilitation.
6. Managers are rewarded for their contributions to learning.

These advantages should encourage more CLOs to use the skills and expertise of managers in the learning and development process. The influence of the management group—especially key operating and support managers—should not be ignored but utilized to improve the quality and image of learning and development initiatives.

Perhaps one of the best illustrations of the payoff involvement comes from Scottish whisky maker Glenmorangie, named learning employer of the year in 2004 by learndirect Scotland (Scottish University for Industry). Glenmorangie's approach is to get everyone involved in the learning process, particularly the managers.

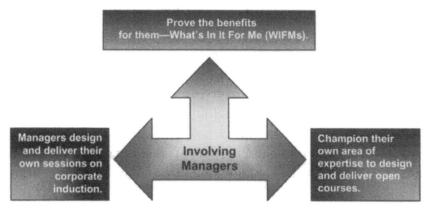

Figure 10-4. Payoff of manager involvement at Glenmorangie.

Figure 10-4 illustrates how managers are involved in their own programs. Serving as champions in their own expertise area, they achieve results, tabulate benefits, and communicate them directly to managers. These efforts help this distillery cut operations costs, increase performance, reduce downtime, and increase operating competency (Mathieson, 2005).

DEVELOPING PARTNERSHIPS WITH MANAGERS

The CLO must create effective partnerships with key business leaders. A partnership relationship can take on several different formats and descriptions. In some situations, it is very informal, loosely defined, and ill structured. In this approach, the CLO may not want to develop partnering relationships at a formal level but may continue to refine it informally. In other situations, the CLO formalizes the process to the extent that particular activities are planned with specific individuals, all for the purpose of improving relationships. The quality of the relationships is a major goal and assessments are sometimes taken to gauge progress. Still, other CLOs make the process very formal where, individuals are discretely identified, and a written plan is developed to improve the partnership. Sometimes a contract is developed with a particular manager. In these situations, assessments are routinely conducted and progress is reported formally. While these approaches represent three distinct levels of formality, it is possible for a CLO to move through these different levels as the partnering process matures and achieves success.

For relationship building to be effective, the CLO must take the initiative to organize, plan, and measure the process, and set the example for others. Key learning and development staff members need to be involved, willingly. Rarely will key managers approach the CLO or other staff members to nurture these relationships. In some organizations, these managers do not want to develop relationships or allocate the time it may take to make the partnership effective. They may see no need for the relationship; perhaps even consider it a waste of time. At best, they are reluctant partners. This situation requires the CLO to properly assess the situation, plan the strategies, and take appropriate actions, routinely and consistently, to ensure that the process is working. The CLO must take the lead and involve others as appropriate and as necessary. While this cannot be a delegated responsibility, it can involve many other members of the learning and development staff. Two critical issues are usually addressed: specific steps necessary to develop an effective relationship, and a set of principles that must be followed when building and nurturing the relationship.

Partnering Steps

An effective, organized approach to building a successful partnership is necessary. The following steps are recommended:

Assess the current status of partnership relationships. The first course of action is to determine the current condition. Table 10-5 shows some of the key issues involved in determining the current status. The self assessment tool should be completed by the CLO and key learning and development team leaders to determine present status and to plan specific issues and activities. In essence, the score provides information for planning and indicates opportunities for in the future.

A score of 15–29 indicates that a partnership is nonexistent and the potential for developing a partnership is very weak; it is probably doomed to fail. If the score is in the 30–44 range, several problems exist with the partnership or anticipated partnership. Progress can be made, but it will be difficult. If the score is in the 45–59 range, the partnership is working effectively or has great potential. A score in the 60–75 range represents a very effective partnership—a model for others. By providing the appropriate upfront attention, it may be possible to assess the potential before spending a significant amount of time on the relationship.

Table 10-5
Assessment of Partnership Potential for Success.

Scale
  1 = definitely no
  2 = more no than yes
  3 = neither yes nor no
  4 = more yes than no
  5 = definitely yes

	Circle One
1. Choice of partners (Is this a strategically valuable partner for learning and development?)	1 2 3 4 5
2. Willingness to become a partner (Does this manager desire to become your partner?)	1 2 3 4 5
3. Trust level (Is there an adequate level of trust or the possibility of achieving it?)	1 2 3 4 5
4. Character and ethics (Does this partner operate in an ethical manner?)	1 2 3 4 5
5. Strategic Purpose (Are the long-term aspirations of both partners compatible?)	1 2 3 4 5
6. Culture fit (Do the partners come from compatible cultures?)	1 2 3 4 5
7. Common goals and interests (Are the goals and interests of the partners shared equally?)	1 2 3 4 5
8. Information sharing (Can both partners freely share information?)	1 2 3 4 5
9. Risks sharing (Are the risks to both partners fairly equal?)	1 2 3 4 5
10. Rewards sharing (Are the rewards and potential gains for both partners fairly equal?)	1 2 3 4 5
11. Resources (Do both partners have adequate resources to support the relationship?)	1 2 3 4 5
12. Duration mutually agreed long-term (Do the partners agree on a long-term partnership?)	1 2 3 4 5
13. Commitment to partnership (Is there a fairly broad level of commitment by both partners?)	1 2 3 4 5
14. Value perceptions (Do both partners have similar perceptions of the value the other brings to the partnership?)	1 2 3 4 5
15. Rules, policies, and measures (Do these issues reinforce the desired partnership behavior?)	1 2 3 4 5
Total Score:	_____

Adapted from Mariotti, 1996.

Identify key individuals for a partnership relationship. Building a partnership works best when it is clearly focused on a few individuals. Not every manager could or should be considered a partner, although a productive relationship should exist with every manager. The key managers that should be targeted for this activity are those who can make the most difference with their involvement. These potential partners may be key business managers whose support or influence is well respected in the organization. There is no prescribed number, only a total amount that is reasonable in terms of the specific activities planned.

Learn and understand the business. An effective partnership relationship cannot be developed unless the learning and development staff understands the operational and strategic issues of the organization. Some time must be devoted to understanding how the organization functions and the major issues, concerns, and problems facing these key managers. In essence, the learning and development staff should view the organization from the perspective of the manager, becoming aware of the issues facing the manager on a daily basis. It is difficult to communicate effectively without this knowledge and understanding. CLOs need to be business partners, and they need to understand the business realities, market pressures, and competitive landscapes.

Consider a written plan. Creating the partnership is often more focused when it is written with specific details. In some organizations, the plan is tailored to a particular manager. Specific activities are undertaken depending on the perceptions, behavior, and influence of that manager. Although this may appear to be awkward to some CLOs, having a written plan ensures that the process receives attention with proper coordination.

Offer assistance to solve problems. The learning and development staff exists to solve business problems and improve performance. An offer of assistance to help solve problems, enhance performance, remove obstacles, and otherwise help the manager achieve departmental, division, and company goals, is an important initiative to begin the relationship. Although the offers may not be accepted early in the relationship building process, eventually they will be, providing an opportunity to deliver assistance. When this happens, it is an excellent opportunity to demonstrate that learning can deliver results.

Show the results of programs and initiatives. It is important to communicate results quickly in order to demonstrate to managers how a program or initiative has achieved success. In addition, the results achieved from other programs or initiatives should be communicated to these key managers. Communication should be rich with data, precise, conclusive, and not very disruptive or time consuming. Routine communications of results build the type of support necessary for managers to change perceptions about learning and development.

Publicize partners' accomplishments and successes. Use every opportunity to give proper credit to the accomplishments of the partner. Focusing attention on the partner's success, even if it was achieved with the assistance of the learning and development staff, helps build the relationship.

Ask the partner to review needs. Whenever a needs assessment is requested or undertaken as part of an overall macro-level assessment, the partner should be asked to review the information and confirm, or add to, the needs. This provides an opportunity to show the extent to which the learning and development staff is attempting to focus on legitimate needs. This supports the "no need/no benefit" philosophy, as adopted by many organizations.

Have the partner serve on an advisory committee. A helpful approach to provide guidance and direction to the learning and development staff is to establish an advisory committee, described earlier. Having the partner serve on this committee provides an excellent chance to build the relationship and enhance the support from the manager.

Shift responsibility to the partner. Although there are multiple responsibilities for learning and development, the primary responsibility must lie with the individual and the management group. Through the partnership relationship, the responsibility for the learning and development should gradually be shifted to the partner. Although the responsibility may already exist, these efforts are designed to get the partner to assume more responsibility and to take a greater role in providing the direction to, and accountability for, learning and development.

Invite input from the partner on key plans and programs. Routinely, these key managers should be asked to provide information on key issues ranging from needs assessment and critical program issues to the implementation of new technology, program design and delivery, and follow-up evaluation. Topics may also include resource requirements and budgeting, and, in some cases, it may involve details, such as the timing of programs and the reporting of information from the learning and development staff.

Ask partner to review program objectives, content, and delivery mechanisms. As a routine activity, these managers should review the objectives, content, and planned delivery for major programs or major redesigns in their area of responsibility. Not only does this help develop a partnership relationship, it provides important input necessary to make this program more successful.

Invite partner to conduct/coordinate program. If appropriate and feasible, the partner should be asked to help coordinate or conduct a part of a program. This action increases buy-in for the process, helps shift responsibility to the manager, and often results in a higher quality outcome. It is difficult for managers to be critical of a process when they are involved in it. Significant involvement activities such as conducting part of the program may be one of the most helpful ways to build the partnership while enhancing the success of the program. Leaders can also use learning programs as an opportunity to communicate executive messages and observe leaders in a learning setting. Many leaders use the classroom as a place to evaluate talent in the organization. It provides exposure to executives, which can help them gain visibility and confidence in their leadership team.

Review progress and replan strategy. The partnership process should be reviewed periodically to check progress and to readjust or replan the strategy. The assessment instrument could be taken again, or the staff could informally review the progress. This review should include a discussion of each partner and the progress that has been made.

While these steps are critical and show a comprehensive approach to developing partnership relationships, there are many other models and frameworks that have proven to be successful. Figure 10-5 shows the strategic business partner model developed by Jim and Dana Robinson. This model focuses on accountability, ensuring that there are open communications, common understandings, common commitments, and, above all, access credibility and trust (Robinson and Robinson, 2005).

Figure 10-5. Strategic business partner model. (Source: Robinson and Robinson, 2005.)

Key Principles

As the specific steps just listed are undertaken, it is important to preserve the nature and quality of the relationship with a partner. Several key principles are essential; they serve as an operating framework to develop, nurture, and refine this critical relationship. Table 10-6 lists these key principles, which should be integrated into each step.

FINAL THOUGHTS

Building effective relationships with management can have a very positive impact on learning and development if the process is utilized properly and the appropriate emphasis is placed on it. Such relationships enhance the respect and credibility for the learning and development staff while helping to ensure success with programs and initiatives. Establishing effective relationships with management is an important role for the CLO—some learning and development staff members may be inhibited in their efforts to make progress, and a few will be intimidated because of the significant changes that must take place to work effectively with the management team. Building relationships requires time, priority, focus, and planning.

Table 10-6
Key Principles When Developing a Partnership Relationship

1. Have patience and persistence throughout the process.
2. Seize win-win opportunities.
3. Address problems and conflicts quickly.
4. Share information regularly and purposefully.
5. Always be honest and display the utmost integrity in all the transactions.
6. Keep high standards of professionalism in each interaction.
7. Give credit and recognition to the partner routinely.
8. Take every opportunity to explain, inform, and educate.
9. Involve managers in as many activities as possible.
10. Eventually, ensure that a balance of power and influence is realized between the two parties.
11. Be very considerate of the partner's time commitments.

Five specific strategies were presented in this chapter: increasing commitment from top executives, improving support from managers, enhancing reinforcement of learning, increasing management involvement, and developing partnerships with key managers. Although these strategies are sometimes overlapping and complementary, they are necessary to add value to the learning and development function.

The driving forces creating this need will continue, challenging the CLO to tap the influence of managers and executives and explore ways to make the process successful. Building partnerships with management is a desired objective for most CLOs, and it is a natural evolution of organizations as they strive for continued success.

CLOs are learning experts, but our primary role is to partner with other business leaders to enhance organizational performance. Successful CLOs understand the business imperatives that drive performance and align learning to support our companies' strategic objectives. Linking learning to the company's performance is critical to build a learning organization that is fully supported by senior management.
Pat Crull, Vice President and Chief Learning Officer,
Time Warner Cable

References

Bates, Stephen. "Linking People Measures to Strategy," *Research Report R-1342-03-RR*. New York, NY: The Conference Board, 2003.

Mathieson, Morag, and Thomas Murry. "Getting Management Buy In," *CIPD Handbook*. London: Chartered Institute of Personnel and Development, 2005.

Mariotti, John L. *The Power of Partnerships: The Next Step Beyond TQM, Reengineering and Lean Production*. Oxford, England: Basil Blackwell, 1996.

Robinson, Jim, and Dana Robinson. *Business Partnering*. San Francisco, CA: Berrett-Koehler, 2005.

CHAPTER 11

The Voices of CLOs

We wanted to conclude this book by providing the expert perspective of 17 leading CLOs. Many of them do not have the official title "CLO"-their titles and responsibilities reflect the broad scope of leaders in the learning and development field. While many of their comments are integrated throughout this book, we thought it might be insightful to read and absorb what they have to say about critical issues involving the role of CLOs and the value they add to their organizations. These leaders exemplify the CLO role. They are role models, thought leaders, and experts in learning and development. They are living the CLO role and leading the profession. Tamar Elkeles interviewed the following CLOs, and their thoughts are shared in this chapter, alphabetically:

Frank Anderson, President, Defense Acquisition University
Susan Burnett, Senior Vice President of People & Organization Effectiveness, The Gap
Tim Conlon, Director of Learning and Chief Learning Officer, Xerox
Bob Corcoran, Vice President of Corporate Citizenship and Chief Learning Officer and President of GE Foundation
Pat Crull, Vice President and Chief Learning Officer, Time Warner Cable
Fred Harburg, Former CLO Motorola & SVP Leadership and Learning, Fidelity Investments
Ted Hoff, Vice President of Learning, IBM
Steve Kerr, Managing Director and Chief Learning Officer, Goldman Sachs
Michael Lee, Executive Vice President of Human Resources, LG Corp.
Donna MacNamara, Vice President of Global Education & Training, Colgate Palmolive

Rick O'Leary, Director, Human Resources & Diversity, Corning
Donnee Ramelli, President, General Motors University
Bonnie Stoufer, Vice President for Learning, Training & Development, Boeing
David Vance, President, Caterpillar University
Allan Weisberg, Vice President of Organization Capability, Johnson & Johnson
Bill Wiggenhorn, Former President, Motorola University and Vice Chairman of Global Ed-Tech Management Group
Kevin Wilde, Vice President and Chief Learning Officer, General Mills

The thoughts reflected in this chapter provide unique insight from some of the leading CLOs around the world. They are exceptional at what they do, well-known, and highly respected for their views. More importantly, they offer realistic perspectives about how the CLO function in the organization is managed. Collectively, they:

1. Show how the learning and development function is an important part of strategy (and often makes a significant influence on strategy).
2. Invest heavily in learning and development and have a mechanism to demonstrate the value of this investment.
3. Take extreme measures to ensure that programs are linked to the business and that they are addressing business issues routinely.
4. Recognize the shift to performance. Many go beyond the traditional learning solutions to provide a variety of nonlearning solutions.
5. Focus on delivering learning at the right time and at the right place, efficiently.
6. Manage the function effectively and efficiently, understanding the costs, working within budgets, and running the learning enterprise like a business.
7. Show the success of major programs, demonstrate value, and communicate value to a variety of stakeholders, ensuring that senior executives and stakeholders understand the value of learning and development.
8. Recognize that talent management is an important responsibility. They manage it, often from the recruiting process to managing retention.
9. Secure tremendous support from executives and, in most cases, the CEO. They have them involved, committed, and serving as role models.

These nine issues represent the focus of this book and are represented in Chapters 2 through 10. Please enjoy and let us know your thoughts.

FRANK ANDERSON, PRESIDENT, DEFENSE ACQUISITION UNIVERSITY

To create an effective learning strategy CLOs should start by understanding what senior leadership is trying to achieve and aligning with their business goals. For a learning organization, the strategy is a subset of what the boss wants to do. CLOs are really "agents for the boss." No organization invests heavily in learning "just because." Training resources are used to achieve the training strategy. CLOs need to ask, "Why do we exist?" "What does success look like?"

Many programs attempt to use return on investment (ROI) analysis to justify their training programs. Too often return on investment is not understood, nor is it being done well by many learning professionals. ROI is usually related to specific programs with specific parameters, working with numbers and assumptions that everyone buys into. At DAU, we do not use ROI as a justification for specific programs. We do not generate numbers to justify assumptions. We gather baseline data so we can identify performance improvements at the individual or organizational level. We measure value more holistically, focusing on our entire learning enterprise.

At DAU, we use value-added contributions (VAC) as our measure of success. We are aligned and connected to senior leadership so that when they think of business strategy, they think of their learning needs. When senior leaders start initiatives, they call us so we can apply the right learning assets to achieve the business strategy. Our VAC is the ability to develop the right skill sets so people can execute the initiative.

For learning programs to be valued by an organization, we believe they need to consistently show contributions to things that are important to the organization. They need to provide learning at the point of need and position the organization with a competitive advantage. Curricula should consistently deliver learning when the learner needs it. The learning and deployment strategy should be to support the workforce at their point of need.

Senior leaders assess the value of the learning organization and must believe there was a VAC. This could be anything from qualitative metrics, relationship building, working agility, or responsiveness. At the end of the day, it's the business leader's role to determine if there was a contribution from learning, not the CLO's.

I also believe that the CLO's role is to communicate and develop tools for the organization to understand how learning contributes to the organization. CLOs need to understand the business, obtain an objective view, and develop learning initiatives for the organization. They need to take the time to talk the language of leadership. CLOs need to understand the issues that senior leaders face. Senior leaders need to see the CLO as a peer—that is the ultimate measure of success.

There are several keys to CLO success:

- Connect to the business.
- Ensure senior leadership views you as a peer.
- Understand what's driving the business.
- Determine how training supports what's important to the senior leadership team.
- Shape training around issues in the organization.
- Use learning assets to enhance the business and ensure all learning products are aligned.

SUSAN BURNETT, SENIOR VICE PRESIDENT OF PEOPLE & ORGANIZATION EFFECTIVENESS, THE GAP

CLOs need to deeply understand and be aligned with their company and line of business strategy. The most effective CLOs are able to "translate business strategy into individual and organization enablers." They define the people implications of the business strategy and work with the executive team to determine the individual and organizational capabilities needed to achieve the strategy. Once these capabilities are defined, CLOs can go to work with their HR partners, creating the people initiatives that will build those capabilities.

Since the job of the CLO in my mind is building capabilities, training should be delivered only when the business needs it. To help my people draw a line of sight from their work to the strategies of the business and company, I like to create a one page matrix that identifies all the business strategies on the left and lists all the capabilities required to achieve those strategies across the top, and then help my people define their deliverables in that context. This guides the learning that we provide to the organization and ensures that we are increasing capabilities that meet business needs.

Business Strategy	Capabilities and People Initiatives			
Grow through acquisitions	Perform cultural due diligence	Design the integrated organization	New people for the new company	Get new teams up and running
	Cultural assessment process	Organization design support	Selection process	Deliver "Fast Start" new team training
Increase supply chain efficiency and effectiveness	Product life cycle reengineering	Vendor assessment and consolidation	Continuous improvement	New supply chain technology
	Business process reengineering and training for the new processes	Vendor assessment process	Six Sigma training	Technology training

Often the CLO will be in a position to drive an enterprise-wide solution to build company capabilities. For example, many times the CEO will use leadership development as a tool to drive new leadership standards and practices. I believe that even with enterprise programs, it's useful to deliver them in the context of the current challenges facing the business. In companies with multiple business units, the context can be different across markets, products, and channels, and it is useful to package and deliver the solution in a way so that it can be a platform to drive specific business objectives.

There are many successful models for organizing the learning and development function. However, I have always believed that it's critical to have learning and development leaders in the businesses they serve. At Gap Inc., we repurposed some of our corporate resources to become the brand and function, learning and development leaders who would support the businesses. The corporate team's role is to design and develop those enterprise programs that will create company capabilities and new practices, and the Brand/Function, learning and development leaders deploy them in the context of their business context and challenges. The Brand learning and development leaders also design and develop solutions required by their business and unique to their success. For example, training store employees on the brand promise they need to deliver for Banana Republic customers is something only needed by this brand. This

model works well, since the learning is close to the business and supported by the business leadership teams.

At The Gap, the people and the budget for learning are also owned
by the brands and functions. The learning and development Directors report to the CLO and their HR leader, and their goals for each
are clear, measurable, and aligned. Most significantly, for the first
time, the total training investment for each business is planned for
and managed by the business learning and development Director, in
collaboration with the CFO. The business executives understand the
cost not only to develop training, but the cost to deliver it to the
target audience. This level of ownership is critical, since it produces
line-owned and supported learning and development investments.

TIM CONLON, DIRECTOR OF LEARNING AND CHIEF LEARNING OFFICER, XEROX

At Xerox our goal is to build talent and high performance in the
organization. After the company turnaround, we had to rebuild the
learning function. Our focus was to build high value, high return
learning capabilities and offerings, meeting the needs in such a way
that created ongoing demand for effective learning solutions. It is
easy for CLOs to demonstrate value when there is a natural business
pull for learning solutions rather than having to push learning programs throughout the enterprise. We determine annually the two or
three vital areas that we can impact and provide opportunities to
meet those critical needs.

The easiest way for a CLO to demonstrate value and business relevance is to connect learning solutions to strategic direction. Helping
leaders deal with what change needs to take place to move themselves,
their people, and organizations from their current state to where they
need to be in the future can demonstrate clear business linkage. An
example of this at Xerox was the Strategy Alignment process, which
engaged the top 385 executives in a series of workshops designed to
internalize the strategy through a structured, cross-organizational
open dialogue of questions and issues with the CEO and Senior Leadership Team. This process not only enabled executives to internalize
the strategic direction, it helped them to translate it into what they
needed to do to lead the changes necessary for success.

Companies will find that their commitment to learning and development increases employee engagement. Employee engagement
should be a direct measurement of the effectiveness of a company's

work environment and is a common metric on many business score-cards. Organizations look to CLOs for learning, employee engagement, integration, and organization/culture change (OD). CLOs need to focus on what's working well across the organization and what is differentiating success in different parts of the company. CLOs are not just focusing on learning programs or applications; they should be driving business success by influencing HR strategy to support organizational performance and effectiveness.

Today's talent management systems include evaluation of capability, assessments of performance, development, and succession. The complexity in the learning function, as in the business environment, is increasing, and CLOs need to be leading talent management in addition to the learning role. Learning is no longer a discrete functional area as it once was. We need to rethink the traditional HR structure and delivery processes.

The CLO's role-including his or her responsibilities for integrating strategy, technology, talent management, and organization effectiveness with learning-is one of the greatest opportunities to create business value, and as such, the strategic direction and impact of the overall HR function.

Bob Corcoran, Vice President of Corporate Citizenship and Chief Learning Officer and President of GE Foundation

The CLO's role is to ensure that the culture supports, drives, and thrives on learning. They must be aware of the inhibitors of learning and ensure that systems are in place to transfer and pull knowledge across the organization.

The learning strategy in any organization must be highly integrated with the long-term business strategy—that is, the learning value proposition. Learning also needs to be integrated into the HR strategic plan. CLOs should understand the culture, knowledge, competencies, and strategies needed to maintain learning in their organization.

Learning is fundamentally a pull process, but CLOs can add value by ensuring that a push process is in place for content. The overall learning curriculum, design, and storage has to be done well. Once the learning systems are in place, the CLO and his or her team can effectively respond to business needs.

CLOs must spend time understanding the culture, values, and leaders in the organization. Ultimately individuals need to learn by themselves. The teaching has to be there, but people have to have the need and desire to learn. CLOs need to focus on reducing and eliminating barriers to learning. Employees should be rewarded for learning, but there should be a consequence for not learning. For example, "If I learn this, then I can perform that." There is an impact on the world if people learn.

The culture at GE is a meritocracy. Rewards are tied to performance. The inhibitor is how fast employees can learn and then apply that new knowledge.

Frequently, those CLOs who have to justify their roles daily are the ones who find themselves in companies with a transaction-based training culture (frequently of their own making). In companies where a true learning culture exists, the CLO doesn't have to justify his or her role but can focus on the task of feeding an insatiable appetite for learning. Those are the companies that understand the value of learning, not training.

In business, it's all about performance, and people in the training community should never forget that. CLOs don't own all levers in the organization that impact performance, and it would be silly to suggest that they do. Systems such as compensation, benefits, and performance management are elements that drive performance and effect change. CLOs need to understand how all these levers work and find ways to align the delivery systems they do control with them to drive performance.

The budget review process for CLOs should be the same as the budget review process for any other business leaders. CLOs can't expect a "free ride" where their budgets go through unquestioned, but neither should they accept a sort of Spanish Inquisition around fundamental training stewardship.

CLOs have to be growth zealots. They must be out there in the organization focusing on learning and growth. The business grows and people grow. If CLOs stop learning themselves and don't grow, then the last days of their careers are close. Every crisis, every problem, every stagnation is a learning opportunity. CLOs must be voracious learners and create a culture of learning for the company. They must be motivated and driven people who can reward learning and provide the systems, the structure, and the environment for learning. They must be zealots for individual and company growth.

PAT CRULL, VICE PRESIDENT AND CHIEF LEARNING OFFICER, TIME WARNER CABLE

CLOs are learning experts, but our primary role is to partner with other business leaders to enhance organizational performance. Successful CLOs understand the business imperatives that drive performance and align learning to support our companies' strategic objectives. Linking learning to the company's performance is critical to build a learning organization that is fully supported by senior management.

Corporations are continually looking for ways to improve their expense ratios and return on investment. So it's crucial to demonstrate the value of learning to management. One way I do that is by setting metrics—with input from business leaders—and committing to impact specific, key aspects of the business as a result of the learning. Critical metrics might include increasing customer or employee satisfaction, reducing errors, or increasing financial returns.

To obtain ongoing support for learning, CLOs must build consensus with the executive team and keep step with their companies' evolving priorities. We repeatedly ask, "Where are we taking our business?" "What do we need to get there?" and "How do you view success?" CLOs who prove that they understand and add value to the business will gain the confidence and backing of leadership. This is particularly important during the budget process when we are competing for limited funding. The ability to draw a clear connection between your work and your company's direction is vital to winning support for learning-based initiatives.

Ongoing collaboration with various groups across the company further strengthens our ability to impact business results. In reality, there is little a learning function can do by itself. To be successful, the CLO needs to collaborate with areas-such as information technology, operations, and marketing-to better understand industry trends, market challenges, and customer relationships. Today's CLOs cannot simply be masters of learning. We must also be knowledgeable business partners.

In my experience, the most effective CLOs are those who are passionate about their work, have a clear vision of learning, and work collaboratively to carry out their vision. They care deeply about people development, individually and collectively. They devise integrated, systematic approaches to organizational learning that meet short- and long-term business and individual development needs.

To implement such a tall order, CLOs must have a strong foundation in designing need-based learning interventions, facilitating learning experiences, assessing individual and organizational needs, and evaluating learning success. We also must possess sound business knowledge and the ability to plan strategically. The most sought-after CLOs successfully balance the dual roles of strategic visionary and effective implementer.

CLOs know their teams have made a significant impact on organizations when employees say, "This changed my life; this taught me what I needed to know." At the enterprise and individual level, the CLOs can make a profound difference for both the organizations they serve, as well as the people who work there.

I believe that CLOs will continue to be in demand, because companies recognize that continuous learning is essential for business success. As the profession evolves, there will be a greater focus on embedding learning into work and applying classroom concepts to real-world issues. With emerging technologies and global expansion, CLOs will continue to use blended approaches for learning—a combination of instructor-led, self-paced, and hands-on training—and will increase their reliance on technology to deliver consistent, timely and effective learning solutions.

My advice to current and aspiring CLOs is to continuously develop yourself and your team, communicate with passion, and have a clear vision of what you want to accomplish.

Here are the guiding principles for CLO success:

- Be grounded in your chosen industry and business.
- Design and deliver training with the business impact in mind.
- Read publications about business and workplace learning. (Remember that CLOs are business professionals as well as learning professionals.)
- Stay active in professional associations. Build and use networks; these are invaluable. Know what's going on in the profession: Who's doing what? How are they doing it better? What's new?
- Attach yourself to the smartest CLOs to learn from them.
- Be open to change! Help make the changes in our profession.

FRED HARBURG, FORMER CLO MOTOROLA & SVP LEADERSHIP AND LEARNING, FIDELITY INVESTMENTS

As a CLO, my driving philosophy has been to assist the business to attain sustained superior results. My efforts have always been aimed at enhancing the business in a manner that is consistent with the values and operating philosophy of the company. In short, it is my responsibility to propel business success and to enable enhanced organizational capability.

Let's say that a business has the goal to increase respect for customers as a way of growing customer loyalty and market share. The CLO in such a business needs to identify the kind of organizational practices and behaviors that will result in increased customer enthusiasm and those that are getting in the way. The next step is to employ the learning and development tools and options that will build the desired customer interaction behaviors while minimizing the barriers to increase customer intimacy among the employee base. This may or may not include providing classes. The job is to build capability.

Implicit in this approach is the need to establish the causal links between behaviors and results. It is critical to gather the evidence that a change in behavior will result in a change in performance and to determine what will most effectively help employees to adapt or adopt the behaviors that drive sustained results while letting go of the offending practices.

There are obvious links between talent management, leadership development, learning, OD, performance management, and succession planning to name a few key elements of the human performance system. Some companies are pulling these things together in an integrated manner and finding that this constellation looks a lot like what they hoped they would get from the CLO's organization.

I have always tried to help my businesses determine profiles for organizational success for their people. I believe this is fundamentally different than competencies since some of this has to do with interests and preferences for circumstances and outcomes. I continue to watch many companies be frustrated by chasing competencies with little to show for all of their efforts. This is a big opportunity for CLOs to offer leadership to a business. Poor job fit is one of the most pervasive and insidious problems facing most organizations. No amount of training and development will make up for a fundamental error in placing people in the wrong jobs. The CLO has a significant opportunity to help individuals learn about themselves and the kind of jobs in which they will flourish and how to navigate around the tempting traps that can seriously damage career choices.

One of the most effective things I have done is to hire performance consultants for each business unit (internal consultant role). These consultants have significant background in learning and organization development. They are focused on the performance of the business unit and are agnostic with respect to the tools for change. They are business centered and make sure that performance solutions meet the needs of the business unit. They work with a team of solution developers in the core who can customize our tool set to meet the unique needs of their client. This model has worked extremely well in a variety of settings.

Determining financial models for learning is a consistent CLO challenge. A common model is that corporate pays for learning infrastructure and the division pays for specific programs for their area. Clear contracting for this with the divisions is critical. The divisions or business units tend to value that which they have a hand in designing and for which they see a specific need. They are far less interested in the generic classes that are offered from the core that do not seem to speak directly to their business needs. Mass customization has proven to be a much better strategy. The units are also interested in learning what is working in the other units, and this is a key role of the core team to act as a conduit for shared learning across the enterprise.

I can't imagine a better role in a company than the CLO role. If you're fascinated by how people and individuals collectively work together to achieve great things, then you can help them make a bigger impact. If you have the passion and have a thick skin, then the CLO role is a great one. The world is beginning to appreciate the role. The CLO role is vital to business continuity; the challenge is credibility and demonstrating value that is self evident not self serving.

Ted Hoff, Vice President of Learning, IBM

The learning strategy in any company should be aligned with the business strategy. It also should be part of the business plan strategy process, since learning is a strategic enabler of growth and performance. A learning strategy must deliver business value, integrate with the HR and talent strategy, and provide a promise of efficiency, effectiveness, and innovation.

To be effective, learning needs to be embedded in the HR strategy. There are many HR challenges in growth and success. A learning strategy should provide strategic value and ensure that it addresses developing an optimal workforce—the right people with the right skills assigned to the right jobs that are aligned with business requirements. Done effectively, this provides a comprehensive talent management and workforce strategy.

Learning should demonstrate efficiency and effectiveness, and in order to do so, it's important to have an effective design at the highest level of productivity. CLOs should focus on providing learning courses at critical points in people's careers through an integrated talent strategy. More learning should be part of the work "embedded learning."

In the on-demand era, the ability to shift learning from the classroom to learning integrated in workflow is a competitive advantage. If organizations can make critical resources—including information, best practice, access to expertise, and dynamic collaboration—available at the exact moment they are needed, the company can leverage learning without having to remove the learner from the workplace.

At IBM, the strategy is to embed learning in real-time workflow. Work Embedded Learning is a newer learning approach in which targeted and measured guidance is delivered to the employee at the exact moment of need, without interrupting the flow of work.

IBM's vision is to create an "on-demand workplace." As work is done, learning opportunities are presented to employees via the on-demand workplace on the IBM intranet. This is a core strategy. As an example, during account planning for clients, a team has "teachable moments." These moments include preparing for account planning, reviewing what's happening in industry, and so on. This demonstrates how work preparation and learning are the same.

The IBM on-demand workplace is customized for sellers, giving them integrated:

- Account and opportunity dashboard
- Embedded guidance for client actions linked to opportunity and account dashboard
- Links to industry and account information
- Links to the people you need to collaborate with about accounts and opportunities

It takes an investment to define the role of people in the company. CLOs need to think about the work processes, IT application integration, what are key learning moments, and how they change. It is a dynamic process with people in businesses. CLOs need to be aware of where the information is flowing throughout the organization.

In addition, we are focused on measures of business value (Level 4). The best evaluation method is leveraging statistical processes with control groups versus participant groups. It's good for CLOs to look for opportunities to conduct a focus group of learning participants versus nonlearning participants. IBM tries to look for ways to evaluate the performance of a group of people who participated in training and to compare those to a group who did not have the training (or who had less of it).

In 2004, IBM Learning took on the responsibility for ensuring that IBMers, including IBM sales people, understood IBM's strategy and differentiated value propositions. We developed and deployed a set of core and common web-based modules which could be leveraged by sellers and all employees across the business globally.

To determine the effectiveness of this program, they organized sellers by geography into 50 clusters. The cluster teams were ranked based on the average number of learning modules completed—from high (taken an average of 19 modules) to low (taken an average of 7 modules).

Quota attainment:

107.7 for the group who completed an average of 19 used more than 15 modules

95.2 for the group who completed an average of 7 used less than 15 modules

Translating this to revenue, the difference in quota attainment had a value of approximately $550 million for the study group of 50 clusters (approximately 550 sellers). The total cost of the learning, design, development, and deployment, for those in the study group is slightly over $1 million, including employee time spent completing the modules.

At IBM, we evaluate the learning by looking at results of those who participated in learning and those who did not. Another example of this is the results of our Role of the Manager Program. We have thirty thousand managers at IBM. It took two years to train all IBM Managers on how to change behaviors in order to create a more positive climate that drives business results. After one year, we looked at statistical differences of employee opinions of managers and looked at who went through the program and who didn't. There were significant statistical differences between what people thought of those managers who participated in the management training and those who did not.

A CLO needs to determine the business value a group is seeking and find out what goals or metrics need to be defined. It's beneficial to think through what solid metrics are available and can be implemented. Two real business measures are quotas and employee opinions. Credible measures are people measures, not learning's measures.

IBM executives still look at participant feedback and the five levels of evaluation based upon knowledge gain, reported behavior change, or business improvement. Sharing metrics is valuable for executives but will not change the mind of those executives who don't believe in training.

As the CLO, I provide an annual report to each business unit talking about learning. In addition, I have a learning leader for each major business unit and geography reporting to me. The learning leaders also present quarterly reports to the businesses that include:

1. Activities that occurred.
2. Measurements—we report these because it does matter, level 1 participant feedback is requested by executives.
3. Business value metrics.

The CLO job is the greatest job in the world with phenomenal opportunities. The role of CLO is to enable the larger HR strategy and to be familiar with the learning business, and it is very helpful if the CLO has access to the senior VPs that run the businesses.

In the last few years, learning and knowledge has become more critical for companies. For CLOs to be effective, knowing about learning must come first, accompanied by an understanding of the company business priorities and knowing how to fit into HR. CLOs need to know how to help change the rest of HR, to help them get a broader perspective, to understand the business, and to create measures of business value.

The CLO of the future needs to have a reasonably high level of knowledge in business, finance, strategy, talent, development, HR, and learning. The role is as big as the CLO wants to make it. CLOs need to have ambition, ability, and executive sponsorship.

Some CLOs are advisors to CEOs, some aren't. Either way, a good CLO needs to have business acumen, integrate with HR strategy, and appreciate how complex the learning field is.

STEVE KERR, MANAGING DIRECTOR AND CHIEF LEARNING OFFICER, GOLDMAN SACHS (THE FIRST CLO IN THE PROFESSION)

TE: Steve, we understand the inception of the CLO title began with you at GE.

SK: *Yes, I originally came up with the name Chief Education Officer (CEO), but Jack Welch said there was only room for one CEO and that title was already taken. Jack thought the title should be reflective of what people do ("learning" is a verb) in the organization instead of what they are ("education" is a noun). Hence, the title CLO.*

The Goldman Sachs strategy for learning is "back of the manual." By that I mean what's on the back of a manual is written for anyone to clearly understand—that's the essence of learning.

I believe the CLO's role is to acquire and assimilate information from the outside and transfer that knowledge within the organization. Bring best practices and ideas to the company. The organization may reject the idea, but the CLO causes others to accept it. I found that incentives and rewards help with this.

CLOs in all organizations are more alike than different; the roles should be primarily the same; it's just how they're applied that is different. CLOs should manage cost, manage heads, and get more output. We need to show that learning is inexpensive. Leaders need to be involved. For superior data, we need to look at benchmarking, but we shouldn't be dependent on third-party reports.

No manager in history has ever asked for a diversity or competency audit—this is what we think is important to provide, not necessarily what the business thinks is important. Problems and opportunities are driven by the firm, and the CLO needs to make them come alive.

People don't share information and knowledge because they don't want to. As CLOs we need to worry about people who prevent knowledge and information from being shared. Evaluate and try to change rewards, politics, and silos that keep people from transferring and communicating ideas and knowledge.

CLOs should evade the questions about ROI. Learning costs are known, benefits are not. It's critical that CLOs ensure that learning is cost efficient. The cost of the learning budget is less than the cost of one senior executive making a bad decision. The goal is to retain talent and enable the organization to make better decisions.

In my role at both GE and Goldman Sachs, eighty percent of courses were taught by senior leaders of the company. When executives are around learning, they understand the value. Clients should also be involved in learning. Both executives and clients need to be around learning to understand the value.

Jack Welch loved learning. He said, "During tough times you need training more rather than less." In other companies, training would be cut during tough times. At GE we increased it.

One way to understand the investment in learning is to look at the cost per student educated: the number of people divided by the cost of learning. If learning is done well, it will have a high ROI. Cost/benefit justifications are silly. You can't figure out what learning is worth because you can't quantify it.

Show that learning is inexpensive, involve leaders, and don't be dependent on third-party reports. Ensure lower costs and more output. CLOs also need to look at "resources in place." A fully employed person in another part of the organization who is interested in learning can design programs, be a spokesperson, and teach programs.

Learning at Goldman Sachs is managed by a senior executive board. I share data with them and provide them with quarterly reports. They meet and are extremely involved in programs. In my role as CLO, I am responding to needs that come from operating units or the board. I test programs in divisions and then release them company-wide. I talk to people who take classes, which gives me good data about the effectiveness of the learning we provide.

CLOs need to convince leaders that learning opportunities are a place to communicate their message. Use learning programs as a pulpit, signify the importance of them, and get information to employees so that programs will be a beneficial use of time. The CLOs role is to move ideas, to create a boundaryless organization. CLOs need to prepare people to move information and barriers. They should create processes to enable decisions and ensure employees are well informed.

Executive development provides a good opportunity to get an assessment of, and focus on, the development of leaders. Executives can evaluate leaders by observing them in development programs. Students often report back to senior leaders about the participants from their classes and their evaluation of their capabilities.

Corporations are prioritizing the connection to succession, focusing on development of the next generation. It is important for CLOs to help the organization use data (good ideas from inside and outside the organization) to develop knowledge throughout the organization. Convert internal and external knowledge into cases, role plays, simulations—tailor and customize the information from other companies.

The greatest possible failure of a CLO is to not move knowledge across the organization. All CLOs are different, but if we can't move knowledge, then we are not doing our jobs.

MICHAEL LEE, EXECUTIVE VICE PRESIDENT OF HUMAN RESOURCES, LG CORP.

The LG Academy, the corporate university of LG is 1) the competency development center for executives and employees where they learn subjects that are directly related to jobs, and 2) the culture building and communication center where we teach courses and programs related to the "LG Way." This is a unique feature of the LG Academy.

This learning model ensures that LG has sustainable long-term competitiveness. We teach core values and management philosophy through an infrastructure for culture building. We develop cases and teach principles and the application of values in our courses.

At the LG Academy, we have mandatory courses, such as new employee orientation and several levels of managerial courses, that are required for promotion to the next rank. We provide a physical place for learning where innovation efforts are shared and discussed. We provide opportunities to discuss future direction and facilitate collaboration. The LG Academy is a symbol of innovation and the values of LG.

The LG Academy enables the business to succeed. The LG Corp., the holding company, provides the "spirit side" of learning programs and links them to the way we do business. In LG, corporate initiatives are mostly conducted by each business subsidiary, and LG Corp. gives only the fundamental guidance.

The LG Way describes our management philosophy, "creating value for customers," and "respect for people." Also, as a company we "compete fairly in the market through innovation and fairness." This is the "integrity" which we believe is the true source of sustainable long-term competitiveness. Our vision is to be the "No. 1 LG." We aspire to be a preferred provider for customers, the preferred corporate entity by investors, a preferred employer, and a company that is envied and revered by our competitors.

As the Chief Human Capital Officer (CHCO) of LG, I have been frustrated with HR metrics. In one way, we use the 9 blocks and quantify the performance and leadership as much as we can. In training, the Level 3 evaluation is practically difficult and the measurement of learning effectiveness is a constant challenge. We don't need fancy methods to come up with new courses. However, the courses need to be aligned with top management philosophy and strategy and must be delivered to have an impact.

The impact analysis of training is for survival and justification. This is, however, secondary to demonstrating value by making sure courses strategically fit with the values we want to instill in our people and the organization. Conviction of top management is much more important than measurement techniques. Do what's important and, in the long run, there will be a big payoff.

Michael Lee's Learning Theory: The Half-Life of Training

To explain, in natural science a radioisotope in a natural condition becomes half in mass in a certain time period. This half-life applies to learning as well. Look at the cases of competency development versus culture and leadership building.

Competency development has a shorter half-life than culture and leadership building. That's because subjects you teach to develop competencies or skills change quickly (accounting rules change, financial schemes change, programming languages change, etc.). There is a constant need for retraining for new competencies. For instance, to become and remain an effective software engineer, retraining on new programming languages is essential. The skills that a new college graduate software engineer learned 6 months ago are already obsolete! The half-life is quite short.

On the other hand, culture building or leadership development doesn't change rapidly. Leadership, values, attitudes, aspirations— all of these tend to be sustained longer than skills related competencies and don't change rapidly. Hence, that half-life is longer.

The investment impact of culture building and leadership development lasts longer, and it doesn't change as quickly as competency or skills training. It is hard to show the effectiveness of culture building efforts and leadership development, but the half-life is much longer, and the investments will accrue much greater return. To look at this from an ROI perspective, culture building has more return on value than competency building since the information retained is used longer and doesn't get outdated as quickly.

Donna MacNamara, Vice President of Global Education & Training, Colgate Palmolive

An effective education and training function is tightly aligned to the priorities, culture, and future directions of the business. My role as CLO is to create a learning strategy that continually meets these criteria and to build the organizational capability required to effectively implement the strategy. Since Colgate Palmolive's mission is to become the best global consumer products company, one of the key alignment factors is also that the education and training strategy be fully global.

Colgate's learning goal is straightforward—to build key skills essential to business success and to support individuals in personal career development. Central to achieving this goal is a global curriculum of 150 programs that span all levels, work functions, and geographies on a world basis. Annually there are 30,000 participants throughout the world. Importantly, line management ownership of both program development and delivery and a pull system coupled with selected corporate mandates for implementation help ensure success.

In terms of beginnings, Colgate's global education and training function was initiated more than a decade ago. The foundation was a single program that very successfully addressed business issues viewed as critical by both the board of directors and the chief operating officer. For education and training to add value to the business, it is essential to align with key priorities, spend time "in the midst of the action," closely partner with business leaders, and consistently provide high quality deliverables.

At Colgate our process includes three-year rolling curriculum plans that are reviewed and updated annually. We work directly with senior leadership to prioritize the most important areas to address based on current and future business directions. Global education and training has a zero-based budget, with all costs and resources associated with new program development and delivery being paid for by the operating units on a line-item basis.

Once it has been decided by senior management that a new program will be developed, the associated costs are paid for by the operating units based on relative revenues. Additionally, a global team of internal subject matter experts is identified to support program development. For program delivery, all costs are paid on a per-use basis by operating units, and all classroom sessions are delivered by line people who have been specifically identified and certified based on the program. This approach ensures a keen focus on priorities, front-end resolution of differences, strong line ownership, and full commitment to follow-through and action. It is also consistent with Colgate's practical, lean approach to management. Without these factors being in place, we don't begin an initiative.

Four principles guide all classroom and e-learning programs:

- *Company specific.* Training is specific to company business issues and opportunities, both current and future. Eighty percent of the courses in the global curriculum are proprietary to the company. In instances where off-the-shelf programs are used, they are selected because of a direct match with company needs.
- *Best practices.* Education and training initiatives are both catalysts for establishing best global practices and are major vehicles for sharing practices from one part of the world to another, from one business category to another, and across work functions. This includes both internal and external best practices.
- *Practical.* Programs are practical, relevant, and directly applicable to job and position responsibilities. All training includes application exercises, action learning, on-the-job tools and resources, or individual action planning.
- *Colgate leaders teach.* All classroom instruction is conducted by line leaders. There is no separate instructional staff. Leaders who are facilitators do this in addition to their primary work responsibility. This includes leaders at all levels of the company and includes both high potential people and seasoned professionals. Becoming an instructor is a prized development opportunity that is inculcated in the culture.

In summary, a CLO needs to understand the business, the learning needs, and how to manage them best in the environment. They should not own learning; the line needs to own it. The role of the CLO is to coach, provide leadership, get the right people, and develop the right opportunities for the organization. The CLO needs to take the responsibility for partnerships, understand client systems, and give the best advice possible to the organization. To be most successful, a CLO needs to act as business person—not just as a business partner—and always be at the top of his or her game professionally.

RICK O'LEARY, DIRECTOR, HUMAN RESOURCES & DIVERSITY, CORNING

At Corning, we focus on learning through a standard platform of courses, experiences, and assignments that are full of content. Our main development areas are the Tuck 20/20 program, a consortium tied to the Dartmouth Executive MBA, a GM program for directors and emerging leaders (300 to 500 people), the Manchester executive development program for 360° and coaching, a manager/supervisor development core curriculum, executive coaches, and Kaplan Devries. Executive support of education is needed to fuel the engine and keep people employed.

To implement effective talent management across the organization, we use forced job rotations for key assignments and support early identification of leaders. Our talent strategy is guided by a management committee of the top six people in the company. We evaluate 40 critical positions and review our global talent with the business unit discussions and management committee review.

Talent discussions are centered around business impact and results. In addition, Corning is a values-driven company; employees need to hit a result and live within our values. We develop leaders and provide coaching so that they attain great results through people. "Did this person produce results and did these results align with our values?" These are the types of questions that guide our discussions about leadership.

In the last few years, companies have been starting to spend money on learning and development again. They've been retreating from formal education, and for the mid-level down, investments have slowed. Lately this trend is turning as the expectation for increased productivity has become a critical focus for global organizations.

At Corning, we use a human capital planning process to create annual learning plans. We look at the people issues that will negatively impact business goals such as staffing, poor management, processes, and skills. We look to determine if the resource is constrained by people and what additional headcount or components are necessary to increase performance.

Our critical initiatives are to map critical competencies and ensure effective hiring. We also include development planning as part of the annual performance process. Development is an objective that is not activity based; it's competency based. Corning has IDPs that are used in talent reviews to support growth in competencies and address critical needs for individual development.

Corning has an inclusive culture and an international global business. To accelerate global productivity, and to enhance language skills and influence skills, we provide a four-month intervention called Creating an Inclusive Culture. Programs like this illustrate that CLOs are in critical positions to impact business productivity and disseminate organizational culture.

DONNEE RAMELLI, PRESIDENT, GENERAL MOTORS UNIVERSITY

Mission. At GMU, our mission is to provide leading edge learning resources to drive technical and business leadership. To make this mission a reality, annual business objectives are used to drive the yearly training plans. Since I get to facilitate the strategic planning meeting for the executive team, I get a first hand perspective about what mission critical learning is required to deliver the needed global performance. By being "at the table," I'm able to link learning to the business needs. In addition, all of the key learning leaders report to Regional Presidents and Global Functional Process Leaders. Business objectives are written collectively with the Chairman and his Automotive Strategy Board who, in turn, determine strategic objectives that drive GM's global training requirements.

Linkage to Business. At GM, the learning strategy is linked to business strategy and business goals. Learning enables business performance through the development of mission critical skills and capability. The business strategy can't be successfully implemented unless the learning strategy is in place and is effective—upgrading skills and performance globally. Sometimes skill development is an issue; sometimes technology is an issue. It's learning's role to enable business success and resolve these issues. Learning is aligned with business results and functional capabilities on a global basis. As is shown in Figure 11-1, it is important to have an effective learning alignment model that engages and integrates learning across the global enterprise.

Learning Alignment Model and How It Works. Since work is done in the functional processes at GM, each Global Functional Process Leader assesses business goals and needs and determines how to enable people to work through performance gaps, decides on areas of change, and creates workforce development requirements. The Global Functional Process Leader, Dean of the functional college, and GMU develop functional learning plans based on business needs. The dean is responsible for the linkage and the efficiency of the learn-

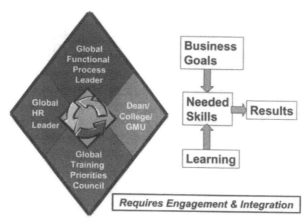

Figure 11-1. Learning alignment model.

ing plan, while GMU manages the design, development, and delivery processes. The Global Priorities Council is made up of operating leaders for the function from each region. The college dean leads the functional training priorities council and provides a bottom-up view of business requirements, gaps, and a learning plan. Together they develop an operational training plan that can be deployed globally for the functional process.

Future of Learning. At GMU, we realize that the next generation workforce will want learning outside the classroom—they want global access 24/7. The classroom provides a connection to the culture and experts. Although extremely valuable, it is slow, costly, and rarely global. Smart people don't need classes for every type of learning. They are quick learners that can "learn by googling," and we will find an increasing use of web sites with job aids and quick e-learning modules in our future. People's learning styles have been, and will continue to be, expanded by technology at the speed we all need to learn to "survive and thrive." CLOs can accelerate and enable this change by building "bite-sized" e-learning modules and "powerful" job aids rather than five day classroom programs.

Leadership Development and Building a Global Network. GMU learning is designed to solve global business problems. In 2001, we created a global leadership development program for high potential global executives to provide a global business understanding of GM. GM's most senior leaders teach in this award winning program and get to engage and dialogue with high performing executives. While the program has high caliber learning content about GM's strategic plan and global operations, the program also creates an environment to leverage global knowledge and solve current business problems. More importantly, this program accelerated global networking and problem solving during our recent global restructuring, allowing one executive to solve two important problems because he was in class with two key executives who helped him break down the right barriers.

ROI. At GM, we have over 2,000 courses. It would take an army to calculate ROI on all of them. Instead, we summarized eight different examples of savings generated by learning programs on a one-page document. These examples in engineering, manufacturing, and sales illustrated how learning has impacted the business and saved over $500 million. Since these examples were connected with critical business operations that had been successful, business leaders usually "get it" and know that learning can enable improved performance. I like to use these examples in front of key business leaders. For instance, "it would have cost $50 million a year to train engineers on our common CAD/CAM systems, but only $20 million on internal development and delivery. Not only did we save $30 million, we created mastery for this new science of math-based design at GM." This financial link to the critical business skills provides clear value to our leaders and eliminates endless ROI calculations and debates.

Summary: What Will Make CLOs Successful Now and in the Future?

Cultivate Leadership Support. It's important for CLOs to work for CEOs and leadership teams who naturally support learning and the development of capability and talent. Engage them in planning, goal setting, and teaching. Advocates are rarely critics.

Link to Business Performance. CLOs must understand the business model and priorities and ensure that learning plans are aligned with business objectives and can sustain growth and development of talent for the future. Adding value is all about improving current performance and results and building smart, agile, world class talent for the enterprise. CLOs need to speak in the language of business leaders that relates to results, performance, and capability that make the business better.

Innovate, Innovate, Innovate. CLOs should find new approaches to leverage learning that are faster, better, cheaper. Challenge everyone to find the latest high-impact practices/technologies. CLOs need to connect learning to business goals and see ahead on learning and technology opportunities. They should enable performance management and focus on driving important business changes. They need to support budget and spending cutbacks across the company to demonstrate their business linkage in tough times, and to quickly leverage global growth and business expansion during those cycles. New ideas can drive success in both areas.

Master the New Mix. CLOs should know how to blend the products and services available to leverage content, technology, and purchasing into an effective and efficient global learning system for their enterprise. Technology is the next big area of focus for CLOs that face global learning challenges—how to use it, exploit it, translate it, and master it for your business model is critical.

Think Like the Boss. CLOs need to think like business leaders so they can naturally integrate the learning strategy into the business model. They need to understand the business challenges and how to use different learning strategies that drive success. CLOs need to be thought leaders that can "think different"—curious, critical, creative, constructive.

BONNIE STOUFER, VICE PRESIDENT FOR LEARNING, TRAINING & DEVELOPMENT, BOEING

A CLO's role revolves around understanding business strategies, challenges, and market drivers. CLOs need to stay closely connected to business leaders, understand the future direction of the Company, and translate what that means for the future capabilities of the workforce.

The business is constantly changing and the CLO needs to be a thought leader who helps architect a learning system that will support that dynamic business environment.

The CLO runs the learning and training function like a business and competes on cost, quality, time, and customer satisfaction. At Boeing, all learning and training services are billed back to the customer and all costs are very visible—not part of overhead. Every year, an Annual Business Plan is developed for the learning services to be provided to each business unit, and affordability targets are identified and agreed upon. In order to maximize the dollars spent, a variety of processes and tools are used to monitor, track, and report services.

In 2005, the Learning and Development Roundtable introduced to the Boeing learning team a simple matrix used by CNA Financial's Knowledge and Learning group to align learning strategies with business strategies. The matrix is a 2 × 2 matrix that allows you to categorize your learning and training dollars either into maintenance or growth on one axis and generic or proprietary investments on the other.

At Boeing, the initiatives and associated budget were mapped into the appropriate quadrant for each of the business units and then the portfolio was reviewed with the leadership teams to discuss if they felt they were spending their monies where they would get the best return. Since each business unit has an affordability target, this portfolio approach is very beneficial in working with them to set priorities and manage trade-offs when unexpected new work is identified.

We also use a robust scorecard for monthly performance reporting to the business units on progress against plan. It includes not only performance on common industry metrics such as cost per hour, annual spending per employee, and percent of payroll but also delivery to schedule, customer satisfaction ratings, productivity metrics, learner satisfaction, supplier evaluation, and impact on learner performance.

To talk the language of the business, CLOs need strong business acumen. They need to demonstrate that they run their organization just like other leaders across the enterprise. They need to constantly be asking the tough questions and be focused on adding value for every dollar spent.

CLOs need to lead change within their own learning function. The pace of modern-day business is so rapid that the traditional models and approaches are not always viable. A wider variety of learning models is being utilized to keep up with business needs—establishing peer-to-peer learning networks, taking the training closer to the workplace, and leveraging knowledge management systems, workplace coaching, and technology based solutions. We're seeing more resources focused on compliance and mandatory training and for a global company, more emphasis on building internal expertise around import and export guidelines as they relate to training.

CLOs need to be learning role models and agile learners. They need to be well-read and stay current with research and benchmarking results. It's important that they establish peer networks that allow them to learn and gain insights from others in the profession. They need to give back to the profession and help develop and prepare others to meet what they see as the challenges for the future of the profession. The CLO's role is more critical and challenging today because businesses are faced with not only complying with new financial and ethical reporting and compliance standards, but also maintaining a competitive workforce that's knowledgeable, adaptive, and entrepreneurial.

DAVID VANCE, PRESIDENT, CATERPILLAR UNIVERSITY

At Caterpillar, learning is aligned to business goals and strategies. We have a very disciplined process to ensure that learning will help the organization achieve its critical success factors (CSFs)—those few things that must go right for the business to succeed. We did this informally the first couple of years by working with the Lead Learning Managers in each of our semiautonomous 28 divisions to identify and prioritize key learning initiatives to support their division CSFs. Three years ago, we formalized the process with Division Learning Plans and an Enterprise Learning Plan, which are basically business plans for learning.

Within each division, the Division Learning Plan is both a top-down and bottom-up process. Senior leadership identifies the business needs to realize the CSFs and the learning staff identifies learning to support them. Plans address needs such as business acumen, change management, and Six Sigma—learning that will apply to many in the division in direct support of the divisions' CSFs. The Division Learning Plan also captures the individual learning needs from employee learning and development plans—this is the bottom-up part. Caterpillar University provides the structure for the process, and each Lead Learning Manager produces their Division Learning Plan, which is their business plan for the year.

Caterpillar University takes their 28 Division Learning Plans and combines them with input from our Executive Office and Caterpillar U. Board of Governors to produce a detailed 100 plus page Enterprise Learning Plan. This document starts with enterprise strategy and CSFs, and identifies the learning initiatives to support them. We make sure to understand the highest priorities for the CEO, our Executive Office and our University Board of Governors. For 2006 these CSFs include quality, safety, production development and distribution, velocity, product availability, and people. Learning has a major role to play in all of these areas in direct support of the company's success. By increasing employee's competency in these areas, we can make a significant contribution to the bottom line.

This more strategic approach is in direct contrast to learning's role in the past. Training was viewed as a perk, as something nice to do for employees when we could afford it. There was no alignment to highest priority business needs and no effort to measure its impact.

Consequently, the training budget was slashed during recessions as a way to improve the bottom line through cost reduction. Learning was not viewed as a productive investment contributing to bottom line success. Yes, learning led to higher employee engagement and, in some cases, made employees more effective on their job, but the consensus seemed to be that training could be scaled back dramatically with little negative impact.

The division and enterprise learning plan process addresses many of these shortcomings. So does running training like a business with focus on measurement, evaluation, and results. Among other things, a CLO must do the following in addition to ensuring proper alignment.

1. *Know the training costs.* Add up all costs for learning, company-wide, and provide credible data about the expenditures.

2. *Manage costs.* Increase efficiency. Reduce spending while increasing effectiveness. Manage the learning budget. Caterpillar has a corporate target for expenditures, which helps set priorities for learning.

3. *Evaluate the investment.* The Board of Governors (Caterpillar's training board) meets quarterly and is provided with a report of Level 1 evaluations. The Board is interested in looking at Level 1 data, so that's what we share. Demand for learning is rising, and the businesses are paying. An increased demand for learning illustrates the value of learning in the businesses. Level 2 is done where appropriate. Levels 3, 4, and 5 evaluations are done on 2 to 3 courses corporate-wide every year using an ROI process model. Results are shared. We use these results to ensure value delivery and to improve our efficiency and effectiveness as well as demonstrate results. We also forecast the value for new programs based on our analysis of previous programs. In 2005 the key programs and processes produced a net dollar benefit in excess of $100 million, primarily through greater productivity and cost reduction. This is real bottom line value.

Executives are comfortable when learning is being managed through an understanding of the costs and benefits. The CLO agenda at Caterpillar is focused on learning, leadership, and change management, not succession planning, talent management, or organization effectiveness. At the present time, that is being done by the organization effectiveness (OE) function; however, integrating organization effectiveness with learning makes sense since there is close collaboration and hand-offs between the functions.

In the future, there will be greater benefits to organizations if the OD/OE function is combined with learning. There are common touch points between learning and OD. It is best to leverage systems and provide clarity to the organization by integrating the two areas. It can be unclear to customers who they go to for services when the two functions are separate. OD/OE and learning professionals have the same language. Business requests may be initiated through learning interventions or OD interventions, and making this seamless for customers is critical.

It is beneficial for CLOs to have a learning background. They also would benefit from a strong business background. Business acumen and P&L responsibility are particularly desirable. It is also important for CLOs to obtain experience outside HR to be more effective. That experience gives more credibility and builds better networks with people outside HR. For CLOs that come from outside the learning function, like myself, it is critical to have close advisors and colleagues who do have expertise and experience in learning.

Not being from the profession does have some benefits, though. You have an opportunity to start fresh, ask anything, and question everything. It is probably easier for an outsider to make dramatic changes and introduce a new approach, like running training as a business.

ALLAN WEISBERG, VICE PRESIDENT OF ORGANIZATION CAPABILITY, JOHNSON & JOHNSON

Johnson & Johnson's learning function is decentralized. We don't have one learning strategy for the company—many groups have their own learning strategy. The corporate strategy is to provide training and development access throughout the company and to understand key passages throughout the organization. This strategy guides access to all learning that is globally available.

The entire learning staff doesn't report into one area but needs to be aligned; we have the same LMS, the same content sharing, the same access to curriculum. Johnson & Johnson (J&J) uses a chargeback model for learning and development costs. Unfortunately training budgets are easy to cut when they are centralized—they become targets to reduce. In a decentralized cost model, the costs are managed locally, which doesn't provide as much of a spotlight on financials, but rather a stronger connection to the business.

Demonstrating the value of the learning function is a challenge for all of us. We've all learned the Kirkpatrick Model (i.e., the four levels), but the reality is that, when you get to Level 3 and Level 4, there are many factors that affect results and it becomes difficult to isolate training. I believe that the most important way to measure impact is through Level 2, or behavior change, because after all, learning application is about behavior change. But it also requires a bit of a leap of faith by leadership to understand that, when applied right, learning is a good investment for a business.

CLOs need to be connected to the business and to the business strategy. There is an aspect of elitism when companies focus on high potentials. Those high potentials get access to development, initiatives, and programs that others may or may not receive. There is growing concern about forming "have" and "have not" groups within companies. It's important for the CLO to stay ahead of this and be an advocate for effectively evaluating and developing talent, not developing an environment where self-fulfilling prophecies exist.

Effective talent management is about assessing and developing people. People excel at different times in their careers and many factors contribute to their performance. Expertise and full performance can occur at different times in a person's career. Labeling someone as high potential at one point in time may not take into account an entire talent pool that may contain individuals "peaking" at different times. CLOs need to be cautious of this and take a leadership role to assess talent at different points in a person's career and at different points in time. This provides a more comprehensive look at the entire talent pool and individual capabilities.

J&J has an OD consulting group to focus on "nontraining" solutions; after all, I think that we all learned earlier on that not everything is a training solution. They charge for services to the business (their rates are typically lower than external consultants) and provide organization design, change management, leadership development and other OD services to internal groups.

The internal consulting groups at J&J have to show value on every project. Their value proposition is to know about J&J and care more about the company than an external consultant. A key difference between internal consultant learning professionals and external consultants is that internal professionals are around for implementation, which enables them to have a broader perspective on all initiatives.

There is an understanding at J&J about the contribution of learning and development across the organization. Culturally, the company is focused on being a learning organization and realizes that to be successful and stay successful, learning is part of the business. The company is able to launch products faster and have successful business initiatives as a result of many parts of a good system, one of them being learning.

Successful CLOs have several skills that are critical differentiators.

- They comprehensively understand the profession—they understand training problems versus work motivation issues. They understand learning and different pieces of learning systems, such as change management, succession, and talent management. Good CLOs are not wedded to e-learning, OD, or the classroom. It is best to be broader and understand all the elements of learning.
- They understand the business and what drives it. R&D at J&J is critical; the goal of the learning organization is to provide resources to help the R&D staff learn. CLOs need to have a coherent way to lay out strategy, be good at presentations, and have good influence skills. They must have knowledge of the field and knowledge of the business.

While many skills are essential for today's CLOs, there are also critical skills for the future.

1. Use of technology, especially nontraditional technology applications, such as mobility applications.
2. Integrating learning into the workflow of the job. In the future, learning will be embedded into work; the lines between formal learning and informal learning will blur. Business leaders will realize that, if they are more effective and efficient, they will win, and learning is a critical element of becoming more effective and efficient. For example, if they can introduce new products faster, they will win over the competition. Learning is the driver of being able to do things better. Getting more information to people and teaching people new ways of doing things will result in more effective and efficient businesses.
3. Emerging markets. In China and India learning plays a critical role in bringing new employees up to speed quickly. Learning and providing information about how to do things in the company are essential. The faster people get it, the better.

Finally, CLOs need to have common sense and logic. CLOs shouldn't try to solve the world's problems; they should go after unique contributions and not be a one trick pony (e.g., only knowing about OD, e-learning, or executive education). Great CLOs need to understand all elements of learning and business.

BILL WIGGENHORN, FORMER PRESIDENT MOTOROLA UNIVERSITY AND VICE CHAIRMAN OF GLOBAL ED-TECH MANAGEMENT GROUP

The learning organization has to be aligned with the strategic intent of the corporation. Learning professionals are responsible for implementing an education and development strategy that is aligned with the institutional strategy. CLOs can then evaluate their success by implementing strategy faster and more completely than would have happened without the education and training support.

Learning functions are a business service center—they should be evaluated like other aspects of the business based on their quality, cost, speed of execution, and service. Their role is to get people developed, not to make a direct buck for shareholders, but to develop people who will make many bucks for the shareholders.

To run learning effectively, there needs to be a good business model. The debate with managing learning as a P&L is to determine if learning is an investment in academics or if it's a service.

Seventeen years ago, George Fisher used the University concept at Motorola as part of an overall strategy for Motorola to enter emerging markets. There was value in global education from a customer and market standpoint, so having a division called a University opened doors for Motorola. It was a business decision to use learning as a way to proliferate new business opportunities for Motorola in China and the other developing markets, and it worked.

Great CLOs must first understand the business. That means they must converse in a business language, understand the numbers of business, and look across the institution to see the enterprise. Next, they must understand educational technology for improving the effectiveness of delivering to the client the skills and knowledge needed on a timely basis. It is important to put learning into the language of the receiver versus the language of the sender.

The job of a CLO is really two roles in one: the CLO role and the leadership development role. The CLO is responsible for the total package of talent management, development, retention programs, consistency of the internal message, competencies, and alignment with the business. They must understand change management, organization design, business and educational technology. This is a large role that is continuously growing.

How fast can the education and training group communicate the strategic initiatives of the company? Leadership development is a forum for communicating messages and standards. This needs to get through the organization and is a critical responsibility of the CLO.

CLOs add value in several areas:

- Creating leadership bench strength for growth and succession. They make critical decisions about external hires or internal transfers/promotions.
- Enabling introduction of new products and services. They provide the opportunity to have trained versus untrained staff.
- Process improvement. They provide measures of training to improve internal operations.

In many companies CLOs provide supplier/customer education (supply chain training in both cases). This ensures consistency in the external and internal messages. CLOs should provide external development to suppliers and customers. These people are part of the supply chain and their knowledge is important to the success of the business. Providing development to them can assist in building greater alignment for the company.

A beneficial application of development for external audiences is using leaders as teachers. Leaders model the company's leadership behaviors and knowledge both inside and outside. Obtaining feedback from suppliers about leaders can provide good information about internal talent in the company.

All external and internal stakeholders are part of the learning system. Ensuring that they all have the same development and message is critical. I believe that suppliers want to supply to, and customers want to buy from, companies that have great leaders and employees (or at least companies that have reputations for having great leaders and employees). That's why it's important to be named to lists that identify great training organizations. If you build a great learning organization, it will help your business work with better suppliers/partners and may help you get better customers. This is a true value add to the business that can be impacted by the CLO and the learning organization.

CLOs need to make sure the education strategy is aligned with the business strategy. A great way to ensure linkage of strategy is to form a learning Board of Directors (BOD) to oversee education investments and represent the internal business groups. These advisory groups or BODs provide approval for learning and development investments and ensure strategic alignment across the company. At the "C" level your peers are the CEO, COO, CFO, and so on. If you don't have a CLO title, the peer group of influence might be different. Having an advisory Board or Board of Directors can provide neutral perspectives and share insights that represent the client, not HR.

Investments in learning are consistent challenges for CLOs. Blended budgets seem to work best. Centralized budgets can create "shadow budgets" where people will create budgets in their areas outside of the corporate budget; and/or people create the budgets themselves and the CLO can't see all of the expenditures. A blended model works best where the corporate budget is centralized and functional areas such as sales, customer service, IT, and division training have a decentralized budget with dotted line oversight to the CLO.

The CLO's charter needs to include "successful implementation of corporate initiatives," "retention of talent," and "helping good executives become great executives." CLOs need to have a portfolio of tools and techniques in change management, OD, coaching, and communication.

Measuring learning effectiveness has been a constant debate among CLOs. It's important to measure the cost of ignorance—it exceeds the investment in people by 10 times. All people should get access to education and training to keep them productive in the work environment. Whether it's academic education or professional development, the company should make the investment. Education discounts should be made available through the employer's connections or relationships with universities. Individual development should focus on the long term, not short term, at the company's expense. CLOs need to maximize tax benefits for the company. There is development that can be a tax write-off if managed correctly and wisely.

Motorola created a brand for its university by going outside to sell training to suppliers. The brand of Motorola University became a significant brand value on the street. The market value of the brand of Motorola University was $500 million. In some market segments, the Motorola University brand was more recognizable than the business brand of Motorola the company. Very few corporate universities sell that brand well. Globalizing the brand drove the HR strategy that was necessary for competitive advantage. The brand of people development was so large that it positively impacted the business. The reputation that was built for Motorola University became a differentiator for the business. Other companies will do business with great businesses, which helped Motorola with customers and suppliers. Our leadership development brand also helped our business. Great leaders provide better organizations. The brand we built for great leadership development generated a reputation for Motorola being a great organization, which enhanced our business with customers and suppliers.

KEVIN WILDE, VICE PRESIDENT AND CHIEF LEARNING OFFICER, GENERAL MILLS

The CLO should be the senior voice for strategic value of learning and its implementation. They should be working with the top of the house on fit, enablers, and strategies. Their focus is on relationship building for implementation of strategic initiatives. CLOs should be business planning people and build alliances with senior business planning people. They need to have interaction with strategic leaders in an organization and assist in removing roadblocks for the learning staff below them.

Our strategy at General Mills is to make sure to fulfill the employees' promise, to be a premium brand. We have an innovation and grow-from-within strategy. We want to create the company as a place for great development through talent acquisition and retention.

Our challenge is to keep moving people and developing people. We need to 1) execute on our strategy, 2) build great leadership, and 3) "be an edge" in the market. learning and development is an "edge" for our business.

Linking learning to the business is a big headache for a company. How does it fit into the business? Link learning to a change agenda. Decentralize training; use councils to get involvement across the company for training; create the leadership and the systems. For many CLOs the problem with centralization of training is how to manage and sell the budget. At General Mills, functional education is in sales, engineering, and finance—not direct line reporting into the CLO. Customer satisfaction goes down when you centralize training, that's why at General Mills sales leads sales training. The benefits to this model are that there is less command and control and the business funds the training.

There are two kinds of elements of training budgets:

1. (End market) FLOW Business provides training on transition, new management, etc. For this training, the per unit cost of training should go down over time.

2. (R&D) INNOVATION Business provides training on personal productivity. This is funded by FLOW business and continuously enhances employee development.

Learning is a variable cost and the trend is that people need it cheaper. It's important for CLOs to continuously work the game of funding. Find what works in the organization and always put learning on the agenda. Make a conscious effort to link learning to the business. The best way to raise quality and reduce price is to have divisions also support training by providing financial commitment. Involve others in the budget.

Don't lead with ROI, do it at the back end, at the front end it's a dialogue. There are many learning professionals who are "activity junkies"—ROI can work if it is done at the end of a program.

For learning to be tied to the business, it's critical to find business issues. For example, if a company wants more innovation, then learning needs to set an agenda on five ways they can help increase innovation.

CLOs need to embed the learning value proposition into business dialogue. It's very relationship and credibility based. Leaders need to value learning. There was a big opportunity in the 1980s for Jack Welch with Crotonville. The CLO needs to find opportunities with executives that will work. Set strategies and prove their worth on the logic of argument. Demonstrate how learning makes a difference.

CLOs should spend 10 percent of their time and budget on follow-up, asking the following questions:

1. Skill gaps—are we choosing the right skills?
2. Is the program well done?
3. Did it happen/occur?

CLOs sometimes overpromise to get others' attention. CLOs should not overcommit. They need to set expectations clearly at the beginning, hire better people, take advantage of external, skilled staff, and not pick up bad contracts that they know they can't deliver, or that may be vague.

A CLO's impact to the company is through HR generalists. Learning can be supported through partners. Learning staff have a comprehensive role that is focused on succession, learning, OD, climate, performance management, individual skill development and organization change. Working with HR can enable greater leverage and business impact.

CLOs need to live the business cases, bring company issues into their curriculum, and use action learning with real issues versus case studies. The business is something to be passionate about. CLOs need to be linked to the business and connect to it at a deep level, bring it to life through perspective.

They need to have a passion for learning. CLOs must have learned new things. Their mission is to build the potential of people and teams and identify and bring out the potential in others. CLOs should always see themselves as professional—"always work your game."

ADDITIONAL QUOTES ABOUT THE CLO . . . FROM UNKNOWN SOURCES

"The CLO's role is to assimilate information and turn knowledge into action, providing meaning and context."

"When you cut learning in a company, you cut the growth of a company. Having a robust learning and development focus enables companies to grow."

"Great CLOs help companies learn faster than their competitors. Learning can be a competitive advantage if effectively managed and implemented."

"The ROI of learning can also be thought of as a measure of company profitability. The more efficient and productive a workforce is, the more profitable the company will be."

Index

Made in the USA
San Bernardino, CA
03 January 2015